Safety Symbols

These symbols appear in laboratory activities. They warn of possible dangers in the laboratory and remind you to work carefully.

 Safety Goggles Wear safety goggles to protect your eyes in any activity involving chemicals, flames or heating, or glassware.

 Lab Apron Wear a laboratory apron to protect your skin and clothing from damage.

 Breakage Handle breakable materials, such as glassware, with care. Do not touch broken glassware.

 Heat-Resistant Gloves Use an oven mitt or other hand protection when handling hot materials such as hot plates or hot glassware.

 Plastic Gloves Wear disposable plastic gloves when working with harmful chemicals and organisms. Keep your hands away from your face, and dispose of the gloves according to your teacher's instructions.

 Heating Use a clamp or tongs to pick up hot glassware. Do not touch hot objects with your bare hands.

 Flames Before you work with flames, tie back loose hair and clothing. Follow instructions from your teacher about lighting and extinguishing flames.

 No Flames When using flammable materials, make sure there are no flames, sparks, or other exposed heat sources present.

 Corrosive Chemical Avoid getting acid or other corrosive chemicals on your skin or clothing or in your eyes. Do not inhale the vapors. Wash your hands after the activity.

 Poison Do not let any poisonous chemical come into contact with your skin, and do not inhale its vapors. Wash your hands when you are finished with the activity.

 Fumes Work in a ventilated area when harmful vapors may be involved. Avoid inhaling vapors directly. Only test an odor when directed to do so by your teacher, and use a wafting motion to direct the vapor toward your nose.

 Sharp Object Scissors, scalpels, knives, needles, pins, and tacks can cut your skin. Always direct a sharp edge or point away from yourself and others.

 Animal Safety Treat live or preserved animals or animal parts with care to avoid harming the animals or yourself. Wash your hands when you are finished with the activity.

 Plant Safety Handle plants only as directed by your teacher. If you are allergic to certain plants, tell your teacher; do not do an activity involving those plants. Avoid touching harmful plants such as poison ivy. Wash your hands when you are finished with the activity.

 Electric Shock To avoid electric shock, never use electrical equipment around water, or when the equipment is wet or your hands are wet. Be sure cords are untangled and cannot trip anyone. Unplug equipment not in use.

 Physical Safety When an experiment involves physical activity, avoid injuring yourself or others. Alert your teacher if there is any reason you should not participate.

 Disposal Dispose of chemicals and other laboratory materials safely. Follow the instructions from your teacher.

 Hand Washing Wash your hands thoroughly when finished with the activity. Use soap and warm water. Rinse well.

 General Safety Awareness When this symbol appears, follow the instructions provided. When you are asked to develop your own procedure in a lab, have your teacher approve your plan before you go further.

Motion, Forces, and Energy

PRENTICE HALL Science Explorer

DISCOVERY CHANNEL SCHOOL

Go Online
sci LINKS NSTA

PEARSON

Boston, Massachusetts
Glenview, Illinois
Shoreview, Minnesota
Upper Saddle River, New Jersey

PRENTICE HALL **Science Explorer**

Motion, Forces, and Energy

Book-Specific Resources
Student Edition
StudentExpress™ CD-ROM
Interactive Textbook Online
Teacher's Edition
All-in-One Teaching Resources
Color Transparencies
Guided Reading and Study Workbook
Student Edition in MP3 Audio
Discovery Channel School® Video
Consumable and Nonconsumable Materials Kits

Program Print Resources
Integrated Science Laboratory Manual
Computer Microscope Lab Manual
Inquiry Skills Activity Books
Progress Monitoring Assessments
Test Preparation Workbook
Test-Taking Tips With Transparencies
Teacher's ELL Handbook
Reading Strategies for Science Content

Differentiated Instruction Resources
Adapted Reading and Study Workbook
Adapted Tests
Differentiated Instruction Guide for Labs and Activities

Program Technology Resources
TeacherExpress™ CD-ROM
Interactive Textbooks Online
PresentationExpress™ CD-ROM
ExamView®, Test Generator CD-ROM
Lab zone™ Easy Planner CD-ROM
Probeware Lab Manual With CD-ROM
Computer Microscope and Lab Manual
Materials Ordering CD-ROM
Discovery Channel School® DVD Library
Lab Activity Video Library—DVD and VHS
Web Site at PearsonSchool.com

Spanish Print Resources
Spanish Student Edition
Spanish Guided Reading and Study Workbook
Spanish Teaching Guide With Tests

Acknowledgments appear on page 244, which constitutes an extension of this copyright page.

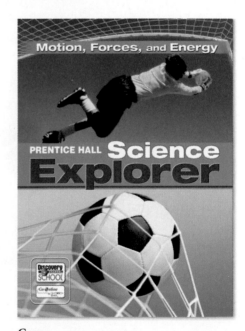

Cover
Both the goalie (top) and the goal net (bottom) change the motion of the soccer ball by exerting a force on it.

PEARSON

13-digit ISBN 978-0-13-365113-3
10-digit ISBN 0-13-365113-4
5 6 7 8 9 10   13 12 11 10 09

Program Authors

Michael J. Padilla, Ph.D.
Associate Dean and Director
Eugene T. Moore School of Education
Clemson University
Clemson, South Carolina

Michael Padilla is a leader in middle school science education. He has served as an author and elected officer for the National Science Teachers Association and as a writer of the National Science Education Standards. As lead author of Science Explorer, Mike has inspired the team in developing a program that meets the needs of middle grades students, promotes science inquiry, and is aligned with the National Science Education Standards.

Ioannis Miaoulis, Ph.D.
President
Museum of Science
Boston, Massachusetts

Originally trained as a mechanical engineer, Ioannis Miaoulis is in the forefront of the national movement to increase technological literacy. As dean of the Tufts University School of Engineering, Dr. Miaoulis spearheaded the introduction of engineering into the Massachusetts curriculum. Currently he is working with school systems across the country to engage students in engineering activities and to foster discussions on the impact of science and technology on society.

Martha Cyr, Ph.D.
Director of K–12 Outreach
Worcester Polytechnic Institute
Worcester, Massachusetts

Martha Cyr is a noted expert in engineering outreach. She has over nine years of experience with programs and activities that emphasize the use of engineering principles, through hands-on projects, to excite and motivate students and teachers of mathematics and science in grades K–12. Her goal is to stimulate a continued interest in science and mathematics through engineering.

Book Author

T. Griffith Jones, Ph.D.
Science Department Chair
P. K. Yonge Developmental Research School
College of Education—University of Florida
Gainesville, Florida

Contributing Writers

Mark Illingworth
Teacher
Hollis Public Schools
Hollis, New Hampshire

Thomas R. Wellnitz
Science Instructor
The Paideia School
Atlanta, Georgia

Consultants

Reading Consultant

Nancy Romance, Ph.D.
Professor of Science
    Education
Florida Atlantic University
Fort Lauderdale, Florida

Mathematics Consultant

William Tate, Ph.D.
Professor of Education and
    Applied Statistics and
    Computation
Washington University
St. Louis, Missouri

Reviewers

Teacher Reviewers

David R. Blakely
Arlington High School
Arlington, Massachusetts

Jane E. Callery
Two Rivers Magnet Middle
    School
East Hartford, Connecticut

Melissa Lynn Cook
Oakland Mills High School
Columbia, Maryland

James Fattic
Southside Middle School
Anderson, Indiana

Dan Gabel
Hoover Middle School
Rockville, Maryland

Wayne Goates
Eisenhower Middle School
Goddard, Kansas

Katherine Bobay Graser
Mint Hill Middle School
Charlotte, North Carolina

Darcy Hampton
Deal Junior High School
Washington, D.C.

Karen Kelly
Pierce Middle School
Waterford, Michigan

David Kelso
Manchester High School Central
Manchester, New Hampshire

Benigno Lopez, Jr.
Sleepy Hill Middle School
Lakeland, Florida

Angie L. Matamoros, Ph.D.
ALM Consulting, INC.
Weston, Florida

Tim McCollum
Charleston Middle School
Charleston, Illinois

Bruce A. Mellin
Brooks School
North Andover, Massachusetts

Ella Jay Parfitt
Southeast Middle School
Baltimore, Maryland

Evelyn A. Pizzarello
Louis M. Klein Middle School
Harrison, New York

Kathleen M. Poe
Fletcher Middle School
Jacksonville, Florida

Shirley Rose
Lewis and Clark Middle School
Tulsa, Oklahoma

Linda Sandersen
Greenfield Middle School
Greenfield, Wisconsin

Mary E. Solan
Southwest Middle School
Charlotte, North Carolina

Mary Stewart
University of Tulsa
Tulsa, Oklahoma

Paul Swenson
Billings West High School
Billings, Montana

Thomas Vaughn
Arlington High School
Arlington, Massachusetts

Susan C. Zibell
Central Elementary
Simsbury, Connecticut

Safety Reviewers

W. H. Breazeale, Ph.D.
Department of Chemistry
College of Charleston
Charleston, South Carolina

Ruth Hathaway, Ph.D.
Hathaway Consulting
Cape Girardeau, Missouri

Douglas Mandt, M.S.
Science Education Consultant
Edgewood, Washington

Activity Field Testers

Nicki Bibbo
Witchcraft Heights School
Salem, Massachusetts

Rose-Marie Botting
Broward County Schools
Fort Lauderdale, Florida

Colleen Campos
Laredo Middle School
Aurora, Colorado

Elizabeth Chait
W. L. Chenery Middle School
Belmont, Massachusetts

Holly Estes
Hale Middle School
Stow, Massachusetts

Laura Hapgood
Plymouth Community
    Intermediate School
Plymouth, Massachusetts

Mary F. Lavin
Plymouth Community
    Intermediate School
Plymouth, Massachusetts

James MacNeil, Ph.D.
Cambridge, Massachusetts

Lauren Magruder
St. Michael's Country
    Day School
Newport, Rhode Island

Jeanne Maurand
Austin Preparatory School
Reading, Massachusetts

Joanne Jackson-Pelletier
Winman Junior High School
Warwick, Rhode Island

Warren Phillips
Plymouth Public Schools
Plymouth, Massachusetts

Carol Pirtle
Hale Middle School
Stow, Massachusetts

Kathleen M. Poe
Fletcher Middle School
Jacksonville, Florida

Cynthia B. Pope
Norfolk Public Schools
Norfolk, Virginia

Anne Scammell
Geneva Middle School
Geneva, New York

Karen Riley Sievers
Callanan Middle School
Des Moines, Iowa

David M. Smith
Eyer Middle School
Allentown, Pennsylvania

Gene Vitale
Parkland School
McHenry, Illinois

Contents

Motion, Forces, and Energy

Careers in Science Understanding Nature's Designs ... xii

Chapter 1 Motion **4**
  1 Describing and Measuring Motion 6
  2 **Integrating Earth Science** Slow Motion on Planet Earth 18
  3 Acceleration 22

VIDEO
Motion

Chapter 2 Forces **34**
  1 The Nature of Force 36
  2 Friction and Gravity 42
  3 Newton's First and Second Laws 51
  4 Newton's Third Law 55
  5 **Integrating Space Science** Rockets and Satellites 64

VIDEO
Forces

Chapter 3 Forces in Fluids **72**
  1 Pressure 74
  2 Floating and Sinking 82
  3 Pascal's Principle 90
  4 **Tech & Design** Bernoulli's Principle 95

VIDEO
Forces in Fluids

Chapter 4 Work and Machines **106**
  1 What Is Work? 108
  2 **Integrating Mathematics** How Machines Do Work 114
  3 Simple Machines 124

VIDEO
Work and Machines

Chapter 5   Energy **144**
1   What Is Energy? 146
2   Forms of Energy 151
3   Energy Transformations and Conservation 158
4   **Integrating Earth Science** Energy and Fossil Fuels 166

Chapter 6   Thermal Energy and Heat **174**
1   Temperature, Thermal Energy, and Heat 176
2   The Transfer of Heat 183
3   **Integrating Chemistry** Thermal Energy and States of Matter .. 190
4   Uses of Heat 195

Interdisciplinary Exploration
Bridges—From Vines to Steel **204**

Reference Section
Skills Handbook 212
Think Like a Scientist 212
Making Measurements 214
Conducting a Scientific Investigation 216
Technology Design Skills 218
Creating Data Tables and Graphs 220
Math Review 223
Reading Comprehension Skills 228

Appendix A Laboratory Safety 232
English and Spanish Glossary 234
Index 240
Acknowledgments 244

VIDEO
Energy

VIDEO
Thermal Energy
and Heat

Activities

Lab zone™ | Chapter **Project** | Opportunities for long-term inquiry

Show Some Motion 5
Newton Scooters 35
Staying Afloat 73

The Nifty Lifting Machine 107
Design and Build a Roller Coaster 145
In Hot Water 175

Lab zone | Discover **Activity** | Exploration and inquiry before reading

How Fast and How Far? 6
How Slow Can It Flow? 18
Will You Hurry Up? 22
Is the Force With You? 36
Which Lands First? 42
What Changes Motion? 51
How Pushy Is a Straw? 55
What Makes an Object Move in a Circle? . .64
Can You Blow Up a Balloon in a Bottle? . .74
What Can You Measure With a Straw? . . .82
How Does Pressure Change? 90
Does the Movement of Air
    Affect Pressure? 95

What Happens When You Pull
    at an Angle? .108
Is It a Machine? .114
How Can You Increase Force? 124
How High Does a Ball Bounce? 146
What Makes a Flashlight Shine? 151
What Would Make a Card Jump? 158
What Is a Fuel? .166
How Cold Is the Water? 176
What Does It Mean to Heat Up? 183
What Happens to Heated Metal? 190
What Happens at the Pump? 195

Lab zone | Try This **Activity** | Reinforcement of key concepts

Spinning Plates 44
Around and Around 52
Colliding Cars 59
Card Trick 76
Dive! 86
Faucet Force 96
Is Work Always the Same? 111
Going Up 116
A Paper Screw 127
Pendulum Swing 162
Feel the Warmth 184
Shake It Up 196

Lab zone — Skills **Activity** — Practice of specific science inquiry skills

Calculating 10
Calculating 47
Communicating .132
Classifying 159
Graphing 168
Inferring 186
Observing 193

Lab zone — Labs — In-depth practice of inquiry skills and science concepts

Skills Lab Inclined to Roll 16
Skills Lab Stopping on a Dime 28
Consumer Lab Sticky Sneakers 40
Skills Lab Forced to Accelerate 62
Design Your Own Lab
    Spinning Sprinklers 81
Skills Lab Sink and Spill 88

Skills Lab Seesaw Science 122
Skills Lab Angling for Access 136
Skills Lab Can You Feel the Power? 156
Skills Lab Soaring Straws 164
Technology Lab Build Your Own
    Thermometer 182
Skills Lab Just Add Water 188

Lab zone — At-Home **Activity** — Quick, engaging activities for home and family

Fingernail Growth .21
House of Cards 39
Swing the Bucket 67
Changing Balloon Density 87
Paper Chimney 99

Machines in the Kitchen 135
Hot Wire 163
Burning Fossils 169
Frosty Balloons 194

• Tech & Design • — Design, build, test, and communicate

Technology and Society Helicopters . . .100
Science and Society Automation in the
    Workplace—Lost Jobs or New Jobs? . .138

Technology Chapter Project Design and
    Build a Roller Coaster 145
Technology Lab Build Your Own
    Thermometer 182

Math
Point-of-use math practice

Analyzing Data

Free Fall 48

Comparing Hydraulic Lifts 93

Calculating Mechanical Advantage 119

Calculating Mechanical Energy 153

Specific Heat of Materials 180

Sample Problems

Calculating Acceleration 25

Calculating Force .53

Calculating Momentum 58

Calculating Power 112

Calculating Efficiency 120

Math Skills

Converting Units 9

Area 75

Exponents 148

Converting Units 179

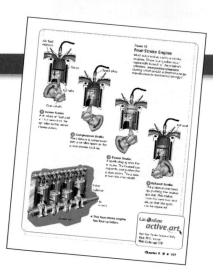

active art
Illustrations come alive online

Graphing Motion .14

Motion of the Continents 20

Conservation of Momentum 60

Hydraulic Devices 92

Types of Pulleys .133

Energy Transformations 160

Four-Stroke Engine 197

Writing in Science

Research and Write 13

News Report 31

Cause-and-Effect Paragraph 50

Descriptive Paragraph 69

Cause-and-Effect Letter 94

News Report 103

Research and Write 131

Proposed Solution 141

Detailed Observation 155

Interview 171

Explanation 187

Cause-and-Effect Paragraph 199

Proposed Solution 201

For Links on Acceleration 24
For Links on Force 38
For Links on Friction 44
For Links on Fluid and Pressure 78
For Links on Bernoulli's Principle 97
For Links on Work 110
For Links on Mechanical Efficiency 120
For Links on Energy 149
For Links on Forms of Energy 152
For Links on Energy Transformations . . .166
For Links on Temperature and Heat 178
For Links on Heat Transfer 184
For Links on Changes of State 191

VIDEO

Enhance understanding through dynamic video.

Preview Get motivated with this introduction to the chapter content.

Field Trip Explore a real-world story related to the chapter content.

Assessment Review content and take an assessment.

Web Links

Get connected to exciting Web resources in every lesson.

$SC\!I\!LINKS_{™}$ Find Web links on topics relating to every section.

Active Art Interact with selected visuals from every chapter online.

Planet Diary® Explore news and natural phenomena through weekly reports.

Science News® Keep up to date with the latest science discoveries.

Experience the complete text-book online and on CD-ROM.

Activities Practice skills and learn content.

Videos Explore content and learn important lab skills.

Audio Support Hear key terms spoken and defined.

Self-Assessment Use instant feedback to help you track your progress.

Understanding Nature's Designs

Ioannis is at the steam-engine exhibit in Boston's Museum of Science.

"This is a biomechanics laboratory," says scientist and engineer Ioannis Miaoulis. "What we study is how animals and plants use energy, motion, and forces." Professor Miaoulis walks over to a network of earthen tunnels built between two panes of glass. The structure has a tube for blowing air over the top.

"This is a cross section of a prairie-dog burrow. There are two entrance holes. One hole is flat, while the other one is built up and rounded. Biologists were wondering why. They thought the prairie dogs wanted a good view, but then why not make both holes high and rounded and get a good view from both?"

Career Path

Ioannis Miaoulis (YAHN is my OW lis) was born in Athens, Greece. He came to the United States to study engineering. He earned a master's degree in engineering at the Massachusetts Institute of Technology. He received a master's degree in economics and a Ph.D. in mechanical engineering at Tufts University in Massachusetts, where he later became the Dean of the School of Engineering. Now he is the president of Boston's Museum of Science.

Miaoulis and his students are learning the likely reason. Wind blowing over a flat surface moves more slowly, because it doesn't have to travel as far as the same breeze going over a rounded surface. "Slow air means high pressure across here" — Miaoulis points to the flat hole. "Fast air going over the rounded hole means low pressure. High pressure here, low pressure there. The holes' shape moves air through the burrow—in the flat hole and out the rounded one. It's prairie-dog air conditioning."

Talking With
Dr. Ioannis Miaoulis

A prairie dog uses its paws to feed itself grass from the western prairie.

? How did you get started in science?

I grew up in Athens, Greece. It's a congested and polluted city, but my school was in the woods and I could do things outdoors. I got to love nature. I dug out anthills to see how they were inside. I found the places where turtles laid their eggs.

In the summers, we lived near the ocean and every day I'd go fishing and snorkeling. I got to know each rock underwater. I didn't even know what a scientist was then, but I was observing and thinking through things because I wanted to catch more fish. If the flow of water was in this direction, where would be a good place for the fish to hang out? I was observing flow patterns to see where, how, and why fish build their nests. I still do it, in part to catch them, because I still like fishing. But now I do it to observe them, to figure them out. I was always curious.

? How is engineering different from science?

Well, I enjoyed doing things with my hands, taking things apart and seeing how they worked, building things and making them work. I found that what I enjoyed about studying was learning science and then doing something with it. And that's engineering. I try to discover something about an animal that nobody ever understood before. Then I'll use that information to design something that will make people's lives easier.

Prairie-Dog Air Conditioning

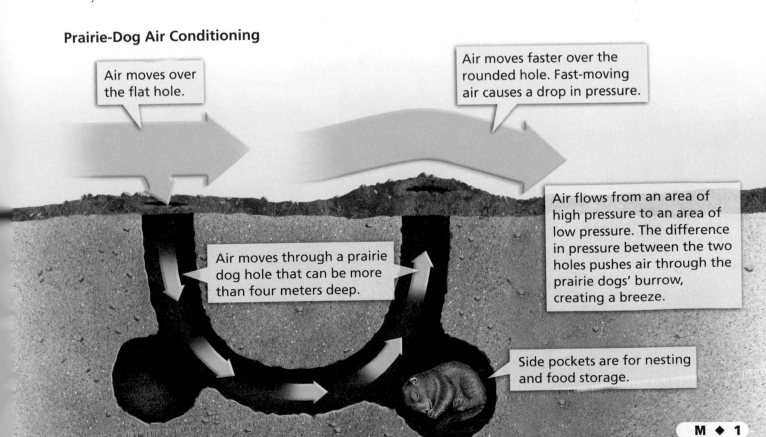

Air moves over the flat hole.

Air moves faster over the rounded hole. Fast-moving air causes a drop in pressure.

Air moves through a prairie dog hole that can be more than four meters deep.

Air flows from an area of high pressure to an area of low pressure. The difference in pressure between the two holes pushes air through the prairie dogs' burrow, creating a breeze.

Side pockets are for nesting and food storage.

? How do you use nature in your engineering designs?

Here's an example. I got interested in how heat travels in the chips that make computers work. They're made in very thin layers or films, thinner than one-hundredth the thickness of your hair. Sometimes, if chips don't heat evenly, they fall apart when you try to make them. I wondered if any plants or animals had solved that problem—using thin films to control how heat was absorbed or reflected. We looked for animals that bask or lie in the sun, or for animals and insects that depend on the warmth of the sun.

If you touch a butterfly, you get a dust on your fingers. When I was little I used to catch butterflies and didn't really understand what the dust was. If you slice those "dust" particles, you find that they are made of many layers. These thin films are little solar collectors. Butterflies can change the amount of heat they catch. They just change the angle at which they hold the thin films on their wings up to the sun. Large areas of butterfly wings heat evenly. So we're looking at the layers on butterfly wings to learn how to make computer chips that will transfer heat more evenly.

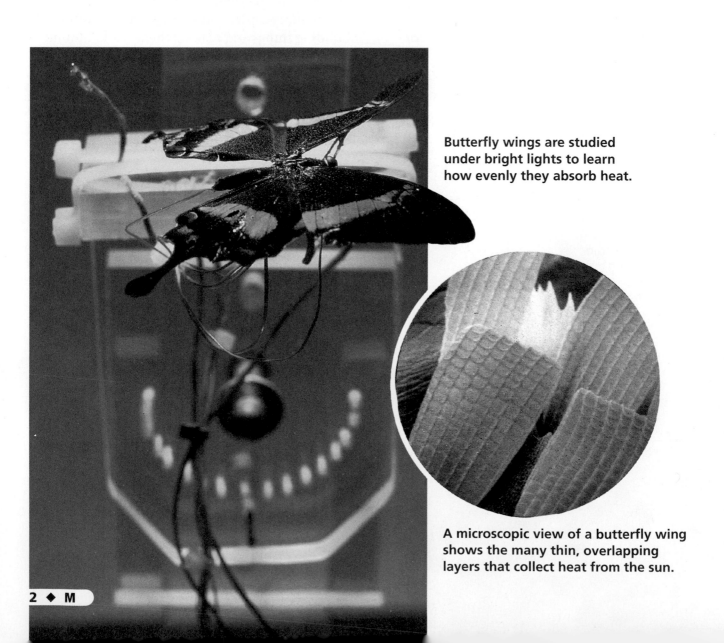

Butterfly wings are studied under bright lights to learn how evenly they absorb heat.

A microscopic view of a butterfly wing shows the many thin, overlapping layers that collect heat from the sun.

Why is a maple seed shaped as it is?

A seed tends to detach when the wind is blowing.

Because of its winglike shape, the seed spirals slowly to the ground. So, in the wind, it travels away from the tree.

A seed that falls away from the roots and shade of the parent tree has a better chance to grow.

Maple seeds can fall to the ground anytime from May to early fall.

? How do you come up with the questions you ask?

It depends. Sometimes it's simply by observing things. If you see a maple seed with wings falling in a fancy way, you might not even think twice about it. But if you start observing and appreciating nature, you start asking questions about how things work. Why would it help the tree to have a seed that could be blown by the wind? I can combine my love of nature from when I was small with what I've learned of science and engineering.

Ioannis shows how water is lost through a plant's leaves.

Writing in Science

Career Link Scientist and engineer Ioannis carefully observes plants and animals and asks himself questions about them. Do you, too, have "a questioning eye"? Think about an animal that you observe often in your environment—a pet, insect, or bird. Write down four *how* or *why* questions about the movement and speed of the animal. In a paragraph, describe steps that you might take to collect data to find possible answers.

Go Online
PHSchool.com
For: More on this career
Visit: PHSchool.com
Web Code: cgb-3000

The BIG Idea
Motion and Forces

 How can an object's motion be described?

Chapter Preview

❶ **Describing and Measuring Motion**
Discover How Fast and How Far?
Math Skills Converting Units
Skills Activity Calculating
Active Art Graphing Motion
Skills Lab Inclined to Roll

❷ **Slow Motion on Planet Earth**
Discover How Slow Can It Flow?
Active Art Continental Drift
At-Home Activity Fingernail Growth

❸ **Acceleration**
Discover Will You Hurry Up?
Skills Lab Stopping on a Dime

The wild horses running across ▶
this meadow are in motion.

Lab zone™ Chapter **Project**

Show Some Motion

Your Goal To identify the motion of several common objects and calculate how fast each one moves

To complete this project, you must
- measure distance and time carefully
- calculate the speed of each object using your data
- prepare display cards of your data, diagrams, and calculations
- follow the safety guidelines in Appendix A

Plan It! With your classmates, brainstorm several examples of objects in motion, such as a feather falling, your friend riding a bicycle, or the minute hand moving on a clock. Choose your examples and have your teacher approve them. Create a data table for each example and record your measurements. For accuracy, repeat your measurements. Then calculate the speed of each object. Make display cards for each example that show data, diagrams, and calculations.

Describing and Measuring Motion

Reading Preview

Key Concepts
- When is an object in motion?
- How do you know an object's speed and velocity?
- How can you graph motion?

Key Terms
- motion • reference point
- International System of Units
- meter • speed • average speed
- instantaneous speed
- velocity • slope

Target Reading Skill

Using Prior Knowledge Before you read, write what you know about motion in a graphic organizer like the one below. As you read, write what you learn.

What You Know
1. A moving object changes position.
2.

What You Learned
1.
2.

Lab zone Discover **Activity**

How Fast and How Far?

1. Using a stopwatch, find out how long it takes you to walk 5 meters at a normal pace. Record your time.
2. Now find out how far you can walk in 5 seconds if you walk at a normal pace. Record your distance.
3. Repeat Steps 1 and 2, walking slower than your normal pace. Then repeat Steps 1 and 2 walking faster than your normal pace.

Think It Over
Inferring What is the relationship between the distance you walk, the time it takes you to walk, and your walking speed?

How do you know if you are moving? If you've ever traveled on a train, you know you cannot always tell if you are in motion. Looking at a building outside the window helps you decide. Although the building seems to move past the train, it's you and the train that are moving.

However, sometimes you may see another train that appears to be moving. Is the other train really moving, or is your train moving? How do you tell?

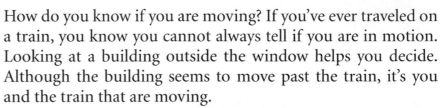

Describing Motion

Deciding if an object is moving isn't as easy as you might think. For example, you are probably sitting in a chair as you read this book. Are you moving? Well, parts of you may be. Your eyes blink and your chest moves up and down. But you would probably say that you are not moving. An object is in **motion** if its distance from another object is changing. Because your distance from your chair is not changing, you could say you are not in motion.

Reference Points To decide if you are moving, you use your chair as a reference point. A **reference point** is a place or object used for comparison to determine if something is in motion. **An object is in motion if it changes position relative to a reference point.**

Objects that we call stationary—such as a tree, a sign, or a building—make good reference points. From the point of view of the train passenger in Figure 1, such objects are not in motion. If the passenger is moving relative to a tree, he can conclude that the train is in motion.

You probably know what happens if your reference point is moving. Have you ever been in a school bus parked next to another bus? Suddenly, you think your bus is moving backward. But, when you look out a window on the other side, you find that your bus isn't moving at all—the other bus is moving forward! Your bus seems to be moving backward because you used the other bus as a reference point.

FIGURE 1
Reference Points
The passenger can use a tree as a reference point to decide if the train is moving. A tree makes a good reference point because it is stationary from the passenger's point of view.
Applying Concepts *Why is it important to choose a stationary object as a reference point?*

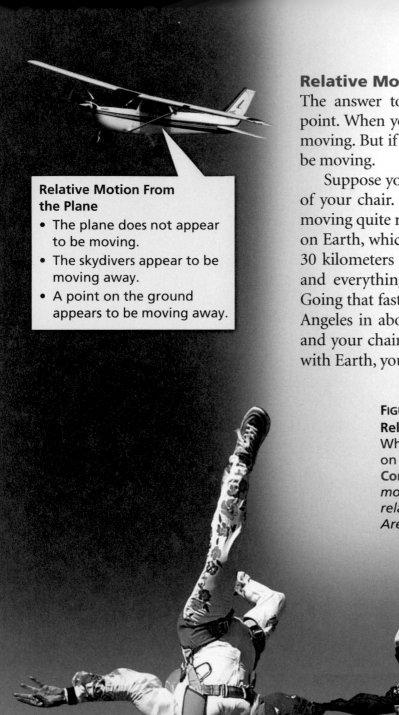

Relative Motion From the Plane
- The plane does not appear to be moving.
- The skydivers appear to be moving away.
- A point on the ground appears to be moving away.

Relative Motion Are you moving as you read this book? The answer to that question depends on your reference point. When your chair is your reference point, you are not moving. But if you choose another reference point, you may be moving.

Suppose you choose the sun as a reference point instead of your chair. If you compare yourself to the sun, you are moving quite rapidly. This is because you and your chair are on Earth, which moves around the sun. Earth moves about 30 kilometers every second. So you, your chair, this book, and everything else on Earth move that quickly as well. Going that fast, you could travel from New York City to Los Angeles in about 2 minutes! Relative to the sun, both you and your chair are in motion. But because you are moving with Earth, you do not seem to be moving.

FIGURE 2
Relative Motion
Whether or not an object is in motion depends on the reference point you choose.
Comparing and Contrasting *Are the skydivers moving relative to each other? Are they moving relative to the airplane from which they jumped? Are they moving relative to the ground?*

Relative Motion From the Skydivers
- The plane appears to be moving away.
- The skydivers do not appear to be moving.
- The ground appears to be moving closer.

Relative Motion From the Ground
- The plane appears to be moving across the sky.
- The skydivers appear to be moving closer.
- The ground does not appear to be moving.

FIGURE 3
Measuring Distance
You can measure distances shorter than 1 meter in centimeters. The wingspan of the butterfly is 7 cm.

Measuring Distance You can use units of measurement to describe motion precisely. You measure in units, or standard quantities of measurement, all the time. For example, you might measure 1 cup of milk for a recipe, run 2 miles after school, or buy 3 pounds of fruit at the store. Cups, miles, and pounds are all units of measurement.

Scientists all over the world use the same system of measurement so that they can communicate clearly. This system of measurement is called the **International System of Units** or, in French, *Système International* (SI).

When describing motion, scientists use SI units to describe the distance an object moves. When you measure distance, you measure length. The SI unit of length is the **meter** (m). A meter is a little longer than a yard. An Olympic-size swimming pool is 50 meters long. A football field is about 91 meters long.

The length of an object smaller than a meter often is measured in a unit called the centimeter (cm). The prefix *centi-* means "one hundredth." A centimeter is one hundredth of a meter, so there are 100 centimeters in a meter. The wingspan of the butterfly shown in Figure 3 can be measured in centimeters. For lengths smaller than a centimeter, the millimeter (mm) is used. The prefix *milli-* means "one thousandth," so there are 1,000 millimeters in a meter. Distances too long to be measured in meters often are measured in kilometers (km). The prefix *kilo-* means "one thousand." There are 1,000 meters in a kilometer.

Scientists also use SI units to describe quantities other than length. You can find more information about SI units in the Skills Handbook at the end of this book.

 **Reading Checkpoint** What system of measurement do scientists use?

Math Skills

Converting Units

Use a conversion factor to convert one metric unit to another. A conversion factor is a fraction in which the numerator and denominator represent equal amounts in different units. Multiply the number you want to convert by the conversion factor.

Suppose you want to know how many millimeters (mm) are in 14.5 meters (m). Since there are 1,000 millimeters in 1 meter, the conversion factor is

$$\frac{1,000 \text{ mm}}{1 \text{ m}}$$

Multiply 14.5 meters by the conversion factor to find millimeters.

$$14.5 \text{ m} \times \frac{1,000 \text{ mm}}{1 \text{ m}}$$
$$= 14.5 \times 1,000 \text{ mm}$$
$$= 14,500 \text{ mm}$$

Practice Problem How many centimeters are in 22.5 meters?

Calculating

Two families meet at the City Museum at 10:00 A.M. Each family uses a different means of transportation to get there. The Gonzalez family leaves at 9:00 A.M. and drives 90 km on a highway. The Browns leave at 9:30 A.M. and ride the train 30 km. What is the average speed for each family's trip? Which family travels at the faster speed?

FIGURE 4

Speed

The cyclists' speeds will vary throughout the cross-country race. However, the cyclist with the greatest average speed will win.

Calculating Speed

A measurement of distance can tell you how far an object travels. A cyclist, for example, might travel 30 kilometers. An ant might travel 2 centimeters. **If you know the distance an object travels in a certain amount of time, you can calculate the speed of the object.** Speed is a type of rate. A rate tells you the amount of something that occurs or changes in one unit of time. The **speed** of an object is the distance the object travels per unit of time.

The Speed Equation To calculate the speed of an object, divide the distance the object travels by the amount of time it takes to travel that distance. This relationship can be written as an equation.

$$\text{Speed} = \frac{\text{Distance}}{\text{Time}}$$

The speed equation consists of a unit of distance divided by a unit of time. If you measure distance in meters and time in seconds, you express speed in meters per second, or m/s. (The slash is read as "per.") If you measure distance in kilometers and time in hours, you express speed in kilometers per hour, or km/h. For example, a cyclist who travels 30 kilometers in 1 hour has a speed of 30 km/h. An ant that moves 2 centimeters in 1 second is moving at a speed of 2 centimeters per second, or 2 cm/s.

Average Speed The speed of most moving objects is not constant. The cyclists shown in Figure 4, for example, change their speeds many times during the race. They might ride at a constant speed along flat ground but move more slowly as they climb hills. Then they might move more quickly as they come down hills. Occasionally, they may stop to fix their bikes.

Although a cyclist does not have a constant speed, the cyclist does have an average speed throughout a race. To calculate **average speed**, divide the total distance traveled by the total time. For example, suppose a cyclist travels 32 kilometers during the first 2 hours. Then the cyclist travels 13 kilometers during the next hour. The average speed of the cyclist is the total distance divided by the total time.

$$\text{Total distance} = 32 \text{ km} + 13 \text{ km} = 45 \text{ km}$$
$$\text{Total time} = 2 \text{ h} + 1 \text{ h} = 3 \text{ h}$$
$$\text{Average speed} = \frac{45 \text{ km}}{3 \text{ h}} = 15 \text{ km/h}$$

The cyclist's average speed is 15 kilometers per hour.

Instantaneous Speed Calculating the average speed of a cyclist during a race is important. However, it is also useful to know the cyclist's instantaneous speed. **Instantaneous speed** is the rate at which an object is moving at a given instant in time.

✓ **Reading Checkpoint** How do you calculate average speed?

FIGURE 5
Measuring Speed
Cyclists use an electronic device known as a cyclometer to track the distance and time that they travel. A cyclometer can calculate both average and instantaneous speed.
Comparing and Contrasting *Explain why the instantaneous speed and the average speed shown below are different.*

DISTANCE
45 km
TIME
3:00:00
h min s

INST. SPEED
22 km/h
AVG. SPEED
15 km/h

Describing Velocity

Knowing the speed at which something travels does not tell you everything about its motion. To describe an object's motion completely, you need to know the direction of its motion. For example, suppose you hear that a thunderstorm is traveling at a speed of 25 km/h. Should you prepare for the storm? That depends on the direction of the storm's motion. Because storms usually travel from west to east in the United States, you need not worry if you live to the west of the storm. But if you live to the east of the storm, take cover.

When you know both the speed and direction of an object's motion, you know the velocity of the object. Speed in a given direction is called **velocity.** You know the velocity of the storm when you know that it is moving 25 km/h eastward.

• Tech & Design in History •

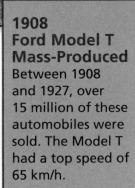

The Speed of Transportation
The speed with which people can travel from one place to another has increased over the years.

**1818
National Road Constructed**
The speed of transportation has been limited largely by the quality of roadways. The U.S. government paid for the construction of a highway named the Cumberland Road. It ran from Cumberland, Maryland, to Wheeling, in present-day West Virginia. Travel by horse and carriage on the roadway was at a speed of about 11 km/h.

**1885
Benz Tricycle Car Introduced**
This odd-looking vehicle was the first internal combustion (gasoline-powered) automobile sold to the public. Although it is an ancestor of the modern automobile, its top speed was only about 15 km/h—not much faster than a horse-drawn carriage.

**1908
Ford Model T
Mass-Produced**
Between 1908 and 1927, over 15 million of these automobiles were sold. The Model T had a top speed of 65 km/h.

1800	1850	1900

At times, describing the velocity of moving objects can be very important. For example, air traffic controllers must keep close track of the velocities of the aircraft under their control. These velocities continually change as airplanes move overhead and on the runways. An error in determining a velocity, either in speed or in direction, could lead to a collision.

Velocity is also important to airplane pilots. For example, stunt pilots make spectacular use of their control over the velocity of their aircrafts. To avoid colliding with other aircraft, these skilled pilots must have precise control of both their speed and direction. Stunt pilots use this control to stay in close formation while flying graceful maneuvers at high speed.

 **Reading Checkpoint** **What is velocity?**

Writing in Science

Research and Write What styles of automobile were most popular during the 1950s, 1960s, and 1970s? Were sedans, convertibles, station wagons, or sports cars the bestsellers? Choose an era and research automobiles of that time. Then write an advertisement for one particular style of car. Be sure to include information from your research.

1934 Zephyr Introduced

The first diesel passenger train in the United States was the *Zephyr*. The *Zephyr* set a long-distance record, traveling from Denver to Chicago at an average speed of 125 km/h for more than 1,600 km.

1956 Interstate Highway System Established

The passage of the Federal-Aid Highway Act established the Highway Trust Fund. This act allowed the construction of the Interstate and Defense Highways. Nonstop transcontinental auto travel became possible. Speed limits in many parts of the system were more than 100 km/h.

2003 Maglev in Motion

The first commercial application of high-speed maglev (magnetic levitation) was unveiled in Shanghai, China. During the 30-km trip from Pudong International Airport to Shanghai's financial district, the train operates at a top speed of 430 km/h, reducing commuting time from 45 minutes to just 8 minutes.

1950   2000   2050

For: Graphing Motion activity
Visit: PHSchool.com
Web Code: cgp-3011

FIGURE 6
Graphing Motion

Distance-versus-time graphs can be used to analyze motion. On the jogger's first day of training, her speed is the same at every point. On the second day of training, her speed varies. **Reading Graphs** *On the first day, how far does the jogger run in 5 minutes?*

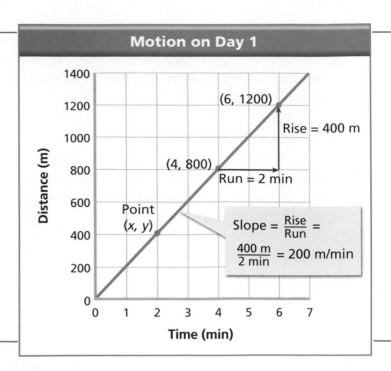

Motion on Day 1

Point (x, y)

$\text{Slope} = \dfrac{\text{Rise}}{\text{Run}} = \dfrac{400 \text{ m}}{2 \text{ min}} = 200 \text{ m/min}$

Rise = 400 m
Run = 2 min
(6, 1200)
(4, 800)

Graphing Motion

You can show the motion of an object on a line graph in which you plot distance versus time. The graphs you see in Figure 6 are distance-versus-time motion graphs. Time is shown on the horizontal axis, or *x*-axis. Distance is shown on the vertical axis, or *y*-axis. A point on the line represents the distance an object has traveled at a particular time. The *x* value of the point is time, and the *y* value is distance.

The steepness of a line on a graph is called **slope.** The slope tells you how fast one variable changes in relation to the other variable in the graph. In other words, slope tells you the rate of change. Since speed is the rate that distance changes in relation to time, the slope of a distance-versus-time graph represents speed. The steeper the slope is, the greater the speed. A constant slope represents motion at constant speed.

Calculating Slope You can calculate the slope of a line by dividing the rise by the run. The rise is the vertical difference between any two points on the line. The run is the horizontal difference between the same two points.

$$\text{Slope} = \frac{\text{Rise}}{\text{Run}}$$

In Figure 6, using the points shown, the rise is 400 meters and the run is 2 minutes. To find the slope, you divide 400 meters by 2 minutes. The slope is 200 meters per minute.

 **Reading Checkpoint** What is the slope of a graph?

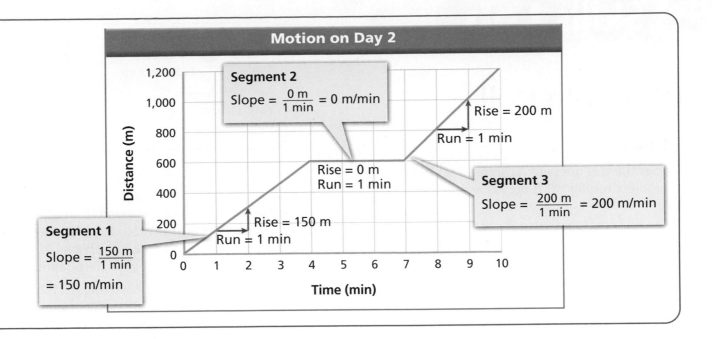

Motion on Day 2

Segment 2
Slope $= \dfrac{0 \text{ m}}{1 \text{ min}} = 0$ m/min

Rise = 200 m
Run = 1 min

Rise = 0 m
Run = 1 min

Segment 3
Slope $= \dfrac{200 \text{ m}}{1 \text{ min}} = 200$ m/min

Rise = 150 m
Run = 1 min

Segment 1
Slope $= \dfrac{150 \text{ m}}{1 \text{ min}}$
$= 150$ m/min

Distance (m): 0, 200, 400, 600, 800, 1,000, 1,200

Time (min): 0 1 2 3 4 5 6 7 8 9 10

Different Slopes Most moving objects do not travel at a constant speed. The graph above shows a jogger's motion on her second day. The line is divided into three segments. The slope of each segment is different. From the steepness of the slopes you can tell that the jogger ran the fastest during the third segment. The horizontal line in the second segment shows that the jogger's distance did not change at all.

Section 1 Assessment

Target Reading Skill
Using Prior Knowledge Review your graphic organizer and revise it based on what you just learned about motion.

Reviewing Key Concepts
1. a. **Reviewing** How do you know if an object is moving?
   b. **Explaining** Why is it important to know if your reference point is moving?
   c. **Applying Concepts** Suppose you are riding in a car. Describe your motion relative to the car, the road, and the sun.
2. a. **Defining** What is speed?
   b. **Describing** What do you know about the motion of an object that has an average speed of 1 m/s?
   c. **Comparing and Contrasting** What is the difference between speed and velocity?

3. a. **Identifying** What does the slope of a distance-versus-time graph show you about the motion of an object?
   b. **Calculating** The rise of a line on a distance-versus-time graph is 600 m and the run is 3 minutes. What is the slope of the line?

Math Practice

This week at swim practice, Jamie swam a total of 1,500 m, while Ellie swam 1.6 km.

4. **Converting Units** Convert Ellie's distance to meters. Who swam the greater distance: Jamie or Ellie?
5. **Converting Units** How many kilometers did Jamie swim?

Inclined to Roll

Go Online
PHSchool.com

For: Data sharing
Visit: PHSchool.com
Web Code: cgd-3012

Problem

How does the steepness of a ramp affect how fast an object rolling off it moves across the floor?

Skills Focus

measuring, calculating, graphing

Materials

- skateboard • meter stick • protractor
- masking tape • flat board, about 1.5 m long
- small piece of sturdy cardboard
- supports to prop up the board (books, boxes)
- two stopwatches

Procedure

1. In your notebook, make a data table like the one below. Include space for five angles.

2. Lay the board flat on the floor. Using masking tape, mark a starting line in the middle of the board. Mark a finish line on the floor 1.5 m beyond one end of the board. Place a barrier after the finish line.

3. Prop up the other end of the board to make a slight incline. Use a protractor to measure the angle that the board makes with the ground. Record the angle in your data table.

4. Working in groups of three, have one person hold the skateboard so that its front wheels are even with the starting line. As the holder releases the skateboard, the other two students should start their stopwatches.

5. One timer should stop his or her stopwatch when the front wheels of the skateboard reach the end of the incline.

6. The second timer should stop his or her stopwatch when the front wheels reach the finish line. Record the times in your data table in the columns labeled Time 1 and Time 2.

7. Repeat Steps 4–6 two more times. If your results for the three times aren't within 0.2 second of one another, carry out more trials.

		Data Table					
Angle (degrees)	Trial Number	Time 1 (to bottom) (s)	Time 2 (to finish) (s)	Avg Time 1 (s)	Avg Time 2 (s)	Avg Time 2 – Avg Time 1 (s)	Avg Speed (m/s)
	1						
	2						
	3						
	1						
	2						
	3						
	1						
	2						

8. Repeat Steps 3–7 four more times, making the ramp gradually steeper each time.

9. For each angle of the incline, complete the following calculations and record them in your data table.
   a. Find the average time the skateboard takes to get to the bottom of the ramp (Time 1).
   b. Find the average time the skateboard takes to get to the finish line (Time 2).
   c. Subtract the average of Time 1 from the average of Time 2.

Analyze and Conclude

1. **Calculating** How can you find the average speed of the skateboard across the floor for each angle of the incline? Determine the average speed for each angle and record it in your data table.

2. **Classifying** Which is your manipulated variable and which is your responding variable in this experiment? Explain. (For a discussion of manipulated and responding variables, see the Skills Handbook.)

3. **Graphing** On a graph, plot the average speed of the skateboard (on the y-axis) against the angle of the ramp (on the x-axis).

4. **Drawing Conclusions** What does your graph show about the relationship between the skateboard's speed and the angle of the ramp?

5. **Measuring** If your measurements for distance, time, or angle were inaccurate, how would your results have been affected?

6. **Communicating** Do you think your method of timing was accurate? Did the timers start and stop their stopwatches exactly at the appropriate points? How could the accuracy of the timing be improved? Write a brief procedure for your method.

Design an Experiment

A truck driver transporting new cars needs to roll the cars off the truck. You offer to design a ramp to help with the task. What measurements would you make that might be useful? Design an experiment to test your ideas. *Obtain your teacher's permission before carrying out your investigation.*

Slow Motion on Planet Earth

Reading Preview

Key Concepts
- How does the theory of plate tectonics explain the movement of Earth's landmasses?
- How fast do Earth's plates move?

Key Terms
- plate • theory of plate tectonics

⟳ Target Reading Skill

Previewing Visuals Before you read, preview Figure 8. Then write two questions that you have about the diagram in a graphic organizer like the one below. As you read, answer your questions.

Motion of the Continents

Q. Why do the continents move over time?
A.
Q.

Lab zone **Discover Activity**

How Slow Can It Flow?

1. Put a spoonful of honey on a plate.
2. Place a piece of tape 4 cm from the bottom edge of the honey.
3. Lift one side of the plate just high enough that the honey starts to flow.
4. Reduce the plate's angle until the honey barely moves. Prop up the plate at this angle.
5. Time how long the honey takes to reach the tape. Calculate the speed of the honey.

Think It Over
Forming Operational Definitions When an object doesn't appear to be moving at first glance, how can you tell if it is?

Have you ever noticed that Earth's landmasses resemble pieces of a giant jigsaw puzzle? It's true. The east coast of South America, for example, would fit nicely into the west coast of Africa. The Arabian Peninsula would fit fairly well with the northeastern coast of Africa. Since the 1600s, people have wondered why Earth's landmasses look as if they would fit together. After all, land can't move. Or can it?

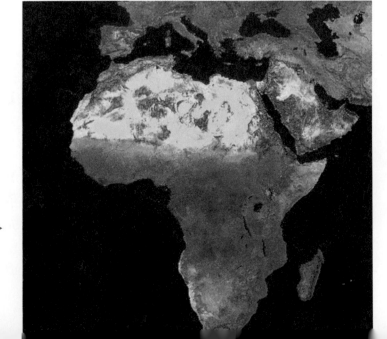

These landmasses would fit fairly well if they were pushed together like puzzle pieces. ▶

Earth's Plates

Earth's rocky outer layer consists of pieces that fit together like a jigsaw puzzle. This outer layer is made of more than a dozen major pieces called **plates.** The boundaries between the plates are cracks in Earth's outer layer. As you can see in Figure 7, plate boundaries do not always lie along the edges of continents. The eastern boundary of the North American plate, for example, lies under the Atlantic Ocean. Many plates have both continents and oceans on them.

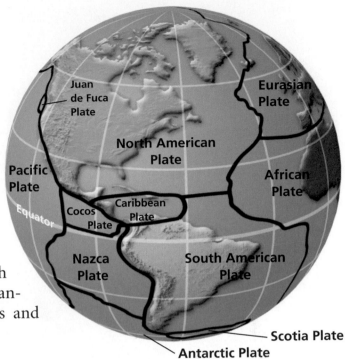

FIGURE 7
Earth's Plates
The black outlines show the boundaries of some of Earth's plates.
Interpreting Maps *Which plates border the Nazca plate?*

The Theory of Plate Tectonics Scientists use the concept of plates to explain how landmasses have changed over time. The **theory of plate tectonics** states that Earth's plates move slowly in various directions. Some plates slowly pull away from each other, some plates push toward each other, and some plates slide past each other. **According to the theory of plate tectonics, Earth's landmasses have changed position over time because they are part of plates that are slowly moving.**

Why Do Earth's Plates Move? Have you ever heated a pot of water and watched what happens? The liquid at the bottom gets hotter faster. The hotter liquid rises upward. At the surface it cools, and then hotter water moving upward pushes it aside. The same type of churning motion drives the movement of Earth's plates.

Underneath Earth's rigid plates is somewhat softer rock that moves similarly to boiling water. Scientists think that heat deep inside Earth causes material there to slowly rise upward. As more heated material rises, it pushes aside cooler material at the top of the layer. Eventually the cooler material sinks downward. The rising and sinking of material creates a slow-moving current beneath Earth's outer layer. It is this current that causes Earth's plates to move.

 **Reading Checkpoint** What causes Earth's plates to move?

225 Million Years Ago

Pangaea

Equator

180-200 Million Years Ago

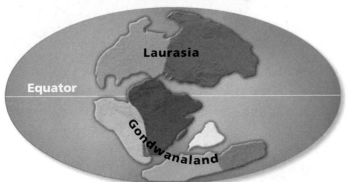

Laurasia

Equator

Gondwanaland

FIGURE 8
Motion of the Continents
The shapes and positions of Earth's continents have changed greatly over time and will continue to change in the future.
Interpreting Maps *Locate Australia on the map. How does its position change over time?*

Go Online
active art

For: Continental Drift activity
Visit: PHSchool.com
Web Code: cfp-1015

135 Million Years Ago

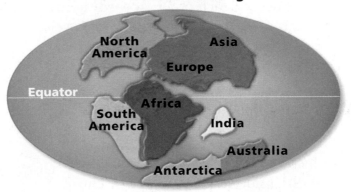

North America

Asia

Europe

Equator

Africa

South America

India

Australia

Antarctica

Present Day

North America

Europe

Asia

Africa

India

Equator

South America

Australia

Antarctica

Scientists have found that South America is moving 10 cm west per year. You can use this speed to predict how far the continent will move in 500 years.

Distance = Speed × Time

Distance = $\frac{10 \text{ cm}}{1 \text{ year}}$ × 500 years = 5,000 cm

South America will move 5,000 cm, or 50 m, in the next 500 years.

Plate Movement

Unless you have experienced an earthquake, you have probably never felt Earth's plates moving. Why not? After all, you live on one of Earth's plates. One reason may be that they move so slowly. **Some plates move at a rate of several centimeters each year. Others move only a few millimeters per year.**

Knowing the average speed of Earth's plates allows scientists to explain how Earth's surface has changed over time. It also helps them predict future changes. Figure 8 shows how scientists think the continents may have looked in the past.

Suppose you study the motion of a plate. You find that the plate moved a distance of 5 centimeters in one year. So, the speed of the plate is 5 cm/yr. You can use this speed to predict how far the plate will move in 1,000 years. Start by rearranging the speed formula to find the distance. Then calculate distance.

$$\text{Distance} = \text{Speed} \times \text{Time}$$

$$\text{Distance} = \frac{5 \text{ cm}}{1 \text{ yr}} \times 1{,}000 \text{ yr} = 5{,}000 \text{ cm}$$

In 1,000 years, the plate will move 5,000 centimeters. You could probably walk the same distance in 30 seconds!

 **Reading Checkpoint** Why are scientists interested in the average speed of Earth's plates?

Section 2 Assessment

Target Reading Strategy Previewing Visuals
Refer to your questions and answers about Figure 8 to help you answer Question 1 below.

Reviewing Key Concepts

1. a. **Defining** What theory explains the movement of pieces of Earth's surface?
   b. **Explaining** Why do Earth's plates move?
   c. **Interpreting Maps** Use the map in Figure 7 to determine which plate contains most of the United States.
2. a. **Reviewing** In general, at what speed do Earth's plates move?
   b. **Calculating** A plate moves at a speed of 45 mm/yr. How far will the plate move in 100 years?
   c. **Predicting** Figure 8 shows that North America and Europe are moving apart from each other. In your lifetime, how will this affect the time it takes to travel between the two continents?

Lab zone **At-Home Activity**

Fingernail Growth Have a family member measure in millimeters the length of the white part of one fingernail. Record the result and which finger you used. In exactly three weeks, again measure the white part of the same fingernail. Then calculate the speed, in millimeters per day, at which the fingernail grew. Discuss with your family member how your results compare with the typical speed of Earth's plates.

Acceleration

Reading Preview

Key Concepts
- What kind of motion does acceleration refer to?
- How is acceleration calculated?
- What graphs can be used to analyze the motion of an accelerating object?

Key Term
- acceleration

Target Reading Skill
Identifying Main Ideas As you read the What Is Acceleration? section, write the main idea in a graphic organizer like the one below. Then write three supporting details that give examples of the main idea.

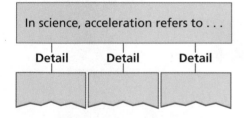

Main Idea

In science, acceleration refers to . . .

Detail	Detail	Detail

Lab zone Discover Activity

Will You Hurry Up?

1. Measure 10 meters in an open area. Mark the distance with masking tape.
2. Walk the 10 meters in such a way that you keep moving faster throughout the entire distance. Have a partner time you.
3. Repeat Step 2, walking the 10 meters in less time than you did before. Then try it again, this time walking the distance in twice the time as the first. Remember to keep speeding up throughout the entire 10 meters.

Think It Over
Inferring How is the change in your speed related to the time in which you walk the 10-meter course?

The pitcher throws. The ball speeds toward the batter. Off the bat it goes. It's going, going, gone! A home run!

Before landing, the ball went through several changes in motion. It sped up in the pitcher's hand, and lost speed as it traveled toward the batter. The ball stopped when it hit the bat, changed direction, sped up again, and eventually slowed down. Most examples of motion involve similar changes. In fact, rarely does any object's motion stay the same for very long.

What Is Acceleration?

Suppose you are a passenger in a car stopped at a red light. When the light changes to green, the driver steps on the accelerator. As a result, the car speeds up, or accelerates. In everyday language, *acceleration* means "the process of speeding up."

Acceleration has a more precise definition in science. Scientists define **acceleration** as the rate at which velocity changes. Recall that velocity describes both the speed and direction of an object. A change in velocity can involve a change in either speed or direction—or both. **In science, acceleration refers to increasing speed, decreasing speed, or changing direction.**

A softball ▲
accelerates
when it is
thrown.

▲ A softball
changes
direction when
it is hit.

A softball ▶
decelerates
when it is
caught.

FIGURE 9
Acceleration
A softball experiences acceleration
when it is thrown, caught, and
hit. **Classifying** *What change in
motion occurs in each example?*

Increasing Speed Whenever an object's speed increases, the object accelerates. A softball accelerates when the pitcher throws it, and again when a bat hits it. A car that begins to move from a stopped position or speeds up to pass another car is accelerating. People can accelerate too. For example, you accelerate when you coast down a hill on your bike.

Decreasing Speed Just as objects can speed up, they can also slow down. This change in speed is sometimes called deceleration, or negative acceleration. For example, a softball decelerates when it lands in a fielder's mitt. A car decelerates when it stops at a red light. A water skier decelerates when the boat stops pulling.

Changing Direction Even an object that is traveling at a constant speed can be accelerating. Recall that acceleration can be a change in direction as well as a change in speed. Therefore, a car accelerates as it follows a gentle curve in the road or changes lanes. Runners accelerate as they round the curve in a track. A softball accelerates when it changes direction as it is hit.

Many objects continuously change direction without changing speed. The simplest example of this type of motion is circular motion, or motion along a circular path. For example, the seats on a Ferris wheel accelerate because they move in a circle.

 **Reading Checkpoint** How can a car be accelerating if its speed is constant at 65 km/h?

0.0s 1.0s   2.0s   3.0s

0 m/s 8 m/s   16 m/s   24 m/s

FIGURE 10

Analyzing Acceleration
The speed of the airplane above increases by the same amount each second. **Interpreting Diagrams** *How does the distance change in each second?*

Calculating Acceleration

Acceleration describes the rate at which velocity changes. If an object is not changing direction, you can describe its acceleration as the rate at which its speed changes. **To determine the acceleration of an object moving in a straight line, you must calculate the change in speed per unit of time.** This is summarized by the following formula.

$$\text{Acceleration} = \frac{\text{Final speed} - \text{Initial speed}}{\text{Time}}$$

If speed is measured in meters per second (m/s) and time is measured in seconds, the SI unit of acceleration is meters per second per second, or m/s^2. Suppose speed is measured in kilometers per hour and time is measured in hours. Then the unit for acceleration is kilometers per hour per hour, or km/h^2.

To understand acceleration, imagine a small airplane moving down a runway. Figure 10 shows the airplane's motion after each of the first five seconds of its acceleration. To calculate the average acceleration of the airplane, you must first subtract the initial speed of 0 m/s from the final speed of 40 m/s. Then divide the change in speed by the time, 5 seconds.

$$\text{Acceleration} = \frac{40 \text{ m/s} - 0 \text{ m/s}}{5 \text{ s}}$$

$$\text{Acceleration} = 8 \text{ m/s}^2$$

The airplane accelerates at a rate of 8 m/s^2. This means that the airplane's speed increases by 8 m/s every second. Notice in Figure 10 that, after each second of travel, the airplane's speed is 8 m/s greater than it was the previous second.

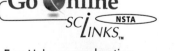

Go Online

SciLINKS NSTA

For: Links on acceleration
Visit: www.SciLinks.org
Web Code: scn-1313

 **Reading Checkpoint** **What must you know about an object moving in a straight line to calculate its acceleration?**

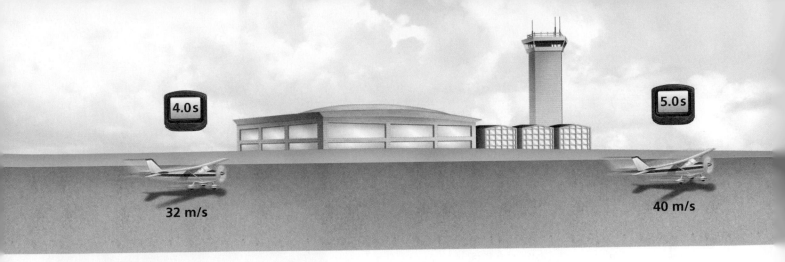

4.0 s

5.0 s

32 m/s

40 m/s

Math ▸ Sample Problem

Calculating Acceleration

As a roller coaster car starts down a slope, its speed is 4 m/s. But 3 seconds later, at the bottom, its speed is 22 m/s. What is its average acceleration?

1 **Read and Understand**
What information are you given?

> Initial speed = 4 m/s
> Final speed = 22 m/s
> Time = 3 s

2 **Plan and Solve**
What quantity are you trying to calculate?

> The average acceleration of the roller coaster car = ∎

What formula contains the given quantities and the unknown quantity?

> $$\text{Acceleration} = \frac{\text{Final speed} - \text{Initial speed}}{\text{Time}}$$

Perform the calculation.

> $$\text{Acceleration} = \frac{22 \text{ m/s} - 4 \text{ m/s}}{3 \text{ s}}$$
> $$\text{Acceleration} = \frac{18 \text{ m/s}}{3 \text{ s}}$$
> $$\text{Acceleration} = 6 \text{ m/s}^2$$

The roller coaster car's average acceleration is 6 m/s².

3 **Look Back and Check**
Does your answer make sense?

> The answer is reasonable. If the car's speed increases by 6 m/s each second, its speed will be 10 m/s after 1 second, 16 m/s after 2 seconds, and 22 m/s after 3 seconds.

Math ▸ Practice

1. **Calculating Acceleration** A falling raindrop accelerates from 10 m/s to 30 m/s in 2 seconds. What is the raindrop's average acceleration?

2. **Calculating Acceleration** A certain car can accelerate from rest to 27 m/s in 9 seconds. Find the car's average acceleration.

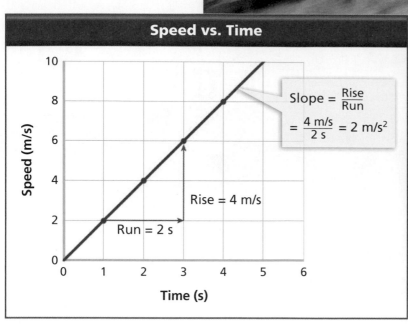

Speed vs. Time

Slope = $\dfrac{\text{Rise}}{\text{Run}}$

$= \dfrac{4 \text{ m/s}}{2 \text{ s}} = 2 \text{ m/s}^2$

Rise = 4 m/s

Run = 2 s

FIGURE 11

Speed-Versus-Time Graph
The slanted, straight line on this speed-versus-time graph tells you that the cyclist is accelerating at a constant rate. The slope of a speed-versus-time graph tells you the object's acceleration.

Predicting *How would the slope of the graph change if the cyclist were accelerating at a greater rate? At a lesser rate?*

Graphing Acceleration

Suppose you ride your bicycle down a long, steep hill. At the top of the hill your speed is 0 m/s. As you start down the hill, your speed increases. Each second, you move at a greater speed and travel a greater distance than the second before. During the five seconds it takes you to reach the bottom of the hill, you are an accelerating object. **You can use both a speed-versus-time graph and a distance-versus-time graph to analyze the motion of an accelerating object.**

Speed-Versus-Time Graph Figure 11 shows a speed-versus-time graph for your bicycle ride down the hill. What can you learn about your motion by analyzing this graph? First, since the line slants upward, the graph shows you that your speed was increasing. Next, since the line is straight, you can tell that your acceleration was constant. A slanted, straight line on a speed-versus-time graph means that the object is accelerating at a constant rate. You can find your acceleration by calculating the slope of the line. To calculate the slope, choose any two points on the line. Then, divide the rise by the run.

$$\text{Slope} = \frac{\text{Rise}}{\text{Run}} = \frac{8 \text{ m/s} - 4 \text{ m/s}}{4 \text{ s} - 2 \text{ s}} = \frac{4 \text{ m/s}}{2 \text{ s}}$$

$$\text{Slope} = 2 \text{ m/s}^2$$

During your bike ride, you accelerated down the hill at a constant rate of 2 m/s^2.

Distance-Versus-Time Graph You can represent the motion of an accelerating object with a distance-versus-time graph. Figure 12 shows a distance-versus-time graph for your bike ride. On this type of graph, a curved line means that the object is accelerating. The curved line in Figure 12 tells you that during each second, you traveled a greater distance than the second before. For example, you traveled a greater distance during the third second than you did during the first second.

The curved line in Figure 12 also tells you that during each second your speed is greater than the second before. Recall that the slope of a distance-versus-time graph is the speed of an object. From second to second, the slope of the line in Figure 12 gets steeper and steeper. Since the slope is increasing, you can conclude that the speed is also increasing. You are accelerating.

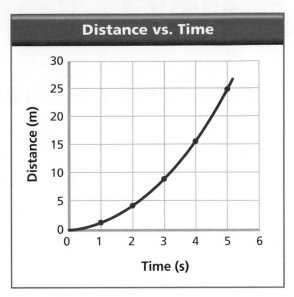

FIGURE 12
Distance-Versus-Time Graph
The curved line on this distance-versus-time graph tells you that the cyclist is accelerating.

 **Reading Checkpoint** What does a curved line on a distance-versus-time graph tell you?

Section 3 Assessment

Target Reading Skill Identifying Main Ideas Use information in your graphic organizer to answer Question 1 below.

Reviewing Key Concepts

1. a. Describing What are the three ways that an object can accelerate?
 b. Summarizing Describe how a baseball player accelerates as he runs around the bases after hitting a home run.
 c. Applying Concepts An ice skater glides around a rink at a constant speed of 2 m/s. Is the skater accelerating? Explain your answer.
2. a. Identifying What is the formula used to calculate the acceleration of an object moving in a straight line?
 b. Calculating A cyclist's speed changes from 0 m/s to 15 m/s in 10 seconds. What is the cyclist's average acceleration?

3. a. Naming What types of graphs can you use to analyze the acceleration of an object?
 b. Explaining How is an object moving if a slanted, straight line on a speed-versus-time graph represents its motion?
 c. Predicting What would a distance-versus-time graph look like for the moving object in part (b)?

Math Practice

4. Calculating Acceleration A downhill skier reaches the steepest part of a trail. Her speed increases from 9 m/s to 18 m/s in 3 seconds. What is her average acceleration?

5. Calculating Acceleration What is a race car's average acceleration if its speed changes from 0 m/s to 40 m/s in 4 seconds?

Stopping on a Dime

Problem

The school will put in a new basketball court in a small area between two buildings. Safety is an important consideration in the design of the court. What is the distance needed between an out-of-bounds line and a wall so that a player can stop before hitting the wall?

Skills Focus

calculating, interpreting data

Materials

- wooden meter stick • tape measure
- 2 stopwatches or watches with second hands

Procedure

PART 1 Reaction Time

1. Have your partner suspend a wooden meter stick, zero end down, between your thumb and index finger, as shown. Your thumb and index finger should be about 3 cm apart.

2. Your partner will drop the meter stick without giving you any warning. Try to grab it with your thumb and index finger.

Reaction Time			
Distance (cm)	Time (s)	Distance (cm)	Time (s)
15	0.175	25	0.226
16	0.181	26	0.230
17	0.186	27	0.235
18	0.192	28	0.239
19	0.197	29	0.243
20	0.202	30	0.247
21	0.207	31	0.252
22	0.212	32	0.256
23	0.217	33	0.260
24	0.221	34	0.263

3. Note the level at which you grabbed the meter stick and use the chart shown to determine your reaction time. Record the time in the class data table.

4. Reverse roles with your partner and repeat Steps 1–3.

PART 2 Stopping Distance

5. On the school field or in the gymnasium, mark off a distance of 25 m. **CAUTION:** *Be sure to remove any obstacles from the course.*

6. Have your partner time how long it takes you to run the course at full speed. After you pass the 25-m mark, come to a stop as quickly as possible and remain standing. You must not slow down before the mark.

7. Have your partner measure the distance from the 25-m mark to your final position. This is the distance you need to come to a complete stop. Enter your time and distance into the class data table.

8. Reverse roles with your partner. Enter your partner's time and distance into the class data table.

Class Data Table			
Student Name	Reaction Time (s)	Running Time (s)	Stopping Distance (m)

Analyze and Conclude

1. **Calculating** Calculate the average speed of the student who ran the 25-m course the fastest.

2. **Interpreting Data** Multiply the speed of the fastest student (calculated in Question 1) by the slowest reaction time listed in the class data table. Why would you be interested in this product?

3. **Interpreting Data** Add the distance calculated in Question 2 to the longest stopping distance in the class data table. What does this total distance represent?

4. **Drawing Conclusions** Explain why it is important to use the fastest speed, the slowest reaction time, and the longest stopping distance in your calculations.

5. **Controlling Variables** What other factors should you take into account to get results that apply to a real basketball court?

6. **Communicating** Suppose you calculate that the distance from the out-of-bounds line to the wall of the basketball court is too short for safety. Write a proposal to the school that describes the problem. In your proposal, suggest a strategy for making the court safer.

More to Explore

Visit a local playground and examine it from the viewpoint of safety. Use what you learned about stopping distance as one of your guidelines, but also try to identify other potentially unsafe conditions. Write a letter to the Department of Parks or to the officials of your town informing them of your findings.

Study Guide

The BIG Idea **Motion and Forces** The motion of an object can be described by its position, speed, direction, and acceleration.

① Describing and Measuring Motion

Key Concepts

- An object is in motion if it changes position relative to a reference point.
- If you know the distance an object travels in a certain amount of time, you can calculate the speed of the object.
- Speed $= \dfrac{\text{Distance}}{\text{Time}}$
- When you know both the speed and direction of an object's motion, you know the velocity of the object.
- You can show the motion of an object on a line graph in which you plot distance versus time.
- Slope $= \dfrac{\text{Rise}}{\text{Run}}$

Key Terms

motion
reference point
International System of Units
meter
speed
average speed
instantaneous speed
velocity
slope

② Slow Motion on Planet Earth

Key Concepts

- According to the theory of plate tectonics, Earth's landmasses have changed position over time because they are part of plates that are slowly moving.
- Some plates move at a rate of several centimeters each year. Others move only a few millimeters per year.

Key Terms

• plate • theory of plate tectonics

③ Acceleration

Key Concepts

- In science, acceleration refers to increasing speed, decreasing speed, or changing direction.
- To determine the acceleration of an object moving in a straight line, you must calculate the change in speed per unit of time.
- Acceleration $= \dfrac{\text{Final speed} - \text{Initial speed}}{\text{Time}}$
- You can use both a speed-versus-time graph and a distance-versus-time graph to analyze the motion of an accelerating object.

Key Term

acceleration

Review and Assessment

Go Online
PHSchool.com
For: Self-Assessment
Visit: PHSchool.com
Web Code: cga-3010

Organizing Information

Concept Mapping Copy the concept map about motion onto a separate sheet of paper. Then complete it and add a title. (For more information on Concept Mapping, see the Skills Handbook.)

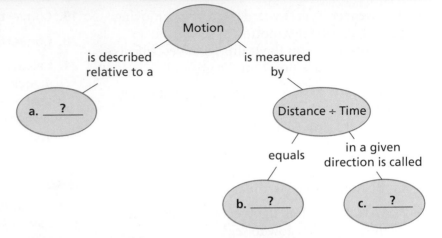

Reviewing Key Terms

Choose the letter of the best answer.

1. A change in position with respect to a reference point is
   a. acceleration.
   b. velocity.
   c. direction.
   d. motion.

2. You do not know an object's velocity until you know its
   a. speed.
   b. reference point.
   c. speed and direction.
   d. acceleration.

3. If you know a car travels 30 km in 20 minutes, you can find its
   a. acceleration.
   b. average speed.
   c. direction.
   d. instantaneous speed.

4. The parts of Earth's outer layer that move are called
   a. reference points.
   b. slopes.
   c. plates.
   d. boundaries.

5. The rate at which velocity changes is called
   a. acceleration. b. constant speed.
   c. average speed. d. velocity.

If the statement is true, write *true*. If it is false, change the underlined word or words to make the statement true.

6. The distance an object travels per unit of time is called <u>acceleration</u>.

7. The basic SI unit of length is the <u>meter</u>.

8. The theory of <u>plate tectonics</u> explains how Earth's landmasses have changed position over time.

9. The <u>slope</u> of a speed-versus-time graph represents acceleration.

10. Both <u>speed</u> and acceleration include the direction of an object's motion.

Writing in Science

News Report Two trucks have competed in a race. Write an article describing the race and who won. Explain the role the average speed of the trucks played. Tell how average speed can be calculated.

Motion
Video Preview
Video Field Trip
▶ Video Assessment

Review and Assessment

Checking Concepts

11. A passenger walks toward the rear of a moving train. Describe her motion as seen from a reference point on the train. Then describe it from a reference point on the ground.

12. Which has a greater speed, a heron that travels 600 m in 60 seconds or a duck that travels 60 m in 5 seconds? Explain.

13. You have a motion graph for an object that shows distance and time. How does the slope of the graph relate to the object's speed?

14. How can you tell if an object is moving when its motion is too slow to see?

15. An insect lands on a compact disc that is put into a player. If the insect spins with the disc, is the insect accelerating? Why or why not?

Thinking Critically

16. **Interpreting Graphs** The graph below shows the motion of a remote-control car. During which segment is the car moving the fastest? The slowest? How do you know?

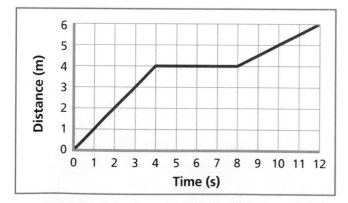

17. **Problem Solving** Two drivers make a 100-km trip. Driver 1 completes the trip in 2 hours. Driver 2 takes 3 hours but stops for an hour halfway. Which driver had a greater average speed? Explain.

18. **Applying Concepts** A family takes a car trip. They travel for an hour at 80 km/h and then for 2 hours at 40 km/h. Find their average speed during the trip.

Math Practice

19. **Converting Units** Convert 119 cm to meters.

20. **Converting Units** Convert 22.4 km to meters.

21. **Calculating Acceleration** During a slap shot, a hockey puck takes 0.5 second to reach the goal. It started from rest and reached a final speed of 35 m/s. What is the puck's average acceleration?

Applying Skills

Use the illustration of the motion of a ladybug to answer Questions 22–24.

22. **Measuring** Measure the distance from the starting line to line B, and from line B to the finish line. Measure to the nearest tenth of a centimeter.

23. **Calculating** Starting at rest, the ladybug accelerated to line B and then moved at a constant speed until it reached the finish line. If the ladybug took 2.5 seconds to move from line B to the finish line, calculate its constant speed during that time.

24. **Interpreting Data** The speed you calculated in Question 21 is also the speed the ladybug had at the end of its acceleration at line B. If it took 2 seconds for the ladybug to accelerate from the start line to line B, what is its average acceleration during that time?

Lab zone Chapter **Project**

Perfomance Assessment Organize your display cards so that they are easy to follow. Remember to put a title on each card stating the speed that you measured. Place the cards in order from the slowest speed to the fastest. Then display them to your class. Compare your results with those of other students.

Standardized Test Prep

Choose the letter of the best answer.

1. Members of the Fairview Track Club are running a 1.5 km race. What is the distance of the race in meters?
   A 0.15 m
   B 15 m
   C 150 m
   D 1,500 m

2. Your father is driving to the beach. He drives at one speed for two hours. He drives at a different speed for another two hours and a third speed for the final hour. How would you find his average speed for all five hours?
   F Divide the total driving time by the total distance.
   G Multiply the total driving time by the total distance.
   H Divide the total distance by the total driving time.
   J Subtract the total driving time from the total distance.

3. Two objects traveling at the same speed have different velocities if they
   A start at different times.
   B travel different distances.
   C have different masses.
   D move in different directions.

4. The graph below shows the distance versus time for a runner moving at a constant 200 m/min. What could the runner do to make the slope of the line rise?

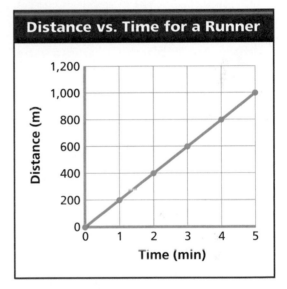

   F stop running
   G decrease speed
   H maintain the same speed
   J increase speed

5. An object used as a reference point to determine motion should be
   A accelerating.
   B stationary.
   C decelerating.
   D changing direction.

Constructed Response

6. Explain how speed, velocity, and acceleration are related.

The BIG Idea
Motion and Forces

Q **What causes an object's motion to change?**

Chapter Preview

❶ The Nature of Force
Discover Is the Force With You?
At-Home Activity House of Cards
Consumer Lab Sticky Sneakers

❷ Friction and Gravity
Discover Which Lands First?
Try This Spinning Plates
Skills Activity Calculating
Analyzing Data Free Fall

❸ Newton's First and Second Laws
Discover What Changes Motion?
Try This Around and Around

❹ Newton's Third Law
Discover How Pushy Is a Straw?
Try This Colliding Cars
Active Art Momentum
Skills Lab Forced to Accelerate

❺ Rockets and Satellites
Discover What Makes an Object Move in a Circle?
At-Home Activity Swing the Bucket

A golfer exerts a force on the golf ball. ▶

Forces
▶ Video Preview
Video Field Trip
Video Assessment

Lab zone™ Chapter **Project**

Newton Scooters

Newton's laws of motion describe the relationship between forces and motion. In this Chapter Project, you will use Newton's third law to design a vehicle that moves without the use of gravity or a power source such as electricity. How can you make an object move without pushing or pulling it?

Your Goal To design and build a vehicle that moves without an outside force acting on it

Your vehicle must

- move forward by pushing back on something
- not be powered by any form of electricity or use gravity in order to move
- travel a minimum distance of 1.5 meters
- be built following the safety guidelines in Appendix A

Plan It! Preview the chapter to find out about Newton's laws of motion. Determine factors that will affect the acceleration of your vehicle. Brainstorm possible designs for your vehicle, but be careful not to lock yourself into a single idea. Remember that a car with wheels is only one type of vehicle.

Think of ways to use household materials to build your vehicle. Draw a diagram of your proposed design and identify the force that will propel your vehicle. Have your teacher approve your design. Then build your vehicle and see if it works!

The Nature of Force

Reading Preview

Key Concepts
• How is a force described?
• How are unbalanced and balanced forces related to an object's motion?

Key Terms
• force
• newton
• net force
• unbalanced forces
• balanced forces

Target Reading Skill
Asking Questions Before you read, preview the red headings. In a graphic organizer like the one below, ask a *what* or *how* question for each heading. As you read, write the answers to your questions.

The Nature of Force

Question	Answer
What is a force?	A force is . . .

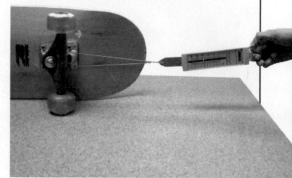

Lab zone Discover Activity

Is the Force With You?
1. Attach a spring scale to each end of a skateboard.
2. Gently pull on one spring scale with a force of 4 N, while your partner pulls on the other with the same force. Observe the motion of the skateboard.
3. Now try to keep your partner's spring scale reading at 2 N while you pull with a force of 4 N. Observe the motion of the skateboard.

Think It Over
Observing Describe the motion of the skateboard when you and your partner pulled with the same force. How was the motion of the skateboard affected when you pulled with more force than your partner?

A hard kick sends a soccer ball shooting down the field toward the goal. Just in time, the goalie leaps forward, stops the ball, and quickly kicks it in the opposite direction. In a soccer game, the ball is rarely still. Its motion is constantly changing. Why? What causes an object to start moving, stop moving, or change direction? The answer is force.

What Is a Force?

In science, the word *force* has a simple and specific meaning. A **force** is a push or a pull. When one object pushes or pulls another object, you say that the first object exerts a force on the second object. You exert a force on a computer key when you push it and on a chair when you pull it away from a table.

Like velocity and acceleration, a force is described by its strength and by the direction in which it acts. If you push on a door, you exert a force in a different direction than if you pull on the door.

The strength of a force is measured in the SI unit called the **newton** (N). This unit is named after the English scientist and mathematician Isaac Newton. You exert about one newton of force when you lift a small lemon.

The direction and strength of a force can be represented by an arrow. The arrow points in the direction of a force. The length of the arrow tells you the strength of a force—the longer the arrow, the greater the force.

 **Reading Checkpoint** What SI unit is used to measure the strength of a force?

Combining Forces

Often, more than a single force acts on an object at one time. The combination of all forces acting on an object is called the **net force.** The net force determines whether an object moves and also in which direction it moves.

When forces act in the same direction, the net force can be found by adding the strengths of the individual forces. In Figure 2, the lengths of the two arrows, which represent two forces, are added together to find the net force.

When forces act in opposite directions, they also combine to produce a net force. However, you must pay attention to the direction of each force. Adding a force acting in one direction to a force acting in the opposite direction is the same as adding a positive number to a negative number. So when two forces act in opposite directions, they combine by subtraction. The net force always acts in the direction of the greater force. If the opposing forces are of equal strength, there is no net force. There is no change in the object's motion,

FIGURE 2
Combining Forces
The strength and direction of the individual forces determine the net force. **Calculating** *How do you find the net force when two forces act in opposite directions?*

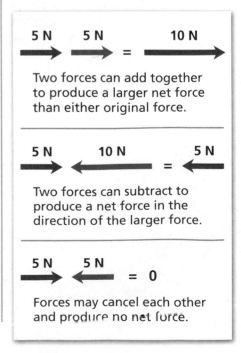

5 N   5 N   10 N
Two forces can add together to produce a larger net force than either original force.

5 N   10 N   5 N
Two forces can subtract to produce a net force in the direction of the larger force.

5 N   5 N   = 0
Forces may cancel each other and produce no net force.

Individual forces

Net force

Individual forces

Net force

Unbalanced Forces in the Same Direction
When two forces act in the same direction, the net force is the sum of the two individual forces. The box moves to the right.

Unbalanced Forces in the Opposite Direction
When two forces act in opposite directions, the net force is the difference between the two individual forces. The box moves to the right.

Unbalanced Forces Whenever there is a net force acting on an object, the forces are unbalanced. **Unbalanced forces** can cause an object to start moving, stop moving, or change direction. **Unbalanced forces acting on an object result in a net force and cause a change in the object's motion.**

Figure 3 shows two people exerting forces on a box. When they both push a box to the right, their individual forces add together to produce a net force in that direction. Since a net, or unbalanced, force acts on the box, the box moves to the right.

When the two people push the box in opposite directions, the net force on the box is the difference between their individual forces. Because the boy pushes with a greater force than the girl, their forces are unbalanced and a net force acts on the box to the right. As a result, the box moves to the right.

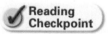 **Reading Checkpoint** What is the result of unbalanced forces acting on an object?

Balanced Forces When forces are exerted on an object, the object's motion does not always change. In an arm wrestling contest, each person exerts a force on the other's arm, but the two forces are exerted in opposite directions. Even though both people push hard, their arm positions may not change.

Equal forces acting on one object in opposite directions are called **balanced forces.** Each force is balanced by the other.

Go Online
SCiLINKS NSTA

For: Links on force
Visit: www.SciLinks.org
Web Code: scn-1321

Individual forces

No net force

Balanced Forces in Opposite Directions
When two equal forces act in opposite directions,
they cancel each other out. The box doesn't move.

FIGURE 3
Balanced and Unbalanced Forces
When the forces acting on an object are
unbalanced, a net force acts on the object.
The object will move. When balanced forces act
on an object, no net force acts on the object.
The object's motion remains unchanged.
Predicting *If both girls pushed the box on the
same side, would the motion of the box change?
Why or why not?*

**Balanced forces acting on an object do not change the
object's motion.** When equal forces are exerted in opposite
directions, there is no net force. In Figure 3, when two people
push on the box with equal force in opposite directions, the
forces balance each other. The box does not move.

Section 1 Assessment

🎯 **Target Reading Skill Asking Questions** Use
the answers to the questions you wrote about the
headings to help you answer the questions below.

Reviewing Key Concepts

1. a. **Defining** What is a force?
   b. **Explaining** How is a force described?
   c. **Interpreting Diagrams** In a diagram, one
   force arrow is longer than the other arrow.
   What can you tell about the forces?
2. a. **Reviewing** How can you find the net force
   if two forces act in opposite directions?
   b. **Comparing and Contrasting** How do
   balanced forces acting on an object affect
   its motion? How do unbalanced forces
   acting on an object affect its motion?

   c. **Calculating** You exert a force of 120 N on a
   desk. Your friend exerts a force of 150 N in
   the same direction. What net force do you
   and your friend exert on the desk?

Lab zone At-Home **Activity**

House of Cards Carefully set two playing
cards upright on a flat surface so that their top
edges lean on each other. The cards should be
able to stand by themselves. In terms of
balanced forces, explain to a family member
why the cards don't move. Then exert a force on
one of the cards. Explain to a family member the
role of unbalanced forces in what happens.

Sticky Sneakers

Problem

Friction is a force that acts in the opposite direction to motion. How does the amount of friction between a sneaker and a surface compare for different brands of sneakers?

Skills Focus

controlling variables, interpreting data

Materials

- three or more different brands of sneakers
- 2 spring scales, 5-N and 20-N, or force sensors
- mass set(s)
- tape
- 3 large paper clips
- balance

Procedure

1. Sneakers are designed to deal with various friction forces, including these:
   - starting friction, which is involved when you start from a stopped position
   - forward-stopping friction, which is involved when you come to a forward stop
   - sideways-stopping friction, which is involved when you come to a sideways stop

2. Prepare a data table in which you can record each type of friction for each sneaker.

3. Place each sneaker on a balance. Then put masses in each sneaker so that the total mass of the sneaker plus the masses is 1,000 g. Spread the masses out evenly inside the sneaker.

4. You will need to tape a paper clip to each sneaker and then attach a spring scale to the paper clip. (If you are using force sensors, see your teacher for instructions.) To measure
   - starting friction, attach the paper clip to the back of the sneaker
   - forward-stopping friction, attach the paper clip to the front of the sneaker
   - sideways-stopping friction, attach the paper clip to the side of the sneaker

Data Table			
Sneaker	Starting Friction (N)	Sideways-Stopping Friction (N)	Forward-Stopping Friction (N)
A			
B			

5. To measure starting friction, pull the sneaker backward until it starts to move. Use the 20-N spring scale first. If the reading is less than 5 N, use a 5-N scale. The force necessary to make the sneaker start moving is equal to the friction force. Record the starting friction force in your data table.

6. To measure either type of stopping friction, use the spring scale to pull each sneaker at a slow, constant speed. Record the stopping friction force in your data table.

7. Repeat Steps 4–6 for the remaining sneakers.

Analyze and Conclude

1. **Controlling Variables** What are the manipulated and responding variables in this experiment? Explain. (See the Skills Handbook to read about experimental variables.)

2. **Observing** Why is the reading on the spring scale equal to the friction force in each case?

3. **Interpreting Data** Which sneaker had the most starting friction? Which had the most forward-stopping friction? Which had the most sideways-stopping friction?

4. **Drawing Conclusions** Do you think that using a sneaker with a small amount of mass in it is a fair test of the friction of the sneakers? Why or why not? (*Hint*: Consider that sneakers are used with people's feet inside them.)

5. **Inferring** Why did you pull the sneaker at a slow speed to test for stopping friction? Why did you pull a sneaker that wasn't moving to test starting friction?

6. **Developing Hypotheses** Can you identify a relationship between the brand of sneaker and the amount of friction you observed? If so, describe the relationship. What do you observe that might cause one sneaker to grip the floor better than another?

7. **Communicating** Draw a diagram for an advertising brochure that shows the forces acting on the sneaker for each type of motion.

Design an Experiment

Wear a pair of your own sneakers. Start running and notice how you press against the floor with your sneaker. How do you think this affects the friction between the sneaker and the floor? Design an experiment that will test for this variable. *Obtain your teacher's permission before carrying out your investigation.*

Friction and Gravity

Reading Preview

Key Concepts
- What factors determine the strength of the friction force between two surfaces?
- What factors affect the gravitational force between two objects?
- Why do objects accelerate during free fall?

Key Terms
- friction • static friction
- sliding friction
- rolling friction • fluid friction
- gravity • mass • weight
- free fall • air resistance
- terminal velocity • projectile

🎯 Target Reading Skill
Comparing and Contrasting As you read, compare and contrast friction and gravity by completing a table like the one below.

	Friction	Gravity
Effect on motion	Opposes motion	
Depends on		
Measured in		

Lab zone Discover **Activity**

Which Lands First?
1. Stack three quarters. Wrap tape around the quarters to hold them tightly together. Place the stack of quarters next to a single quarter near the edge of a desk.
2. Put a ruler flat on the desk behind the coins. Line it up parallel to the edge of the desk and just touching the coins.
3. Keeping the ruler parallel to the edge of the desk, push the coins over the edge at the same time. Observe how long the coins take to land.

Think It Over
Predicting Did you see a difference in the time the coins took to fall? Use what you observed to predict whether a golf ball will fall more quickly than a table tennis ball. Will a pencil fall more quickly than a book? How can you test your predictions?

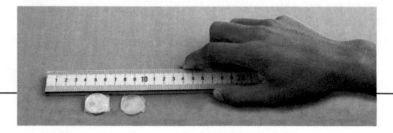

What happens when you jump on a sled on the side of a snow-covered hill? You can predict that the sled will slide down the hill. Now think about what happens at the bottom of the hill. Does the sled keep sliding? You can predict that the sled will slow down and stop.

Why does the sled's motion change on the side of the hill and then again at the bottom? In each case, unbalanced forces act on the sled. The force of gravity causes the sled to accelerate down the hill. The force of friction eventually causes the sled to stop. These two forces affect many motions on Earth.

◀ Friction and gravity both act on the sled.

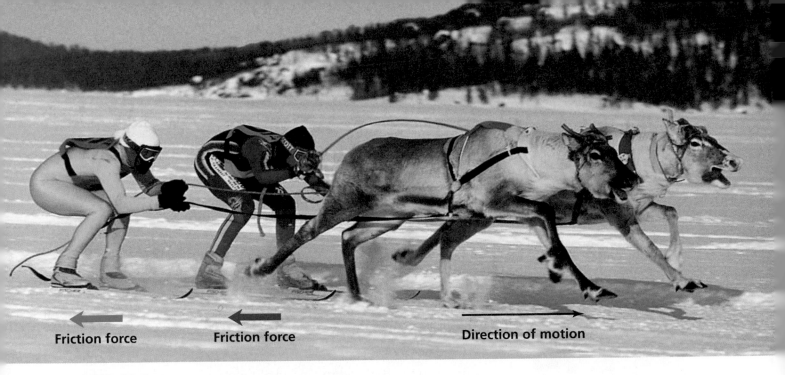

Friction force   Friction force   Direction of motion

FIGURE 4
Friction and Smooth Surfaces The smooth surfaces of
the skis make for a fast ride for these Finnish skiers.
Relating Diagrams and Photos *How does the direction
of friction compare to the direction of motion?*

Friction

When a sled moves across snow, the bottom of the sled rubs
against the surface of the snow. In the same way, the skin of a
firefighter's hands rubs against the polished metal pole during
the slide down the pole. The force that two surfaces exert on
each other when they rub against each other is called **friction.**

The Causes of Friction In general, smooth surfaces produce less friction than rough surfaces. **The strength of the
force of friction depends on two factors: how hard the
surfaces push together and the types of surfaces involved.**
The skiers in Figure 4 get a fast ride because there is very little
friction between their skis and the snow. The reindeer would
not be able to pull them easily over a rough surface such as
sand. Friction also increases if surfaces push hard against each
other. If you rub your hands together forcefully, there is more
friction than if you rub your hands together lightly.

A snow-packed surface or a metal firehouse pole may seem
quite smooth. But, as you can see in Figure 5, even the smoothest
objects have irregular, bumpy surfaces. When the irregularities
of one surface come into contact with those of another surface,
friction occurs. Friction acts in a direction opposite to the direction of the object's motion. Without friction, a moving object
might not stop until it strikes another object.

FIGURE 5
A Smooth Surface?
If you look at the polished surface
of an aluminum alloy under a
powerful microscope, you'll find
that it is actually quite rough.

Lab zone Try This **Activity**

Spinning Plates

You can compare rolling friction to sliding friction.

1. Stack two identical pie plates together. Try to spin the top plate.

2. Now separate the plates and fill the bottom of one pie plate loosely with marbles.

3. Place the second plate in the plate with marbles.

4. Try to spin the top plate again. Observe the results.

Drawing Conclusions What applications can you think of for the rolling friction modeled in this activity?

Go Online
SciLINKS NSTA

For: Links on friction
Visit: www.SciLinks.org
Web Code: scn-1322

Static Friction Four types of friction are shown in Figure 6. The friction that acts on objects that are not moving is called **static friction.** Because of static friction, you must use extra force to start the motion of stationary objects. For example, think about what happens when you try to push a heavy desk across a floor. If you push on the desk with a force less than the force of static friction between the desk and the floor, the desk will not move. To make the desk move, you must exert a force greater than the force of static friction. Once the desk is moving, there is no longer any static friction. However, there is another type of friction—sliding friction.

Sliding Friction Sliding friction occurs when two solid surfaces slide over each other. Sliding friction can be useful. For example, you can spread sand on an icy path to improve your footing. Ballet dancers apply a sticky powder to the soles of their ballet slippers so they won't slip on the dance floor. And when you stop a bicycle with hand brakes, rubber pads slide against the tire surfaces, causing the wheels to slow and eventually stop. On the other hand, sliding friction is a problem if you fall off your bike and skin your knee!

Rolling Friction When an object rolls across a surface, **rolling friction** occurs. Rolling friction is easier to overcome than sliding friction for similar materials. This type of friction is important to engineers who design certain products. For example, skates, skateboards, and bicycles need wheels that move freely. So engineers use ball bearings to reduce the friction between the wheels and the rest of the product. These ball bearings are small, smooth steel balls that reduce friction by rolling between moving parts.

Fluid Friction Fluids, such as water, oil, or air, are materials that flow easily. **Fluid friction** occurs when a solid object moves through a fluid. Like rolling friction, fluid friction is easier to overcome than sliding friction. This is why the parts of machines that must slide over each other are often bathed in oil. In this way, the solid parts move through the fluid instead of sliding against each other. When you ride a bike, fluid friction occurs between you and the air. Cyclists often wear streamlined helmets and specially designed clothing to reduce fluid friction.

 Reading Checkpoint **What are two ways in which friction can be useful?**

FIGURE 6
Types of Friction

Types of friction include static, sliding, rolling, and fluid friction. **Making Generalizations** *In what direction does friction act compared to an object's motion?*

Static Friction ▼
To make the sled move, the athlete first has to overcome the force of static friction. Static friction acts in the opposite direction to the intended motion.

Direction of motion   Sliding friction

Sliding Friction ▲
Once the sled is moving, it slides over the floor. Sliding friction acts between the sled and the floor in the opposite direction to the sled's motion.

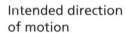

Intended direction of motion   Static friction

Rolling Friction ▼
Rolling friction occurs when an object rolls over a surface. For the skateboarder, rolling friction acts in the direction opposite to the skateboard's motion.

Direction of motion   Rolling friction

Fluid friction   Direction of motion

Fluid Friction ▲
When an object pushes fluid aside, friction occurs. The surfer must overcome the fluid friction of the water.

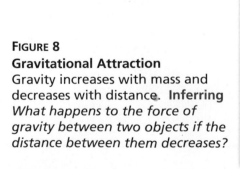

FIGURE 7
Gravity and Acceleration
Divers begin accelerating as soon as they leap from the platform.

Gravity

Would you be surprised if you let go of a pen you were holding and it did not fall? You are so used to objects falling that you may not have thought about why they fall. One person who thought about it was Isaac Newton. He concluded that a force acts to pull objects straight down toward the center of Earth. **Gravity** is a force that pulls objects toward each other.

Universal Gravitation Newton realized that gravity acts everywhere in the universe, not just on Earth. It is the force that makes an apple fall to the ground. It is the force that keeps the moon orbiting around Earth. It is the force that keeps all the planets in our solar system orbiting around the sun.

What Newton realized is now called the law of universal gravitation. The law of universal gravitation states that the force of gravity acts between all objects in the universe. This means that any two objects in the universe, without exception, attract each other. You are attracted not only to Earth but also to all the other objects around you. Earth and the objects around you are attracted to you as well. However, you do not notice the attraction among objects because these forces are small compared to the force of Earth's attraction.

Factors Affecting Gravity Two factors affect the gravitational attraction between objects: mass and distance. **Mass** is a measure of the amount of matter in an object. The SI unit of mass is the kilogram. One kilogram is the mass of about 400 modern pennies. Everything that has mass is made up of matter.

FIGURE 8
Gravitational Attraction
Gravity increases with mass and decreases with distance. **Inferring** *What happens to the force of gravity between two objects if the distance between them decreases?*

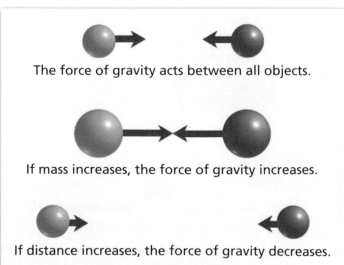

The force of gravity acts between all objects.

If mass increases, the force of gravity increases.

If distance increases, the force of gravity decreases.

The more mass an object has, the greater its gravitational force. Because the sun's mass is so great, it exerts a large gravitational force on the planets. That's one reason why the planets orbit the sun.

In addition to mass, gravitational force depends on the distance between the objects. The farther apart two objects are, the lesser the gravitational force between them. For a spacecraft traveling toward Mars, Earth's gravitational pull decreases as the spacecraft's distance from Earth increases. Eventually the gravitational pull of Mars becomes greater than Earth's, and the spacecraft is more attracted toward Mars.

Weight and Mass Mass is sometimes confused with weight. Mass is a measure of the amount of matter in an object; weight is a measure of the gravitational force exerted on an object. The force of gravity on a person or object at the surface of a planet is known as **weight.** So, when you step on a bathroom scale, you are determining the gravitational force Earth is exerting on you.

Weight varies with the strength of the gravitational force but mass does not. Suppose you weighed yourself on Earth to be 450 newtons. Then you traveled to the moon and weighed yourself again. You might be surprised to find out that you weigh only about 75 newtons—the weight of about 8 kilograms on Earth! You weigh less on the moon because the moon's mass is only a fraction of Earth's.

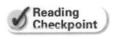

Reading Checkpoint **What is the difference between weight and mass?**

Lab zone Skills Activity

Calculating

You can determine the weight of an object if you measure its mass.

1. Estimate the weight of four objects. (*Hint:* A small lemon weighs about 1 N.)
2. Use a balance to find the mass of each object. If the measurements are not in kilograms, convert them to kilograms.
3. Multiply each mass by 9.8 m/s^2 to find the weight in newtons.

How close to actual values were your estimates?

FIGURE 9

Mass and Weight This astronaut jumps easily on the moon. **Comparing and Contrasting** *How do his mass and weight on the moon compare to his mass and weight on Earth?*

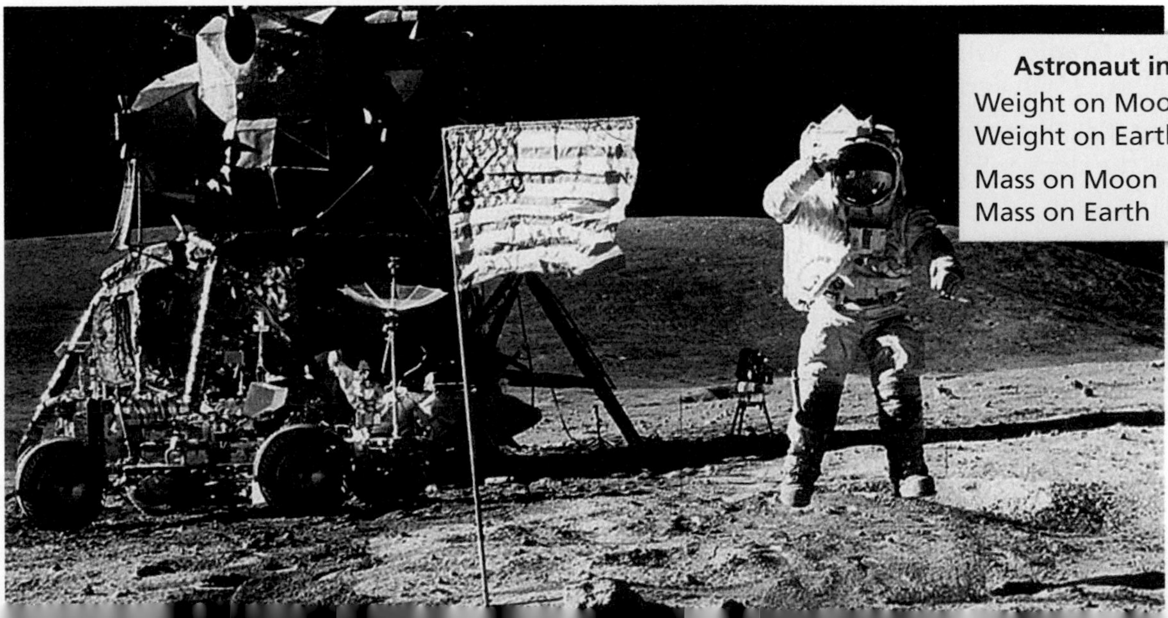

Astronaut in Spacesuit

Weight on Moon	=	270 N
Weight on Earth	=	1,617 N
Mass on Moon	=	165 kg
Mass on Earth	=	165 kg

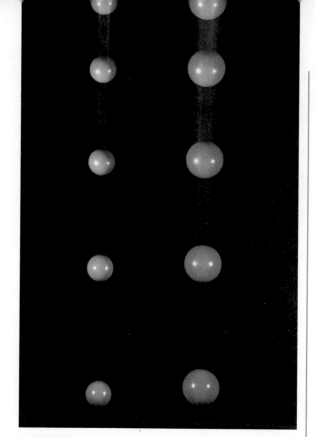

FIGURE 10
Free Fall
In the absence of air, two objects with different masses fall at exactly the same rate.

Gravity and Motion

On Earth, gravity is a downward force that affects all objects. When you hold a book, you exert a force that balances the force of gravity. When you let go of the book, gravity becomes an unbalanced force and the book falls.

Free Fall When the only force acting on an object is gravity, the object is said to be in **free fall**. An object in free fall is accelerating. Do you know why? **In free fall, the force of gravity is an unbalanced force, which causes an object to accelerate.**

How much do objects accelerate as they fall? Near the surface of Earth, the acceleration due to gravity is 9.8 m/s^2. This means that for every second an object is falling, its velocity increases by 9.8 m/s. For example, suppose an object is dropped from the top of a building. Its starting velocity is 0 m/s. After one second, its velocity has increased to 9.8 m/s. After two seconds, its velocity is 19.6 m/s (9.8 m/s + 9.8 m/s). The velocity continues to increase as the object falls.

While it may seem hard to believe at first, all objects in free fall accelerate at the same rate regardless of their masses. The two falling objects in Figure 10 demonstrate this principle.

Math Analyzing Data

Free Fall

Use the graph to answer the following questions.

1. **Interpreting Graphs** What variable is on the horizontal axis? The vertical axis?

2. **Calculating** Calculate the slope of the graph. What does the slope tell you about the object's motion?

3. **Predicting** What will be the speed of the object at 6 seconds?

4. **Drawing Conclusions** Suppose another object of the same size but with a greater mass was dropped instead. How would the speed values change?

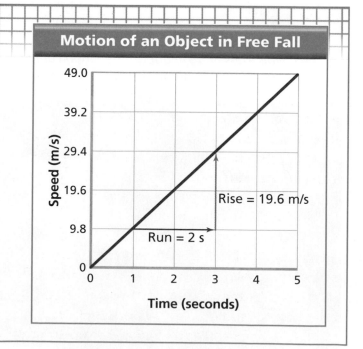

Motion of an Object in Free Fall

Rise = 19.6 m/s
Run = 2 s

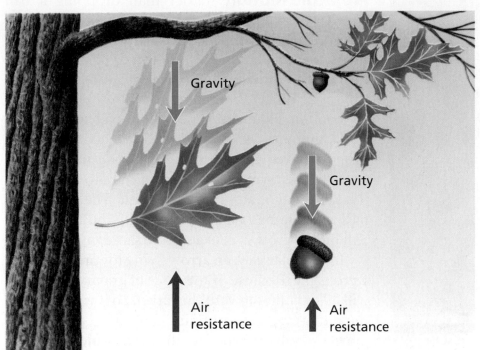

Air Resistance
Falling objects with a greater
surface area experience more air
resistance. If the leaf and the acorn
fall from the tree at the same time,
the acorn will hit first. **Comparing
and Contrasting** *If the objects fall
in a vacuum, which one will hit
first? Why?*

Air Resistance Despite the fact that all objects are supposed
to fall at the same rate, you know that this is not always the case.
For example, an oak leaf flutters slowly to the ground, while an
acorn drops straight down. Objects falling through air experience a type of fluid friction called **air resistance.** Remember that
friction is in the direction opposite to motion, so air resistance is
an upward force exerted on falling objects. Air resistance is not
the same for all objects. Falling objects with a greater surface area
experience more air resistance. That is why a leaf falls more
slowly than an acorn. In a vacuum, where there is no air, all
objects fall with exactly the same rate of acceleration.

You can see the effect of air resistance if you drop a flat
piece of paper and a crumpled piece of paper at the same time.
Since the flat paper has a greater surface area, it experiences
greater air resistance and falls more slowly. In a vacuum, both
pieces of paper would fall at the same rate.

Air resistance increases with velocity. As a falling object
speeds up, the force of air resistance becomes greater and greater.
Eventually, a falling object will fall fast enough that the upward
force of air resistance becomes equal to the downward force of
gravity acting on the object. At this point the forces on the object
are balanced. Remember that when forces are balanced, there is
no acceleration. The object continues to fall, but its velocity
remains constant. The greatest velocity a falling object reaches is
called its **terminal velocity.** Terminal velocity is reached when
the force of air resistance equals the weight of the object.

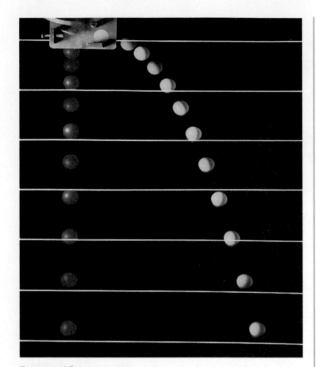

FIGURE 12
Projectile Motion
One ball is dropped vertically and a second ball is thrown horizontally at the same time.
Making Generalizations *Does the horizontal velocity of the ball affect how fast it falls?*

Projectile Motion Rather than dropping a ball straight down, what happens if you throw it horizontally? An object that is thrown is called a **projectile** (pruh JEK tul). Will a projectile that is thrown horizontally land on the ground at the same time as an object that is dropped?

Look at Figure 12. The yellow ball was given a horizontal push at the same time as the red ball was dropped. Even though the yellow ball moves horizontally, the force of gravity continues to act on it in the same way it acts on the red ball. The yellow ball falls at the same rate as the red ball. Thus, both balls will hit the ground at exactly the same time.

In a similar way, an arrow flying toward a target is a projectile. Because of the force of gravity, the arrow will fall as it flies toward the target. So if you try to hit the bull's-eye, you must aim above it to account for gravity's pull. When you throw a projectile at an upward angle, the force of gravity reduces its vertical velocity. Eventually, the upward motion of the projectile will stop, and gravity will pull it back toward the ground. From this point, the projectile will fall at the same rate as any dropped object.

 **Reading Checkpoint** **How does gravity affect objects that are moving horizontally?**

Section 2 Assessment

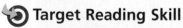 **Target Reading Skill**

Comparing and Contrasting Use the information in your table about friction and gravity to help you answer the questions below.

Reviewing Key Concepts

1. a. **Listing** What are the four types of friction?
   b. **Summarizing** What factors affect the friction force between two surfaces?
   c. **Classifying** What types of friction occur when you ride a bike through a puddle?
2. a. **Identifying** What is the law of universal gravitation?
   b. **Explaining** How do mass and distance affect the gravitational attraction between objects?
   c. **Predicting** How would your weight change on the surface of an Earth-sized planet whose mass was greater than Earth's? Why?

3. a. **Reviewing** Why does an object accelerate when it falls toward Earth's surface?
   b. **Describing** How does the mass of an object affect its acceleration during free fall?
   c. **Applying Concepts** What force changes when a sky diver's parachute opens? What force stays the same?

Writing in Science

Cause-and-Effect Paragraph Suppose Earth's gravitational force were decreased by half. How would this change affect a game of basketball? Write a paragraph explaining how the motion of the players and the ball would be different.

Newton's First and Second Laws

Reading Preview

Key Concepts
- What is Newton's first law of motion?
- What is Newton's second law of motion?

Key Term
- inertia

Target Reading Skill
Outlining As you read, make an outline about Newton's first and second laws. Use the red headings for the main topics and the blue headings for the subtopics.

Newton's First and Second Laws
I. The First Law of Motion
A. Inertia
B.
II. The Second Law of Motion
A.

Isaac Newton ▼

Lab zone Discover **Activity**

What Changes Motion?

1. Stack several metal washers on top of a toy car.
2. Place a heavy book on the floor near the car.
3. Predict what will happen to both the car and the washers if you roll the car into the book. Test your prediction.

Think It Over
Observing What happened to the car when it hit the book? What happened to the washers? What might be the reason for any difference between the motions of the car and the washers?

How and why objects move as they do has fascinated scientists for thousands of years. In the early 1600s, the Italian astronomer Galileo Galilei suggested that, once an object is in motion, no force is needed to keep it moving. Force is needed only to change the motion of an object. Galileo's ideas paved the way for Isaac Newton. Newton proposed the three basic laws of motion in the late 1600s.

The First Law of Motion

Newton's first law restates Galileo's ideas about force and motion. **Newton's first law of motion states that an object at rest will remain at rest, and an object moving at a constant velocity will continue moving at a constant velocity, unless it is acted upon by an unbalanced force.**

If an object is not moving, it will not move until a force acts on it. Clothes on the floor of your room, for example, will stay there unless you pick them up. If an object is already moving, it will continue to move at a constant velocity until a force acts to change either its speed or direction. For example, a tennis ball flies through the air once you hit it with a racket. If your friend doesn't hit the ball back, the forces of gravity and friction will eventually stop the ball. On Earth, gravity and friction are unbalanced forces that often change an object's motion.

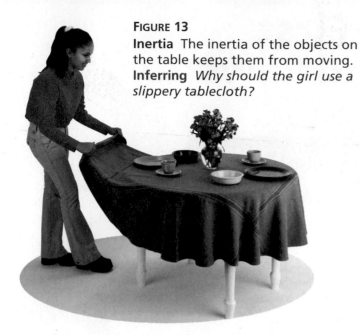

FIGURE 13
Inertia The inertia of the objects on the table keeps them from moving.
Inferring *Why should the girl use a slippery tablecloth?*

Inertia Whether an object is moving or not, it resists any change to its motion. Galileo's concept of the resistance to a change in motion is called inertia. **Inertia** (in UR shuh) is the tendency of an object to resist a change in motion. Newton's first law of motion is also called the law of inertia.

Inertia explains many common events, such as why you move forward in your seat when a car stops suddenly. When the car stops, inertia keeps you moving forward. A force, such as the pull of a seat belt, is required to change your motion.

Inertia Depends on Mass Some objects have more inertia than other objects. For example, suppose you needed to move an empty aquarium and an aquarium full of water. Obviously, the full aquarium is harder to move than the empty one, because it has more mass. The greater the mass of an object is, the greater its inertia, and the greater the force required to change its motion. The full aquarium is more difficult to move because it has more inertia than the empty aquarium.

 **Reading Checkpoint** How is mass related to inertia?

The Second Law of Motion

Suppose you are baby-sitting two children who love wagon rides. Their favorite part is when you accelerate quickly. When you get tired and sit in the wagon, one of the children pulls you. He soon finds he cannot accelerate the wagon nearly as fast as you can. How is the wagon's acceleration related to the force pulling it? How is the acceleration related to the wagon's mass?

Lab zone Try This **Activity**

Around and Around

An object moving in a circle has inertia.

1. Tape one end of a length of thread (about 1 m) to a table tennis ball.
2. Suspend the ball in front of you and swing it in a horizontal circle, keeping it 2–3 cm above the floor.
3. Let go of the thread and observe the direction in which the ball rolls.
4. Repeat this several times, letting go of the thread at different points.

Inferring At what point do you need to let go of the thread if you want the ball to roll directly away from you? Toward you? Draw a diagram as part of your answer.

Determining Acceleration According to Newton's second law of motion, acceleration depends on the object's mass and on the net force acting on the object. This relationship can be written as an equation.

$$\text{Acceleration} = \frac{\text{Net force}}{\text{Mass}}$$

Acceleration is measured in meters per second per second (m/s^2), and mass is measured in kilograms (kg). According to Newton's second law, then, force is measured in kilograms times meters per second per second ($kg \cdot m/s^2$). The short form for this unit of force is the newton (N). Recall that a newton is the SI unit of force. You can think of 1 newton as the force required to give a 1-kg mass an acceleration of $1 \ m/s^2$.

Go Online
PHSchool.com

For: More on Newton's laws
Visit: PHSchool.com
Web Code: cgd-3023

Math Sample Problem

Calculating Force

A speedboat pulls a 55-kg water-skier. The force causes the skier to accelerate at $2.0 \ m/s^2$. Calculate the net force that causes this acceleration.

1 Read and Understand
What information are you given?
> Mass of the water-skier (m) = **55 kg**
> Acceleration of the water-skier (a) = **2.0 m/s²**

2 Plan and Solve
What quantity are you trying to calculate?
> The net force (F_{net}) = ■

What formula contains the given quantities and the unknown quantity?

$$a = \frac{F_{net}}{m} \quad \text{or} \quad F_{net} = m \times a$$

Perform the calculation.
> $F_{net} = m \times a = $ **55 kg × 2.0 m/s²**
> $F = $ **110 kg · m/s²**
> $F = $ **110 N**

3 Look Back and Check
Does your answer make sense?
> A net force of 110 N is required to accelerate the water-skier. This may not seem like enough force, but it does not include the force of the speedboat's pull that overcomes friction.

Math Practice

1. **Calculating Force** What is the net force on a 1,000-kg object accelerating at $3 \ m/s^2$?
2. **Calculating Force** What net force is needed to accelerate a 25-kg cart at $14 \ m/s^2$?

FIGURE 14
Force and Mass
The force of the boy's pull and the mass of the wagon determine the wagon's acceleration.

Changes in Force and Mass How can you increase the acceleration of the wagon? Look again at the equation. One way to increase acceleration is by changing the force. If the mass is constant, acceleration and force change in the same way. So to increase the acceleration of the wagon, you can increase the force used to pull it.

Another way to increase acceleration is to change the mass. According to the equation, acceleration and mass change in opposite ways. If the force is constant, an increase in mass causes a decrease in acceleration. The opposite is also true: A decrease in mass causes an increase in acceleration with a constant force. To increase the acceleration of the wagon, you can decrease its mass. So, instead of you, the children should ride in the wagon.

 **Reading Checkpoint** **What are two ways to increase the acceleration of an object?**

Section 3 Assessment

Target Reading Skill Outlining Use the information in your outline about Newton's first and second laws of motion to help you answer the questions below.

Reviewing Key Concepts

1. a. **Reviewing** What does Newton's first law of motion state?
   b. **Explaining** Why is Newton's first law of motion sometimes called the law of inertia?
   c. **Inferring** Use what you know about inertia to explain why you feel pressed back into the seat of a car when it accelerates.
2. a. **Defining** State Newton's second law of motion in your own words.
   b. **Problem Solving** How could you keep an object's acceleration the same if the force acting on the object were doubled?

c. **Applying Concepts** Using what you know about Newton's second law, explain why a car with a large mass might use more fuel than a car with a smaller mass. Assume both cars drive the same distance.

Math Practice

3. **Calculating Force** Find the force it would take to accelerate an 800-kg car at a rate of 5 m/s^2.
4. **Calculating Force** What is the net force acting on a 0.15-kg hockey puck accelerating at a rate of 12 m/s^2?

Newton's Third Law

Reading Preview

Key Concepts
- What is Newton's third law of motion?
- How can you determine the momentum of an object?
- What is the law of conservation of momentum?

Key Terms
- momentum
- law of conservation of momentum

🎯 Target Reading Skill

Previewing Visuals Before you read, preview Figure 18. Then write two questions that you have about the diagram in a graphic organizer like the one below. As you read, answer your questions.

Conservation of Momentum

Q.	What happens when two moving objects collide?
A.	
Q.	

How Pushy Is a Straw?

1. Stretch a rubber band around the middle of the cover of a medium-size hardcover book.
2. Place four marbles in a small square on a table. Place the book on the marbles so that the cover with the rubber band is on top.
3. Hold the book steady by placing one index finger on the binding. Then, as shown, push a straw against the rubber band with your other index finger.
4. Push the straw until the rubber band stretches about 10 cm. Then let go of both the book and the straw at the same time.

Think It Over

Developing Hypotheses What did you observe about the motion of the book and the straw? Write a hypothesis to explain what happened in terms of the forces on the book and the straw.

Have you ever tried to teach a friend how to roller-skate? It's hard if you are both wearing skates. When your friend pushes against you to get started, you move too. And when your friend runs into you to stop, you both end up moving! To understand these movements you need to know Newton's third law of motion and the law of conservation of momentum.

Newton's Third Law of Motion

Newton proposed that whenever one object exerts a force on a second object, the second object exerts a force back on the first object. The force exerted by the second object is equal in strength and opposite in direction to the first force. Think of one force as the "action" and the other force as the "reaction." **Newton's third law of motion states that if one object exerts a force on another object, then the second object exerts a force of equal strength in the opposite direction on the first object.** Another way to state Newton's third law is that for every action there is an equal but opposite reaction.

When the gymnast does a flip, he pushes down on the vaulting horse. The reaction force of the vaulting horse pushes him up to complete the flip.

Action force

Reaction force

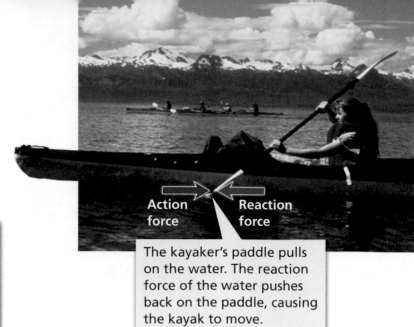

Action force   Reaction force

The kayaker's paddle pulls on the water. The reaction force of the water pushes back on the paddle, causing the kayak to move.

When the dog leaps, it pushes down on the ground. The reaction force of the ground pushes the dog into the air.

Action force

Reaction force

FIGURE 15
Action-Reaction Pairs
Action-reaction pairs explain how a gymnast can flip over a vaulting horse, how a kayaker can move through the water, and how a dog can leap off the ground. *Observing Name some other action-reaction pairs that you have observed.*

Action-Reaction Pairs You're probably familiar with many examples of Newton's third law. Pairs of action and reaction forces are all around you. When you jump, you push on the ground with your feet. This is an action force. The ground pushes back on your feet with an equal and opposite force. This is the reaction force. You move upward when you jump because the ground is pushing you! In a similar way, a kayaker moves forward by exerting an action force on the water with a paddle. The water pushes back on the paddle with an equal reaction force that propels the kayak forward.

Now you can understand what happens when you teach your friend to roller-skate. Your friend exerts an action force when he pushes against you to start. You exert a reaction force in the opposite direction. As a result, both of you move in opposite directions.

Detecting Motion Can you always detect motion when paired forces are in action? The answer is no. For example, when Earth's gravity pulls on an object, you cannot detect Earth's equal and opposite reaction. Suppose you drop your pencil. Gravity pulls the pencil downward. At the same time, the pencil pulls Earth upward with an equal and opposite reaction force. You don't see Earth accelerate toward the pencil because Earth's inertia is so great that its acceleration is too small to notice.

Do Action-Reaction Forces Cancel? Earlier you learned that if two equal forces act in opposite directions on an object, the forces are balanced. Because the two forces add up to zero, they cancel each other out and produce no change in motion. Why then don't the action and reaction forces in Newton's third law of motion cancel out as well? After all, they are equal and opposite.

The action and reaction forces do not cancel out because they are acting on different objects. Look at the volleyball player on the left in Figure 16. She exerts an upward action force on the ball. In return, the ball exerts an equal but opposite downward reaction force back on her wrists. The action and reaction forces act on different objects.

On the other hand, the volleyball players on the right are both exerting a force on the *same* object—the volleyball. When they hit the ball from opposite directions, each of their hands exerts a force on the ball equal in strength but opposite in direction. The forces on the volleyball are balanced and the ball does not move either to the left or to the right.

 Reading Checkpoint) **Why don't action and reaction forces cancel each other?**

Force on wrists

Force on ball

FIGURE 16
Action-Reaction Forces
In the photo on the left, the player's wrists exert the action force. In the photo below, the ball exerts reaction forces on both players.
Interpreting Diagrams *In the photo below, which forces cancel each other out? What force is not cancelled? What will happen to the ball?*

Forces on hands

Force on ball

Force on ball

Momentum

All moving objects have what Newton called a "quantity of motion." What is this quantity of motion? Today we call it momentum. **Momentum** (moh MEN tum) is a characteristic of a moving object that is related to the mass and the velocity of the object. **The momentum of a moving object can be determined by multiplying the object's mass and velocity.**

> **Momentum = Mass × Velocity**

Since mass is measured in kilograms and velocity is measured in meters per second, the unit for momentum is kilogram-meters per second (kg·m/s). Like velocity, acceleration, and force, momentum is described by its direction as well as its quantity. The momentum of an object is in the same direction as its velocity.

Math Sample Problem

Calculating Momentum

Which has more momentum: a 3.0-kg sledgehammer swung at 1.5 m/s, or a 4.0-kg sledgehammer swung at 0.9 m/s?

1 Read and Understand
What information are you given?
> Mass of smaller sledgehammer = **3.0 kg**
> Velocity of smaller sledgehammer = **1.5 m/s**
> Mass of larger sledgehammer = **4.0 kg**
> Velocity of larger sledgehammer = **0.9 m/s**

2 Plan and Solve
What quantities are you trying to calculate?
> The momentum of each sledgehammer = ■

What formula contains the given quantities and the unknown quantity?
> Momentum = Mass × Velocity

Perform the calculations.
> Smaller sledgehammer: 3.0 kg × 1.5 m/s = 4.5 kg·m/s
> Larger sledgehammer: 4.0 kg × 0.9 m/s = 3.6 kg·m/s

3 Look Back and Check
Does your answer make sense?
> The 3.0-kg hammer has more momentum than the 4.0-kg one. This answer makes sense because it is swung at a greater velocity.

Math Practice

1. **Calculating Momentum**
   A golf ball travels at 16 m/s, while a baseball moves at 7 m/s. The mass of the golf ball is 0.045 kg and the mass of the baseball is 0.14 kg. Which has greater momentum?

2. **Calculating Momentum**
   What is the momentum of a bird with a mass of 0.018 kg flying at 15 m/s?

FIGURE 17
Momentum
An object's momentum depends on velocity and mass.
Problem Solving *If both dogs have the same velocity, which one has the greater momentum?*

The more momentum a moving object has, the harder it is to stop. The mass of an object affects the amount of momentum the object has. For example, you can catch a baseball moving at 20 m/s, but you cannot stop a car moving at the same speed. The car has more momentum because it has a greater mass. The velocity of an object also affects the amount of momentum an object has. For example, an arrow shot from a bow has a large momentum because, although it has a small mass, it travels at a high velocity.

Reading Checkpoint What must you know to determine an object's momentum?

Conservation of Momentum

In everyday language, conservation means saving resources. You might conserve water or fossil fuels, for example. The word *conservation* has a more specific meaning in physical science. In physical science, conservation refers to the conditions before and after some event. An amount that is conserved is the same amount after an event as it was before.

The total amount of momentum objects have is conserved when they collide. Momentum may be transferred from one object to another, but none is lost. This fact is called the law of conservation of momentum.

The **law of conservation of momentum** states that, in the absence of outside forces, the total momentum of objects that interact does not change. The amount of momentum is the same before and after they interact. **The total momentum of any group of objects remains the same, or is conserved, unless outside forces act on the objects.** Friction is an example of an outside force.

FIGURE 18
Conservation of Momentum

In the absence of friction, momentum is conserved when two train cars collide. **Interpreting Diagrams** *In which diagram is all of the momentum transferred from the blue car to the green car?*

Ⓐ Two Moving Objects

Before

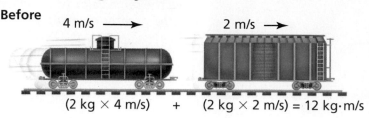

4 m/s →   2 m/s →

(2 kg × 4 m/s) + (2 kg × 2 m/s) = 12 kg·m/s

Before the collision, the blue car moves faster than the green car. Afterward, the green car moves faster. The total momentum stays the same.

After

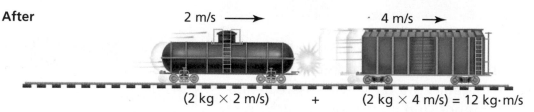

2 m/s →   4 m/s →

(2 kg × 2 m/s) + (2 kg × 4 m/s) = 12 kg·m/s

Ⓑ One Moving Object

When the green car is at rest before the collision, all of the blue car's momentum is transferred to it. Momentum is conserved.

Before

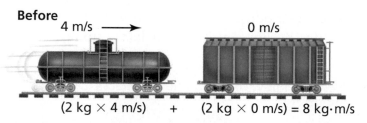

4 m/s →   0 m/s

(2 kg × 4 m/s) + (2 kg × 0 m/s) = 8 kg·m/s

After

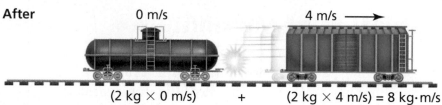

0 m/s   4 m/s →

(2 kg × 0 m/s) + (2 kg × 4 m/s) = 8 kg·m/s

Ⓒ Two Connected Objects

Before

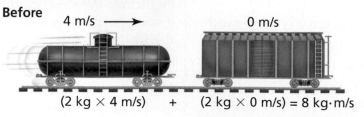

4 m/s →   0 m/s

(2 kg × 4 m/s) + (2 kg × 0 m/s) = 8 kg·m/s

If the two cars couple together, momentum is still conserved. Together, the cars move slower than the blue car did before the collision.

After

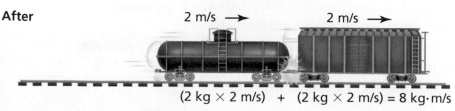

2 m/s →   2 m/s →

(2 kg × 2 m/s) + (2 kg × 2 m/s) = 8 kg·m/s

Collisions With Two Moving Objects In Figure 18A, a train car travels at 4 m/s down the same track as another train car traveling at only 2 m/s. The two train cars have equal masses. The blue car catches up with the green car and bumps into it. During the collision, the speed of each car changes. The blue car slows down to 2 m/s, and the green car speeds up to 4 m/s. Momentum is conserved—the momentum of one train car decreases while the momentum of the other increases.

Collisions With One Moving Object In Figure 18B, the blue car travels at 4 m/s but the green car is not moving. Eventually the blue car hits the green car. After the collision, the blue car is no longer moving, but the green car travels at 4 m/s. Even though the situation has changed, momentum is conserved. All of the momentum has been transferred from the blue car to the green car.

Collisions With Connected Objects Suppose that, instead of bouncing off each other, the two train cars couple together when they hit. Is momentum still conserved in Figure 18C? After the collision, the coupled train cars make one object with twice the mass. The velocity of the coupled trains is 2 m/s—half the initial velocity of the blue car. Since the mass is doubled and the velocity is divided in half, the total momentum remains the same.

 **Reading Checkpoint** What happens to the momentum of two objects after they collide?

Section 4 Assessment

⟳ **Target Reading Skill Previewing Visuals** Refer to your questions and answers about Figure 18 to help you answer Question 3 below.

Reviewing Key Concepts

1. a. **Reviewing** State Newton's third law of motion.
   b. **Summarizing** According to Newton's third law of motion, how are action and reaction forces related?
   c. **Applying Concepts** What would happen if you tried to catch a ball when you were standing on roller skates?
2. a. **Defining** What is momentum?
   b. **Predicting** What is the momentum of a parked car?
   c. **Relating Cause and Effect** Why is it important for drivers to allow more distance between their cars when they travel at faster speeds?

3. a. **Identifying** What is conservation of momentum?
   b. **Inferring** The total momentum of two marbles before a collision is 0.06 kg·m/s. No outside forces act on the marbles. What is the total momentum of the marbles after the collision?

Math ▸ Practice

4. **Calculating Momentum** What is the momentum of a 920-kg car moving at a speed of 25 m/s?
5. **Calculating Momentum** Which has more momentum: a 250-kg dolphin swimming at 4 m/s, or a 350-kg manatee swimming at 2 m/s?

Forced to Accelerate

Problem

How is the acceleration of a skateboard related to the force that is pulling it?

Skills Focus

calculating, graphing, interpreting data

Materials

- skateboard   • meter stick   • string
- stopwatch   • masking tape
- spring scale, 5-N
- several bricks or other large mass(es)

Procedure

1. Attach a loop of string to a skateboard. Place the bricks on the skateboard.

2. Using masking tape, mark off a one-meter distance on a level floor. Label one end "Start" and the other "Finish."

3. Attach a spring scale to the loop of string. Pull it so that you maintain a force of 2.0 N. Be sure to pull with the scale straight out in front. Practice applying a steady force to the skateboard as it moves.

4. Copy the data table into your notebook.

5. Find the smallest force needed to pull the skateboard at a slow, constant speed. Do not accelerate the skateboard. Record this force on the first line of the table.

6. Add 0.5 N to the force in Step 5. This will be enough to accelerate the skateboard. Record this force on the second line of the table.

7. Have one of your partners hold the front edge of the skateboard at the starting line. Then pull on the spring scale with the force you found in Step 6.

8. When your partner says "Go" and releases the skateboard, maintain a constant force until the skateboard reaches the finish line. A third partner should time how long it takes the skateboard to go from start to finish. Record the time in the column labeled Trial 1.

9. Repeat Steps 7 and 8 twice more. Record your results in the columns labeled Trial 2 and Trial 3.

10. Repeat Steps 7, 8, and 9 using a force 1.0 N greater than the force you found in Step 5.

11. Repeat Steps 7, 8, and 9 twice more. Use forces that are 1.5 N and 2.0 N greater than the force you found in Step 5.

Data Table							
Force (N)	Trial 1 Time (s)	Trial 2 Time (s)	Trial 3 Time (s)	Average Time (s)	Average Speed (m/s)	Final Speed (m/s)	Acceleration (m/s^2)

Analyze and Conclude

1. **Calculating** For each force, find the average of the three times that you measured. Record the average time in your data table.

2. **Calculating** For each force, find the average speed of the skateboard. Use this formula:

   Average speed = 1 m ÷ Average time

   Record this value for each force.

3. **Calculating** To obtain the final speed of the skateboard, multiply each average speed by 2. Record the result in your data table.

4. **Calculating** To obtain the acceleration, divide each final speed you found by the average time. Record the acceleration in your data table.

5. **Graphing** Make a line graph. Show the acceleration on the y-axis and the force on the x-axis. The y-axis scale should go from 0 m/s^2 to about 1 m/s^2. The x-axis should go from 0 N to 3.0 N. If your data points seem to form a straight line, draw a line through them.

6. **Interpreting Data** Your first data point is the force required for an acceleration of zero. How do you know the force for an acceleration of zero?

7. **Interpreting Data** According to your graph, how is the acceleration of the skateboard related to the pulling force?

8. **Communicating** Write a paragraph in which you identify the manipulated variable and the responding variable in this experiment. Describe other variables that might have affected the outcome of this experiment. (See the Skills Handbook to read about experimental variables.)

Design an Experiment

Design an experiment to test how the acceleration of the loaded skateboard depends on its mass. Think about how you would vary the mass of the skateboard. What quantity would you need to measure that you did not measure in this experiment? Do you have the equipment to make that measurement? If not, what other equipment would you need? *Obtain your teacher's permission before carrying out your investigation.*

Rockets and Satellites

Reading Preview

Key Concepts
- How does a rocket lift off the ground?
- What keeps a satellite in orbit?

Key Terms
- satellite
- centripetal force

Target Reading Skill
Identifying Main Ideas As you read the What Is a Satellite? section, write the main idea in a graphic organizer like the one below. Then write three supporting details that further explain the main idea.

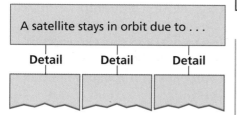

Main Idea

A satellite stays in orbit due to . . .

Detail	Detail	Detail

Lab zone Discover Activity

What Makes an Object Move in a Circle?

1. Tie a small mass, such as an empty thread spool, to the end of a string no more than one meter long.
2. Swing the object rapidly around in a circle that is perpendicular to the floor. Make sure no one is near the swinging object, and don't let it go!
3. Predict what will happen if you decrease the speed of the object. Test your prediction.
4. Predict how the length of the string affects the object's motion. Test your prediction.

Think It Over
Forming Operational Definitions Describe the object's motion. How do you know that the string exerts a force?

In October 1957, 14-year-old Homer Hickam looked upward and saw a speck of light move across the sky. It was the Russian satellite *Sputnik*, the first artificial satellite. It was propelled into space by a powerful rocket. This sight inspired Homer and his friends. They spent the next three years designing, building, and launching rockets in their hometown of Coalwood, West Virginia. Many of their first attempts failed, but they did not give up. Eventually, they built a rocket that soared to a height of almost ten kilometers. Their hard work paid off. In 1960, they won first place in the National Science Fair. Since then, rocket launches have become more familiar, but they are still an awesome sight.

◀ **Homer Hickam holds a rocket that he and his friends designed.**

How Do Rockets Lift Off?

A space shuttle like the one in Figure 19 has a mass of more than 2 million kilograms when loaded with fuel. To push the shuttle away from the pull of Earth's gravity and into space requires an incredible amount of force. How is this force generated? Rockets and space shuttles lift into space using Newton's third law of motion. As they lift off, they burn fuel and push the exhaust gases downward at a high velocity. In turn, the gases push upward on the rocket with an equal but opposite force. **A rocket can rise into the air because the gases it expels with a downward action force exert an equal but opposite reaction force on the rocket.** As long as this upward pushing force, called thrust, is greater than the downward pull of gravity, there is a net force in the upward direction. As a result, the rocket accelerates upward into space.

What Is a Satellite?

Rockets are often used to carry satellites into space. A **satellite** is any object that orbits another object in space. An artificial satellite is a device that is launched into orbit. Artificial satellites are designed for many purposes, such as communications, military intelligence, weather analysis, and geographical surveys. The International Space Station is an example of an artificial satellite. It was designed for scientific research.

Circular Motion Artificial satellites travel around Earth in an almost circular path. Recall that an object traveling in a circle is accelerating because it constantly changes direction. If an object is accelerating, a force must be acting on it. Any force that causes an object to move in a circular path is a **centripetal force** (sen TRIP ih tul). The word *centripetal* means "center-seeking."

In the Discovery Activity, the string supplies the centripetal force. The string acts to pull the object toward the center, and thereby keeps it moving in a circular path. For a satellite, the centripetal force is the gravitational force that pulls the satellite toward the center of Earth.

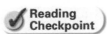 **Reading Checkpoint** What type of force causes an object to move in a circular path?

Action force

Reaction force

FIGURE 19
A Rocket Launch
The action force pushes the rocket's exhaust gases downward. The reaction force of the gases sends the rocket into space. **Predicting** *As the rocket ascends, how will its mass change?*

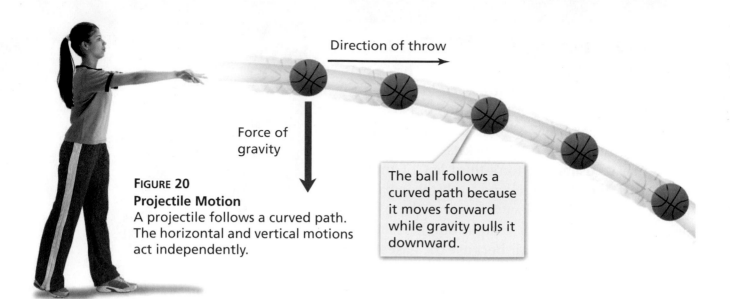

Direction of throw

Force of
gravity

FIGURE 20
Projectile Motion
A projectile follows a curved path.
The horizontal and vertical motions
act independently.

The ball follows a
curved path because
it moves forward
while gravity pulls it
downward.

FIGURE 21
Satellite Motion
The faster a projectile is thrown, the farther
it travels before it hits the ground. A
projectile with enough velocity moves in a
circular orbit. **Interpreting Diagrams** *How
does the direction of gravity compare to the
direction of the orbiting projectile's motion
at any point?*

Satellite Motion Gravity pulls satellites toward Earth.
So why don't satellites fall to the ground, as a ball thrown
through the air would? The answer is that satellites have a
greater horizontal velocity than a ball would have. Instead
of falling to Earth, satellites fall around Earth.

If you throw a ball horizontally, as shown in
Figure 20, the ball will move away from you at the same
time that it is pulled to the ground because of gravity.
The horizontal and vertical motions act independently,
and the ball follows a curved path toward the ground. If
you throw the ball faster, it will land even farther in
front of you. The faster you throw a projectile, the farther it travels before it lands.

Now suppose, as Isaac Newton did, what would happen if you were on a high mountain and could throw a
ball as fast as you wanted. The faster you threw it, the
farther away it would land. But, at a certain speed, the
path of the ball would match the curve of Earth.
Although the ball would keep falling due to gravity,
Earth's surface would curve away from the ball at the
same rate. Thus the ball would fall around Earth in a
circle, as shown in Figure 21.

**Satellites in orbit around Earth continuously fall
toward Earth, but because Earth is curved they travel
around it.** In other words, a satellite is a falling projectile
that keeps missing the ground! It falls around Earth
rather than into it. A satellite does not need fuel because
it continues to move ahead due to its inertia. At the same
time, gravity continuously changes the satellite's direction. The speed with which an object must be thrown in
order to orbit Earth turns out to be about 7,900 m/s!

Satellite Location Some satellites, such as mapping and observation satellites, are put into low orbits of less than 1,000 kilometers. In a low orbit, satellites complete a trip around Earth in less than two hours. Other satellites are sent into higher orbits. At those distances, a satellite travels more slowly, taking longer to circle Earth. For example, communications satellites travel about 36,000 kilometers above Earth's surface. At that height, they circle Earth once every 24 hours. Because Earth rotates once every 24 hours, a satellite above the equator always stays at the same point above Earth as it orbits.

Reading Checkpoint How does gravity help keep satellites in orbit?

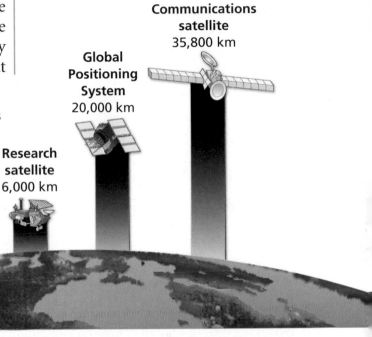

FIGURE 22
Satellite Locations
Depending on their uses, artificial satellites orbit at different heights.

Communications satellite 35,800 km

Global Positioning System 20,000 km

Research satellite 6,000 km

Space shuttle 400 km

Section 5 Assessment

Target Reading Skill Identifying Main Ideas Use your graphic organizer to help you answer Question 2 below.

Reviewing Key Concepts

1. **a. Identifying** Which of Newton's three laws of motion explains how a rocket lifts off?
   b. Explaining How do action-reaction pairs explain how a rocket lifts off?
   c. Applying Concepts As a rocket travels upward from Earth, air resistance decreases along with the force of gravity. The rocket's mass also decreases as its fuel is used up. If thrust remains the same, how do these factors affect the rocket's acceleration?

2. **a. Defining** What is a satellite?
   b. Relating Cause and Effect What causes satellites to stay in orbit rather than falling toward Earth?

   c. Inferring In Figure 21, a projectile is thrown with enough velocity to orbit Earth. What would happen if the projectile were thrown with a greater velocity?

Lab zone At-Home Activity

Swing the Bucket Fill a small plastic bucket halfway with water and take it outdoors. Challenge a family member to swing the bucket in a vertical circle. Explain that the water won't fall out at the top if the bucket is moving fast enough. Tell your family member that if the bucket falls as fast as the water, the water will stay in the bucket. Relate this activity to a satellite that also falls due to gravity, yet remains in orbit.

① The Nature of Force

Key Concepts

- A force is described by its strength and by the direction in which it acts.
- Unbalanced forces acting on an object result in a net force and a change in the object's motion.
- Balanced forces acting on an object do not change the object's motion.

Key Terms

- force • newton • net force
- unbalanced forces • balanced forces

② Friction and Gravity

Key Concepts

- The strength of the force of friction depends on two factors: how hard the surfaces push together and the types of surfaces involved.
- Two factors affect the gravitational attraction between objects: mass and distance.
- In free fall, the force of gravity is an unbalanced force, which causes an object to accelerate.

Key Terms

friction	mass
static friction	weight
sliding friction	free fall
rolling friction	air resistance
fluid friction	terminal velocity
gravity	projectile

③ Newton's First and Second Laws

Key Concepts

- An object at rest will remain at rest, and an object moving at a constant velocity will continue moving at a constant velocity, unless it is acted upon by an unbalanced force.
- Acceleration depends on the object's mass and on the net force acting on the object.
- $\text{Acceleration} = \dfrac{\text{Net force}}{\text{Mass}}$

Key Term

inertia

④ Newton's Third Law

Key Concepts

- If one object exerts a force on another object, then the second object exerts a force of equal strength in the opposite direction on the first object.
- The momentum of a moving object is equal to its mass times its velocity.

$$\text{Momentum} = \text{Mass} \times \text{Velocity}$$

- The total momentum of any group of objects remains the same, or is conserved, unless outside forces act on the objects.

Key Terms

momentum
law of conservation of momentum

⑤ Rockets and Satellites

Key Concepts

- A rocket can rise into the air because the gases it expels with a downward action force exert an equal but opposite reaction force on the rocket.
- Satellites in orbit around Earth continuously fall toward Earth, but because Earth is curved they travel around it.

Key Terms

satellite   centripetal force

Review and Assessment

Organizing Information

Contrasting Copy the table about the different types of friction onto a sheet of paper. Then complete it and add a title. (For more on Comparing and Contrasting, see the Skills Handbook.)

Type of Friction	Occurs When	Example
Static	An object is not moving	a. ___?___
Sliding	b. ___?___	c. ___?___
Rolling	d. ___?___	e. ___?___
Fluid	f. ___?___	g. ___?___

Reviewing Key Terms

Choose the letter of the best answer.

1. When an unbalanced force acts on an object, the force
   a. changes the motion of the object.
   b. is canceled by another force.
   c. does not change the motion of the object.
   d. is equal to the weight of the object.

2. Air resistance is a type of
   a. rolling friction.
   b. sliding friction.
   c. centripetal force.
   d. fluid friction.

3. Which of the following is not a projectile?
   a. a satellite
   b. a thrown ball
   c. a ball on the ground
   d. a soaring arrow

4. The resistance of an object to any change in its motion is called
   a. inertia.
   b. friction.
   c. gravity.
   d. weight.

5. The product of an object's mass and its velocity is called the object's
   a. net force.
   b. weight.
   c. momentum.
   d. gravitation.

If the statement is true, write _true_. If it is false, change the underlined word or words to make the statement true.

6. <u>Balanced forces</u> are equal forces acting on an object in opposite directions.

7. <u>Rolling friction</u> occurs when two solid surfaces slide over each other.

8. The greatest velocity a falling object reaches is called its <u>momentum</u>.

9. The <u>law of universal gravitation</u> states that the total momentum of objects that interact does not change.

10. The type of force that causes a satellite to orbit Earth is a <u>centripetal force.</u>

Writing in Science

Descriptive Paragraph Suppose you have been asked to design a new amusement park ride. Write a description of how you will design it. Explain the role that friction and gravity will play in the ride's design.

Discovery CHANNEL SCHOOL

Forces
Video Preview
Video Field Trip
▶ Video Assessment

Review and Assessment

Checking Concepts

11. Four children pull on the same toy at the same time, yet there is no net force on the toy. How is that possible?

12. Why do slippery fluids such as oil reduce sliding friction?

13. Will a flat sheet of paper dropped from a height of 2 m accelerate at the same rate as a piece of paper crumpled into a ball? Why or why not?

14. Explain how force, mass, and acceleration are related by Newton's second law of motion.

15. Suppose you are an astronaut making a space walk outside your space station when your jet pack runs out of fuel. How can you use your empty jet pack to get you back to the station?

16. Draw a diagram showing the motion of a satellite around Earth. Label the forces acting on the satellite. Is the satellite accelerating?

Thinking Critically

17. Classifying What kind of friction allows you to walk without slipping?

18. Applying Concepts You are moving fast on a skateboard when your wheel gets stuck in a crack on the sidewalk. Using the term *inertia*, explain what happens.

19. Problem Solving Look at the diagram below of two students pulling a bag of volleyball equipment. The friction force between the bag and the floor is 15 N. What is the net force acting on the bag? What is the acceleration of the bag?

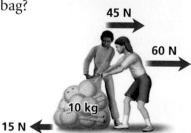

20. Relating Cause and Effect When you drop a golf ball to the pavement, it bounces up. Is a force needed to make it bounce up? If so, what exerts the force?

Math Practice

21. Calculating Force A 7.3-kg bowling ball accelerates at a rate of 3.7 m/s². What force acts on the bowling ball?

22. Calculating Momentum A 240-kg snow-mobile travels at 16 m/s. The mass of the driver is 75 kg. What is the momentum of the snowmobile and driver?

Applying Skills

Use the illustration showing a collision between two balls to answer Questions 23–25.

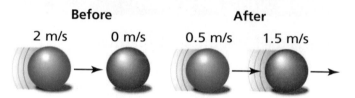

23. Calculating Use the formula for momentum to find the momentum of each ball before and after the collision. Assume the mass of each ball is 0.4 kg.

24. Inferring Find the total momentum before and after collision. Is the law of conservation of momentum satisfied in this collision? Explain.

25. Designing Experiments Design an experiment in which you could show that momentum is not conserved between the balls when friction is strong.

Lab zone Chapter **Project**

Performance Assessment Test your vehicle to make sure it will work on the type of floor in your classroom. Will the vehicle stay within the bounds set by your teacher? Identify all the forces acting on the vehicle. What was the most significant source of friction for your vehicle? List at least three features you included in the design of the vehicle that led to an improvement in its performance. For example, did you give it a smooth shape for low air resistance?

Standardized Test Prep

Choose the letter of the best answer.

1. In the balloon diagram above, why don't the two forces cancel each other out?
   A They are not equal.
   B They both act on the air.
   C They both act on the balloon.
   D They act on different objects.

2. What force makes it less likely for a person to slip on a dry sidewalk as opposed to an icy sidewalk?
   F air resistance
   G friction
   H inertia
   J momentum

3. Which of the following is determined by the force of gravity?
   A weight
   B momentum
   C mass
   D distance

4. The table below shows the mass and velocity of four animals. Which animal has the greatest momentum?

Mass and Velocity of Animals		
Animal	Mass (kg)	Velocity (m/s)
Cheetah	45	20
Grizzly bear	200	13
Hyena	70	18
Wild turkey	11	7

   F cheetah
   G grizzly bear
   H hyena
   J wild turkey

5. A 50-car freight train and an 8-car passenger train are stopped on parallel tracks. It is more difficult to move the freight train than the passenger train. What accounts for this fact?
   A terminal velocity
   B inertia
   C centripetal force
   D speed

Constructed Response

6. Write a short paragraph explaining how a parachute works in terms of forces.

Chapter 3

Forces in Fluids

The BIG Idea
Science and Technology

Q How can you predict if an object will sink or float?

Chapter Preview

❶ **Pressure**
Discover Can You Blow Up a Balloon in a Bottle?
Math Skills Area
Try This Card Trick
Design Your Own Lab Spinning Sprinklers

❷ **Floating and Sinking**
Discover What Can You Measure With a Straw?
Try This Cartesian Diver
At-Home Activity Changing Balloon Density
Skills Lab Sink and Spill

❸ **Pascal's Principle**
Discover How Does Pressure Change?
Active Art Hydraulic Systems
Analyzing Data Comparing Hydraulic Lifts

❹ **Bernoulli's Principle**
Discover Does the Movement of Air Affect Pressure?
Try This Faucet Force
At-Home Activity Paper Chimney

The force of air pushing on a hang glider's wing helps to keep the glider aloft. ▶

Forces in Fluids

▶ **Video Preview**
Video Field Trip
Video Assessment

Staying Afloat

Whether an object sinks or floats depends on more than just its weight. In this Chapter Project, you will design and build a boat that can float in water and carry cargo. You will find out what forces in fluids make an object sink or float.

Your Goal To construct a boat that can float in water and carry cargo

Your boat must

- be made of metal only
- support a cargo of 50 pennies without allowing any water to enter for at least 10 seconds
- travel at least 1.5 meters
- be built following the safety guidelines in Appendix A

Plan It! Before you design your boat, think about the shape of real ships. Preview the chapter to find out what makes an object float. Then look for simple metal objects that you can form into a boat. Compare different materials and designs to build the most efficient boat you can. After your teacher approves your design, build your boat and test it.

Lab zone™ Chapter **Project**

Pressure

Reading Preview

Key Concepts
• What does pressure depend on?
• How do fluids exert pressure?
• How does fluid pressure change with elevation and depth?

Key Terms
• pressure • pascal • fluid
• barometer

Target Reading Skill
Previewing Visuals Before you read, preview Figure 5. Then write two questions that you have about the diagram in a graphic organizer like the one below. As you read, answer your questions.

Pressure Variations

Q.	Why does pressure change with elevation and depth?
A.	
Q.	

Lab zone Discover **Activity**

Can You Blow Up a Balloon in a Bottle?

1. Insert a balloon into the neck of an empty bottle. Try to blow up the balloon.
2. Now insert a straw into the bottle, next to the balloon. Keep one end of the straw sticking out of the bottle. Try again to blow up the balloon.

Think It Over
Developing Hypotheses Did using the straw make a difference? If it did, develop a hypothesis to explain why.

Outside, deep snow covers the ground. You put on your sneakers and head out, shovel in hand. When you step outside, your foot sinks deep into the snow. It's nearly up to your knees! Nearby, a sparrow hops across the surface of the snow. Unlike you, the bird does not sink. In fact, it barely leaves a mark! Why do you sink into the snow while the sparrow rests on the surface?

What Is Pressure?

The word *pressure* is related to the word *press*. It refers to a force exerted over an area on the surface of an object. You may recall that Earth's gravity pulls you downward with a force equal to your weight. Due to gravity, your feet exert a force on the surface of Earth over an area the size of your feet. In other words, your feet exert pressure on the ground.

Exerting pressure on snow ▶

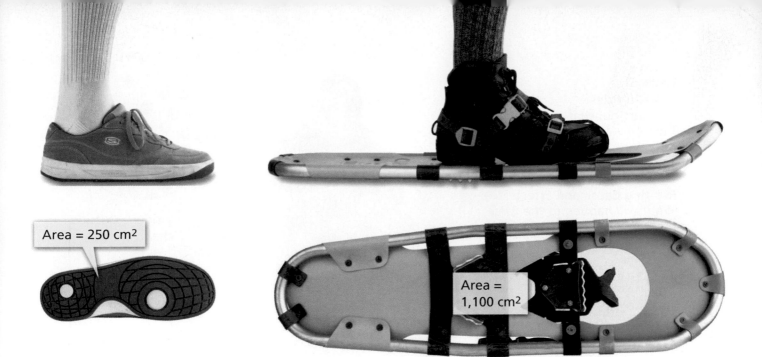

Area = 250 cm²

Area = 1,100 cm²

Pressure and Area Force and pressure are closely related, but they are not the same thing. **Pressure decreases as the area over which a force is distributed increases.** The larger the area over which the force is distributed, the less pressure is exerted. In order to stand on snow without sinking, you can't make yourself weigh the same as a bird. However, you can change the area over which you exert the force of your weight.

If you wear sneakers, like those shown in Figure 1, your weight is distributed over the soles of both shoes. You'll exert pressure over an area of about 500 cm² and sink into the snow. But if you wear snowshoes, you'll exert pressure over a much greater area—about 2,200 cm². Because the force of your weight is distributed over a greater area, the overall pressure exerted on the snow is much less. Like a sparrow, you can stand on the snow without sinking!

Calculating Pressure The relationship of force, area, and pressure is summarized by a formula.

$$\text{Pressure} = \frac{\text{Force}}{\text{Area}}$$

Pressure is equal to the force exerted on a surface divided by the total area over which the force is exerted. Force is measured in newtons (N). Area is measured in square meters (m²). Since force is divided by area, the SI unit of pressure is the newton per square meter (N/m²). This unit of pressure is also called the **pascal** (Pa): 1 N/m² = 1 Pa.

 **Reading Checkpoint** What is the SI unit of pressure called?

FIGURE 1
Pressure and Area
Pressure depends on the area over which a force is distributed.
Inferring *Which type of shoe would you use to keep from sinking into deep snow?*

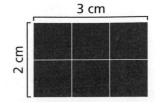

Area
The area of a surface is the number of square units that it covers. To find the area of a rectangle, multiply its length by its width. The area of the rectangle below is 2 cm × 3 cm, or 6 cm².

3 cm

2 cm

Practice Problem Which has a greater area: a rectangle that is 4 cm × 20 cm, or a square that is 10 cm × 10 cm?

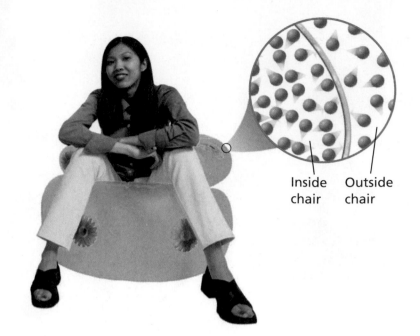

FIGURE 2
Fluid Particles
The particles that make up a fluid move constantly in all directions. When a particle collides with a surface, it exerts a force on the surface.
Relating Cause and Effect
What will happen to the force exerted by the particles in the chair when you add more air to the chair?

Inside chair   Outside chair

Lab zone Try This Activity

Card Trick

1. Fill a small plastic cup to the brim with water. Gently place an index card over the top of the cup.

2. Hold the card in place and slowly turn the cup upside down. Let go of the card. What happens? Without touching the card, turn the container on its side.

Inferring Why does the water stay in the cup when you turn the cup upside down?

Fluid Pressure

Solids such as sneakers are not the only materials that exert pressure. Fluids also exert pressure. A **fluid** is a material that can easily flow. As a result, a fluid can change shape. Liquids such as water and oil and gases such as air and helium are examples of fluids.

What Causes Fluid Pressure? To understand how fluids exert forces that can result in pressure, think about the tiny particles that make up the fluid. Particles in a fluid constantly move in all directions, as shown in Figure 2. As they move, the particles collide with each other and with any surface that they meet.

As each particle in a fluid collides with a surface, it exerts a force on the surface. **All of the forces exerted by the individual particles in a fluid combine to make up the pressure exerted by the fluid.** Because the number of particles is large, you can consider the fluid as a whole. So, the fluid pressure is the total force exerted by the fluid divided by the area over which the force is exerted.

Air Pressure Did you know that you live at the bottom of 100 kilometers of fluid that surrounds Earth? This fluid, called air, is the mixture of gases that makes up Earth's atmosphere. These gases press down on everything on Earth's surface, all the time. Air exerts pressure because it has mass. You may forget that air has mass, but each cubic meter of air around you has a mass of about 1 kilogram. Because the force of gravity pulls down on this mass of air, the air has weight. The weight of the air is the force that produces air pressure, or atmospheric pressure.

Balanced Pressure Hold out your hand, palm up. You are holding up air. At sea level, atmospheric pressure is about 10.13 N/cm^2. The surface area of your hand is about 100 cm^2. So, the weight supported by the surface area of your hand is about 1,000 newtons, or about the same weight as that of a large washing machine!

How could your hand possibly support that weight and not feel it? In a stationary fluid, pressure at a given point is exerted equally in all directions. The weight of the atmosphere does not just press down on your hand. It presses on your hand from every direction. The pressures balance each other.

Balanced pressures also explain why the tremendous air pressure pushing on you from all sides does not crush you. Your body contains fluids that exert outward pressure. For example, your lungs and sinus cavities contain air. Your cells and blood vessels contain liquids. So pressure from fluids inside your body balances the air pressure outside your body.

What happens when air pressure becomes unbalanced? Look at Figure 4. When the can is full of air, the air pressure inside the can balances the atmospheric pressure outside the can. When air is removed from the can, the unbalanced force of the outside air pressure crushes the can.

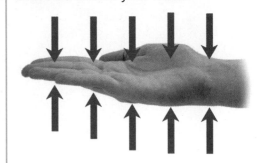

 Reading Checkpoint) **How is the pressure on your hand balanced?**

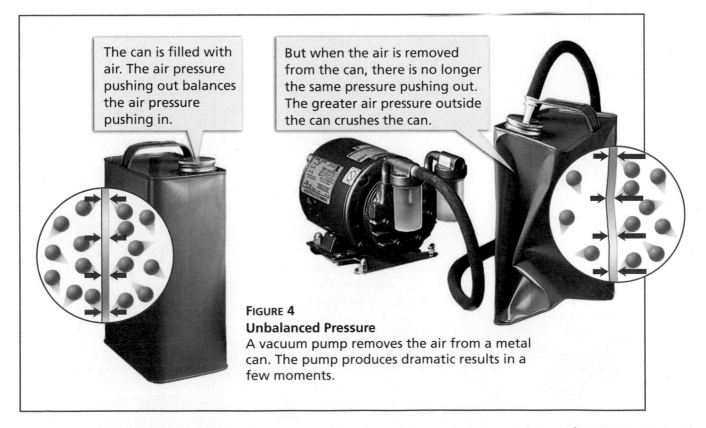

The can is filled with air. The air pressure pushing out balances the air pressure pushing in.

But when the air is removed from the can, there is no longer the same pressure pushing out. The greater air pressure outside the can crushes the can.

FIGURE 4
Unbalanced Pressure
A vacuum pump removes the air from a metal can. The pump produces dramatic results in a few moments.

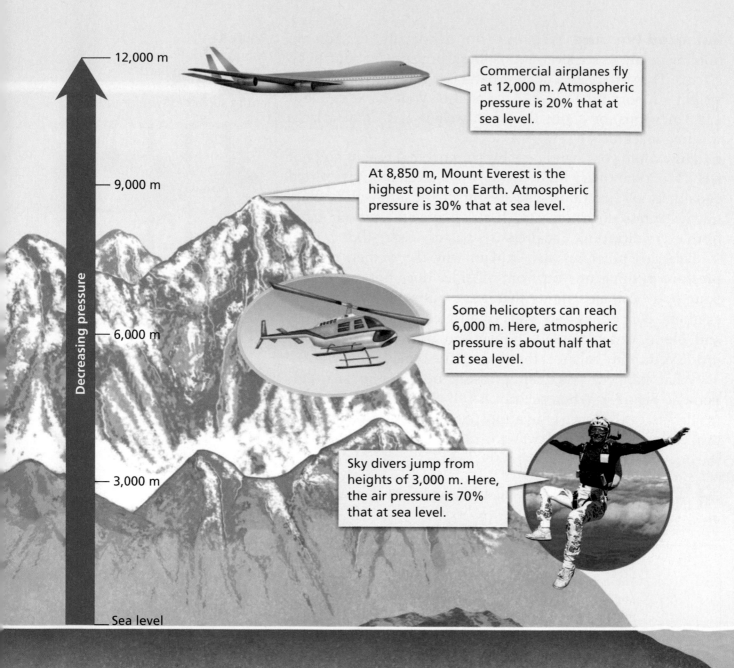

12,000 m —— Commercial airplanes fly at 12,000 m. Atmospheric pressure is 20% that at sea level.

9,000 m —— At 8,850 m, Mount Everest is the highest point on Earth. Atmospheric pressure is 30% that at sea level.

Decreasing pressure

6,000 m —— Some helicopters can reach 6,000 m. Here, atmospheric pressure is about half that at sea level.

3,000 m —— Sky divers jump from heights of 3,000 m. Here, the air pressure is 70% that at sea level.

Sea level

Go Online
SCiLINKS NSTA
For: Links on fluids and pressure
Visit: www.SciLinks.org
Web Code: scn-1331

FIGURE 5
Pressure Variations
Atmospheric pressure decreases gradually as the elevation above sea level increases. Water pressure increases rapidly as the water depth increases. **Applying Concepts** *Why do airplanes have pressurized cabins?*

Variations in Fluid Pressure

Does the pressure of a fluid ever change? What happens to pressure as you climb to a higher elevation or sink to a lower depth within a fluid? Figure 5 shows how pressure changes depending on where you are.

Atmospheric Pressure and Elevation Have you ever felt your ears "pop" as you rode up in an elevator? The "popping" has to do with changing air pressure. At higher elevations, there is less air above you and therefore less air pressure. **As your elevation increases, atmospheric pressure decreases.**

The fact that air pressure decreases as you move up in elevation explains why your ears pop. When the air pressure outside your body changes, the air pressure inside adjusts, but more slowly. So, for a moment, the air pressure behind your eardrums is greater than it is in the air outside. Your body releases this pressure with a "pop," balancing the pressures.

Water Pressure and Depth Fluid pressure depends on depth. The pressure at one meter below the surface of a swimming pool is the same as the pressure one meter below the surface of a lake. But if you dive deeper into either body of water, pressure becomes greater as you descend. The deeper you swim, the greater the pressure you feel. **Water pressure increases as depth increases.**

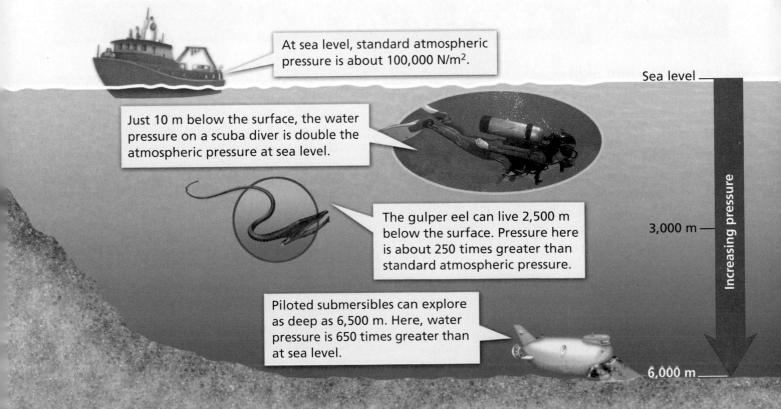

At sea level, standard atmospheric pressure is about 100,000 N/m².

Just 10 m below the surface, the water pressure on a scuba diver is double the atmospheric pressure at sea level.

The gulper eel can live 2,500 m below the surface. Pressure here is about 250 times greater than standard atmospheric pressure.

Piloted submersibles can explore as deep as 6,500 m. Here, water pressure is 650 times greater than at sea level.

Sea level

3,000 m

6,000 m

Increasing pressure

FIGURE 6

Aneroid Barometer
An aneroid barometer measures atmospheric pressure.
Interpreting Photographs *What type of weather might be coming when atmospheric pressure decreases?*

As with air, you can think of water pressure as being due to the weight of the water above a particular point. At greater depths, there is more water above that point and therefore more weight to support. In addition, air in the atmosphere pushes down on the water. Therefore, the total pressure at a given point beneath the water results from the weight of the water plus the weight of the air above it. In the deepest parts of the ocean, the pressure is more than 1,000 times the air pressure you experience every day.

Measuring Pressure You can measure atmospheric pressure with an instrument called a **barometer.** There are two types of barometers: a mercury barometer and an aneroid barometer. The aneroid barometer is the barometer you usually see hanging on a wall. Weather forecasters use the pressure reading from a barometer to help forecast the weather. Rapidly decreasing atmospheric pressure usually means a storm is on its way. Increasing pressure is often a sign of fair weather. You may hear barometric pressure readings expressed in millimeters, inches, or another unit called a millibar. For example, the standard barometric pressure at sea level may be reported as 760 millimeters, 29.92 inches, or 1,013.2 millibars.

Reading Checkpoint What instrument measures atmospheric pressure?

Section 1 Assessment

Target Reading Skill
Previewing Visuals Refer to your questions and answers about Figure 5 to help you answer Question 3 below.

Reviewing Key Concepts

1. **a. Reviewing** What two factors does pressure depend on?
   b. Comparing and Contrasting Who exerts more pressure on the ground—a 50-kg woman standing in high heels, or a 50-kg woman standing in work boots?
2. **a. Summarizing** How do fluids exert pressure?
   b. Explaining Since most of the weight of the atmosphere is above you, why aren't you crushed by it?
   c. Inferring How is your body similar to the can containing air shown in Figure 4?

3. **a. Describing** How does atmospheric pressure change as you move away from the surface of Earth?
   b. Comparing and Contrasting Compare the change in atmospheric pressure with elevation to the change in water pressure with depth.
   c. Applying Concepts Why must an astronaut wear a pressurized suit in space?

Math Practice

4. **Area** Find the area of a rectangular photo that is 20 cm long and 15 cm wide.

5. **Area** Which has a greater area: a square table that measures 120 cm × 120 cm, or a rectangular table that measures 200 cm × 90 cm?

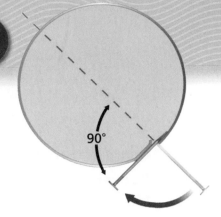

90°

Lab zone Design Your Own Lab

Spinning Sprinklers

Problem

What factors affect the speed of rotation of a lawn sprinkler?

Skills Focus

designing experiments, controlling variables

Materials

- empty soda can
- fishing line, 30 cm
- waterproof marker
- wide-mouth jar or beaker
- stopwatch
- nails of various sizes
- large basin

Procedure

PART 1 Making a Sprinkler

1. Fill the jar with enough water to completely cover a soda can. Place the jar in the basin.

2. Bend up the tab of a can and tie the end of a length of fishing line to it. **CAUTION:** *The edge of the can opening can be sharp.*

3. Place a mark on the can to help you keep track of how many times the can spins.

4. Using the small nail, make a hole in the side of the can about 1 cm up from the bottom. Poke the nail straight in. Then twist the nail until it makes a right angle with the radius of the can as shown in the figure above. **CAUTION:** *Nails are sharp and should be used only to puncture the cans.*

5. Submerge the can in the jar and fill the can to the top with water.

6. Quickly lift the can with the fishing line so that it is 1–2 cm above the water level in the jar.

7. Practice counting how many spins the can completes in 15 seconds.

PART 2 What Factors Affect Spin?

8. How does the size of the hole affect the number of spins made by the can? Propose a hypothesis and then design an experiment to test the hypothesis. Obtain your teacher's approval before carrying out your experiment. Record all your data.

9. How does the number of holes affect the number of spins made by the can? Propose a hypothesis and then design an experiment to test the hypothesis. Obtain your teacher's approval before carrying out your experiment. Record all your data.

Analyze and Conclude

1. **Designing Experiments** How does the size of the hole affect the rate of spin of the can? How does the number of holes affect the rate of spin of the can?

2. **Controlling Variables** What other variables might affect the number of spins made by the can?

3. **Interpreting Data** Explain the motion of the can in terms of water pressure.

4. **Classifying** Which of Newton's three laws of motion could you use to explain the motion of the can? Explain.

5. **Communicating** Use the results of your experiment to write a paragraph that explains why a spinning lawn sprinkler spins.

More to Explore

Some sprinkler systems use water pressure to spin. Examine one of these sprinklers to see the size, direction of spin, and number of holes. What would happen if you connected a second sprinkler to the first with another length of hose? If possible, try it.

Floating and Sinking

Reading Preview

Key Concepts
- What is the effect of the buoyant force?
- How can you use density to determine whether an object will float or sink in a fluid?

Key Terms
- buoyant force
- Archimedes' principle
- density

Target Reading Skill
Relating Cause and Effect
As you read, identify the reasons why an object sinks. Write the information in a graphic organizer like the one below.

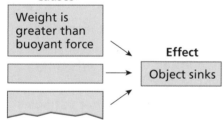

Causes

Weight is greater than buoyant force

Effect

Object sinks

Lab zone Discover **Activity**

What Can You Measure With a Straw?
1. Cut a plastic straw to a 10-cm length.
2. Use a waterproof marker to make marks on the straw that are 1 cm apart.
3. Roll some modeling clay into a ball about 1.5 cm in diameter. Stick one end of the straw in the clay. You have built a device known as a hydrometer.
4. Place the hydrometer in a glass of water. About half of the straw should remain above water. If it sinks, remove some of the clay. Make sure no water gets into the straw.
5. Dissolve 10 spoonfuls of sugar in a glass of water. Try out your hydrometer in this liquid.

Think It Over
Predicting Compare your observations in Steps 4 and 5. Then predict what will happen if you use 20 spoonfuls of sugar in a glass of water. Test your prediction.

In April 1912, the *Titanic* departed from England on its first and only voyage. At the time, it was the largest ship afloat—nearly three football fields long. The *Titanic* was also the most technologically advanced ship in existence. Its hull was divided into compartments, and it was considered to be unsinkable.

Yet a few days into the voyage, the *Titanic* struck an iceberg. One compartment after another filled with water. Less than three hours later, the bow of the great ship slipped under the waves. As the stern rose high into the air, the ship broke in two. Both pieces sank to the bottom of the Atlantic Ocean. More than a thousand people died.

◀ **The bow section of the *Titanic* resting on the ocean floor**

Buoyancy

Ships are designed to have buoyancy—the ability to float. How is it possible that a huge ship can float easily on the surface of water under certain conditions, and then in a few hours become a sunken wreck? To answer this question, you need to understand the buoyant force.

Gravity and the Buoyant Force You have probably experienced the buoyant force. If you have ever picked up an object under water, you know that it seems much lighter in water than in air. Water and other fluids exert an upward force called the **buoyant force** that acts on a submerged object. **The buoyant force acts in the direction opposite to the force of gravity, so it makes an object feel lighter.**

As you can see in Figure 7, a fluid exerts pressure on all surfaces of a submerged object. Since the pressure in a fluid increases with depth, the upward pressure on the bottom of the object is greater than the downward pressure on the top. The result is a net force acting upward on the submerged object. This is the buoyant force.

Remember that the weight of a submerged object is a downward force. If an object's weight is greater than the buoyant force, a net force acts downward on the object. The object will sink. If the weight of an object is equal to the buoyant force, no net force acts on the object. The object will not sink. A submerged object whose weight is equal to the buoyant force also has no net force acting on it. The object will not sink. For example, both the jellyfish and the turtle shown in Figure 8 have balanced forces acting on them. Neither animal will rise or sink.

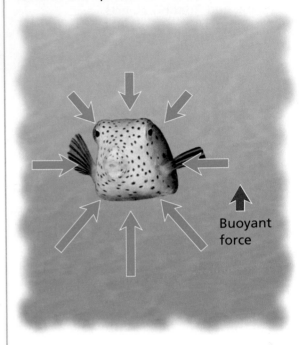

FIGURE 7
Buoyant Force
The pressure on the bottom of a submerged object is greater than the pressure on the top. The result is a net force in the upward direction.

Buoyant force

Weight

Buoyant force

Weight

FIGURE 8
Buoyant Force and Weight
The weight of an object is a force that works opposite the buoyant force on the object. **Comparing and Contrasting** *Why does the lobster sink?*

Weight

Buoyant force

Weight

Buoyant force

FIGURE 9
Archimedes' Principle
Archimedes' principle applies to sinking and floating objects.
Predicting *If you press down on the floating film can, what will happen to the volume of the displaced fluid in the small beaker?*

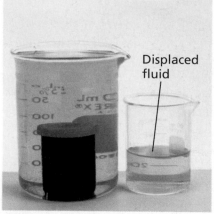

Displaced fluid

Sinking
When the film can has film in it, it sinks. The volume of fluid displaced by the can is equal to the volume of the can.

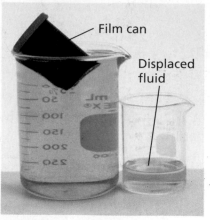

Film can

Displaced fluid

Floating
When the film can is empty, it floats. The volume of displaced fluid is equal to the volume of the submerged portion of the can.

Archimedes' Principle You know that all objects take up space. A submerged object displaces, or takes the place of, a volume of fluid equal to its own volume. A partly submerged object, however, displaces a volume of fluid equal to the volume of its submerged portion only. You can see this in Figure 9.

Archimedes, a mathematician of ancient Greece, discovered a connection between the weight of a fluid displaced by an object and the buoyant force acting on it. This connection is known as Archimedes' principle. **Archimedes' principle** states that the buoyant force acting on a submerged object is equal to the weight of the fluid the object displaces. To understand what this means, think about swimming in a pool. Suppose your body displaces 50 liters of water. The buoyant force exerted on you will be equal to the weight of 50 liters of water, or about 500 N.

You can use Archimedes' principle to explain why a ship floats on the surface. Since the buoyant force equals the weight of the displaced fluid, the buoyant force will increase if more fluid is displaced. A large object displaces more fluid than a small object. A greater buoyant force acts on the larger object even if the large object has the same weight as the small object.

Look at Figure 10. The shape of a ship's hull causes the ship to displace a greater volume of water than a solid piece of steel with the same mass. A ship displaces a volume of water equal in weight to the submerged portion of the ship. According to Archimedes' principle, the weight of the displaced water is equal to the buoyant force. Since a ship displaces more water than a block of steel, a greater buoyant force acts on the ship. A ship floats on the surface as long as the buoyant force acting on it is equal to its weight.

Reading Checkpoint Does a greater buoyant force act on a large object or a small object?

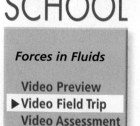

Forces in Fluids

Video Preview
▶ Video Field Trip
Video Assessment

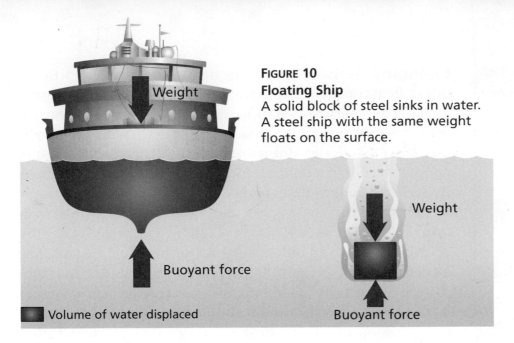

FIGURE 10
Floating Ship
A solid block of steel sinks in water. A steel ship with the same weight floats on the surface.

Weight

Buoyant force

Weight

Buoyant force

Volume of water displaced

Density

Exactly why do some objects float and others sink? To find the answer, you must relate an object's mass to its volume. In other words, you need to know the object's density.

What Is Density? The **density** of a substance is its mass per unit volume.

$$\text{Density} = \frac{\text{Mass}}{\text{Volume}}$$

For example, one cubic centimeter (cm³) of lead has a mass of 11.3 grams, so its density is 11.3 g/cm³. In contrast, one cubic centimeter of cork has a mass of only about 0.25 gram. So the density of cork is about 0.25 g/cm³. Lead is more dense than cork. The density of water is 1.0 g/cm³. So water is less dense than lead but more dense than cork.

Comparing Densities of Substances In Figure 11, several liquids and other materials are shown along with their densities. Notice that liquids can float on top of other liquids. (You may have seen salad oil floating on top of vinegar.) The liquids and materials with the greatest densities are near the bottom of the cylinder.

By comparing densities, you can predict whether an object will float or sink in a fluid. An object that is more dense than the fluid in which it is immersed sinks. An object that is less dense than the fluid in which it is immersed floats to the surface. And if the density of an object is equal to the density of the fluid in which it is immersed, the object neither rises nor sinks in the fluid. Instead, it floats at a constant depth.

FIGURE 11
Densities of Substances
You can use density to predict whether an object will sink or float when placed in a liquid. **Interpreting Data** *Will a rubber washer sink or float in corn oil?*

Substance	Density (g/cm³)
Wood	0.7
Corn oil	0.925
Plastic	0.93
Water	1.00
Tar ball	1.02
Glycerin	1.26
Rubber washer	1.34
Corn syrup	1.38
Copper wire	8.8
Mercury	13.6

Dive!

1. Fill a plastic jar or bottle almost completely with water.

2. Bend a plastic straw into a U shape and cut the ends so that each side is 4 cm long. Attach the ends with a paper clip. Drop the straw in the jar, paper clip first.

3. Attach more paper clips to the first one until the straw floats with its top about 0.5 cm above the surface. This is the diver.

4. Put the lid on the jar. Observe what happens when you slowly squeeze and release the jar several times.

Drawing Conclusions
Explain the behavior of the diver.

Changing Density Changing density can explain why an object floats or sinks. For example, you can change the density of water by freezing it into ice. Since water expands when it freezes, ice occupies more space than water. That's why ice is less dense than water. But it's just a little less dense! So most of an ice cube floating on the surface is below the water's surface. An iceberg like the one shown in Figure 12 is really a very large ice cube. The part that you see above water is only a small fraction of the entire iceberg.

You can make an object sink or float in a fluid by changing its density. Look at Figure 13 to see how this happens to a submarine. The density of a submarine is increased when water fills its flotation tanks. The overall mass of the submarine increases. Since its volume remains the same, its density increases when its mass increases. So the submarine will dive. To make the submarine float to the surface, water is pumped out of it, decreasing its mass. Its density decreases, and it rises toward the surface.

You can also explain why a submarine dives and floats by means of the buoyant force. Since the buoyant force is equal to the weight of the displaced fluid, the buoyant force on the submerged submarine stays the same. Changing the water level in the flotation tanks changes the weight of the submarine. The submarine dives when its weight is greater than the buoyant force. It rises to the surface when its weight is less than the buoyant force.

Don't forget that air is also a fluid. If you decrease the density of an object, such as a balloon, the object will float and not sink in air. Instead of air, you can fill a balloon with helium gas. A helium balloon rises because helium is less dense than air. A balloon filled with air, however, is denser than the surrounding air because the air inside it is under pressure. The denser air inside, along with the weight of the balloon, make it fall to the ground.

 Reading Checkpoint   **Why does a helium balloon float in air?**

FIGURE 12
Iceberg
An iceberg is dangerous to ships because most of it is under water.

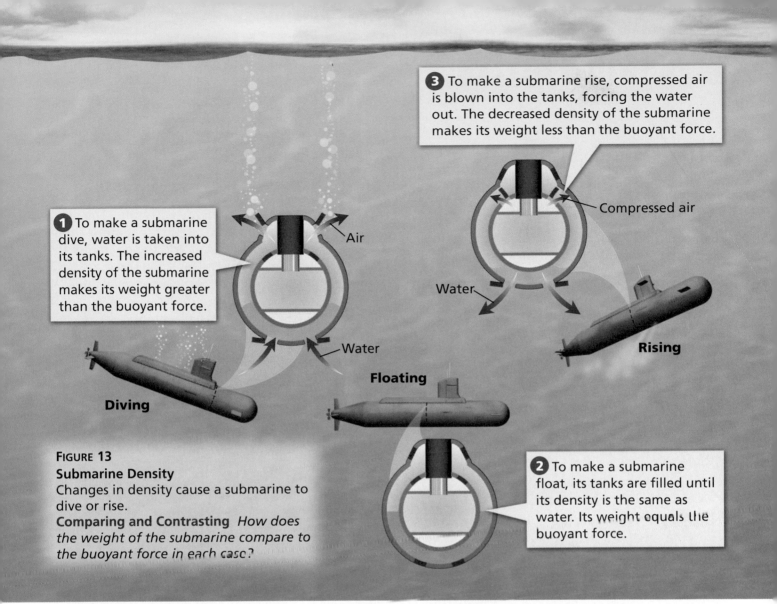

③ To make a submarine rise, compressed air is blown into the tanks, forcing the water out. The decreased density of the submarine makes its weight less than the buoyant force.

Compressed air

① To make a submarine dive, water is taken into its tanks. The increased density of the submarine makes its weight greater than the buoyant force.

Air

Water

Water

Rising

Diving

Floating

FIGURE 13
Submarine Density
Changes in density cause a submarine to dive or rise.
Comparing and Contrasting *How does the weight of the submarine compare to the buoyant force in each case?*

② To make a submarine float, its tanks are filled until its density is the same as water. Its weight equals the buoyant force.

Section 2 Assessment

Target Reading Skill

Relating Cause and Effect Refer to your graphic organizer to help you answer the questions below.

Reviewing Key Concepts

1. a. **Explaining** How does the buoyant force affect a submerged object?
   b. **Summarizing** How does Archimedes' principle relate the buoyant force acting on an object to the fluid displaced by the object?
   c. **Calculating** An object that weighs 340 N floats on a lake. What is the weight of the displaced water? What is the buoyant force?
2. a. **Defining** What is density?
   b. **Explaining** How can you use the density of an object to predict whether it will float or sink in water?

c. **Applying Concepts** Some canoes have compartments on either end that are hollow and watertight. These canoes won't sink, even when they capsize. Explain why.

Lab zone At-Home **Activity**

Changing Balloon Density Attach paper clips to the string of a helium balloon. Ask a family member to predict how many paper clips you will need to attach to make the balloon sink to the floor. How many paper clips can you attach and still keep the helium balloon suspended in the air? Explain how adding paper clips changes the overall density of the balloon.

Skills Lab

Sink and Spill

Problem

How is the buoyant force acting on a floating object related to the weight of the water it displaces?

Skills Focus

controlling variables, interpreting data, drawing conclusions

Materials

- paper towels • pie pan
- triple-beam balance • beaker, 600-mL
- jar with watertight lid, about 30-mL
- table salt

Procedure

1. Preview the procedure and copy the data table into your notebook.

2. Find the mass, in grams, of a dry paper towel and the pie pan together. Multiply the mass by 0.01. This gives you the weight in newtons. Record it in your data table.

3. Place the 600-mL beaker, with the dry paper towel under it, in the middle of the pie pan. Fill the beaker to the very top with water.

4. Fill the jar about halfway with salt. (The jar and salt must be able to float in water.) Then find the mass of the salt and the dry jar (with its cover on) in grams. Multiply the mass by 0.01. Record this weight in your data table.

5. Gently lower the jar into the 600-mL beaker. (If the jar sinks, take it out and remove some salt. Repeat Steps 2, 3, and 4.) Estimate the fraction of the jar that is underwater, and record it.

6. Once all of the displaced water has been spilled, find the total mass of the paper towel and pie pan containing the water. Multiply the mass by 0.01 and record the result in your data table.

7. Empty the pie pan. Dry off the pan and the jar.

8. Repeat Steps 3 through 7 several more times. Each time fill the jar with a different amount of salt, but make sure the jar still floats.

9. Calculate the buoyant force for each trial and record it in your data table. (*Hint*: When an object floats, the buoyant force is equal to the weight of the object.)

10. Calculate the weight of the displaced water in each case. Record it in your data table.

Data Table						
Jar	Weight of Empty Pie Pan and Dry Paper Towel (N)	Weight of Jar, Salt, and Cover (N)	Weight of Pie Pan With Displaced Water and Paper Towel (N)	Fraction of Jar Submerged in Water	Buoyant Force (N)	Weight of Displaced Water (N)
1						
2						
3						

Analyze and Conclude

1. **Controlling Variables** In each trial, the jar had a different weight. How did this affect the way that the jar floated?

2. **Interpreting Data** The jar had the same volume in every trial. Why did the volume of displaced water vary?

3. **Drawing Conclusions** What can you conclude about the relationship between the buoyant force and the weight of the displaced water?

4. **Drawing Conclusions** If you put too much salt in the jar, it will sink. What can you conclude about the buoyant force in this case? How can you determine the buoyant force for an object that sinks?

5. **Communicating** Write a paragraph suggesting places where errors may have been introduced into the experiment. Propose some ways to control the errors.

Design an Experiment

How do you think your results would change if you used a liquid that is more dense or less dense than water? Design an experiment to test your hypothesis. What liquid or liquids will you use? Will you need equipment other than what you used for this experiment? If so, what will you need? *Obtain your teacher's permission before carrying out your investigation.*

Pascal's Principle

Reading Preview

Key Concepts
- What does Pascal's principle say about change in fluid pressure?
- How does a hydraulic system work?

Key Terms
- Pascal's principle
- hydraulic system

Target Reading Skill

Asking Questions Before you read, preview the red headings. In a graphic organizer like the one below, ask a *what* or *how* question for each heading. As you read, write the answers to your questions.

Pascal's Principle

Question	Answer
How is pressure transmitted in a fluid?	Pressure is transmitted . . .

Discover **Activity**

How Does Pressure Change?

1. Fill an empty 2-liter plastic bottle with water. Then screw on the cap. There should be no bubbles in the bottle (or only very small bubbles).
2. Lay the bottle on its side. At one spot, push in the bottle with your left thumb.
3. With your right thumb, push in fairly hard on a spot at the other end, as shown. What does your left thumb feel?
4. Pick another spot on the bottle for your left thumb and repeat Step 3.

Think It Over

Observing When you push in with your right thumb, does the water pressure in the bottle increase, decrease, or remain the same? How do you know?

At first, you hesitate, but then you hold out your hand. The aquarium attendant places the sea star in your palm. You can feel motion on your skin. The many tiny "feet" on the animal's underside look something like suction cups, and they tickle just a bit! The attendant explains that the sea star has a system of tubes containing water in its body. As the water moves around in the tubes, it creates fluid pressure that allows the sea star to move. The sea star also uses this system to obtain its food.

A sea star uses fluid ▶
pressure to move.

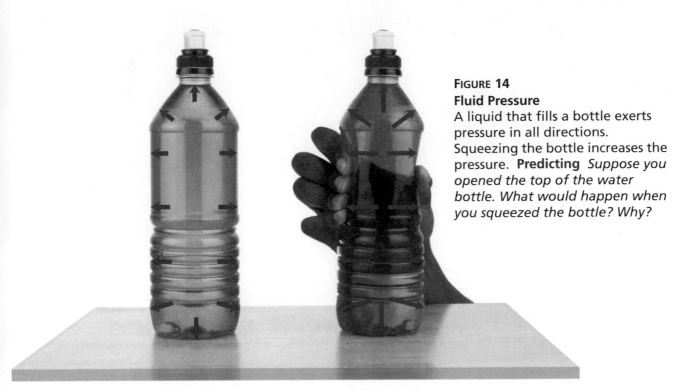

FIGURE 14
Fluid Pressure
A liquid that fills a bottle exerts pressure in all directions. Squeezing the bottle increases the pressure. **Predicting** *Suppose you opened the top of the water bottle. What would happen when you squeezed the bottle? Why?*

Transmitting Pressure in a Fluid

If you did the Discover Activity, you may be surprised to learn that a sea star's water-filled tube system is like the closed bottle you pushed your thumb against. Recall that the fluid pressure in the closed container increased when you pushed against its side. By changing the fluid pressure at any spot in the closed container, you transmitted pressure throughout the container. In the 1600s, a French mathematician named Blaise Pascal developed a principle to explain how pressure is transmitted in a fluid. Pascal's name is used for the unit of pressure.

What Is Pascal's Principle? As you may recall, fluid exerts pressure on any surface it touches. For example, the water in each bottle shown in Figure 14 exerts pressure on the entire surface of the bottle—up, down, and sideways.

What happens if you squeeze the bottle when its top is closed? The water has nowhere to go, so it presses harder on the inside surface of the bottle. The water pressure increases everywhere in the bottle. This is shown by the increased length of the arrows on the right in Figure 14.

Pascal discovered that pressure increases by the same amount throughout an enclosed or confined fluid. **When force is applied to a confined fluid, the change in pressure is transmitted equally to all parts of the fluid.** This relationship is known as **Pascal's principle.**

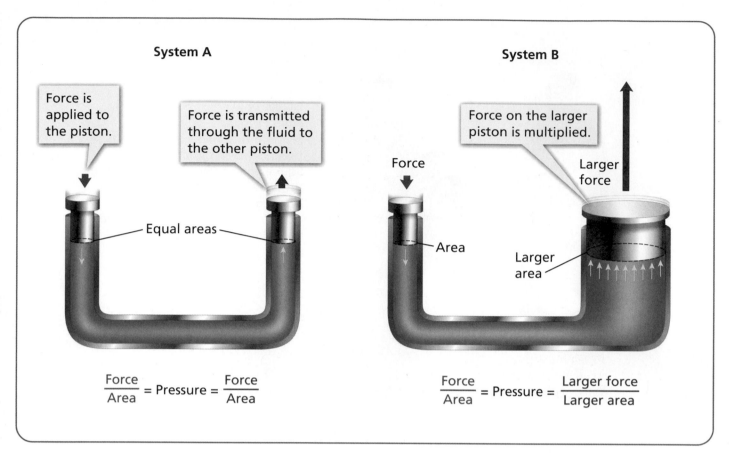

System A

Force is applied to the piston.

Force is transmitted through the fluid to the other piston.

Equal areas

$$\frac{\text{Force}}{\text{Area}} = \text{Pressure} = \frac{\text{Force}}{\text{Area}}$$

System B

Force on the larger piston is multiplied.

Force

Larger force

Area

Larger area

$$\frac{\text{Force}}{\text{Area}} = \text{Pressure} = \frac{\text{Larger force}}{\text{Larger area}}$$

FIGURE 15
Hydraulic Devices
In a hydraulic device, a force applied to one piston increases the fluid pressure equally throughout the fluid. By changing the area of the pistons, the force can be multiplied.
Problem Solving *To multiply the force applied to the left piston four times, how large must the area of the right piston be?*

For: Hydraulic Systems activity
Visit: PHSchool.com
Web Code: cgp-3033

Using Pascal's Principle You can see Pascal's principle at work in Figure 15, which shows a model of a hydraulic device. A hydraulic device works by applying a force to an enclosed fluid. The device consists of two pistons, one at each end of a U-shaped tube. A piston is like a stopper that slides up and down in a tube.

Suppose you fill System A with water and then push down on the left piston. The increase in fluid pressure will be transmitted to the right piston. According to Pascal's principle, both pistons experience the same fluid pressure. So, because both pistons have the same surface area, they will experience the same force.

Now look at System B. The right piston has a greater surface area than the left piston. Suppose the area of the small piston is 1 square centimeter and the area of the large piston is 9 square centimeters. The right piston has an area nine times greater than the area of the left piston. If you push down on the left piston, pressure is transmitted equally to the right piston. The force you exert on the left piston is multiplied nine times on the right piston. By changing the area of the pistons, you can multiply force by almost any amount you wish.

 **Reading Checkpoint** How is force multiplied in System B?

Hydraulic Systems

Hydraulic systems make use of hydraulic devices to perform a variety of functions. A **hydraulic system** uses liquids to transmit pressure in a confined fluid. **A hydraulic system multiplies force by applying the force to a small surface area. The increase in pressure is then transmitted to another part of the confined fluid, which pushes on a larger surface area.** You have probably seen a number of hydraulic systems at work, including lift systems and the brakes of a car. Because they use fluids to transmit pressure, hydraulic systems have few moving parts that can jam, break, or wear down.

Hydraulic Lifts Hydraulic lift systems are used to raise cars off the ground so mechanics can repair them with ease. You may be surprised to learn that hydraulic systems are also used to lift the heavy ladder on a fire truck to reach the upper windows of a burning building. In addition, hydraulic lifts are used to operate many pieces of heavy construction equipment such as dump trucks, backhoes, snowplows, and cranes. Next time you see a construction vehicle at work, see if you can spot the hydraulic pistons in action.

 Reading Checkpoint **What are some uses of hydraulic systems?**

Math ▶ Analyzing Data

Comparing Hydraulic Lifts

In the hydraulic device in Figure 15, a force applied to the piston on the left produces a lifting force in the piston on the right. The graph shows the relationship between the applied force and the lifting force for two hydraulic lifts.

1. **Reading Graphs** Suppose a force of 1,000 N is applied to both lifts. Use the graph to determine the lifting force of each lift.

2. **Reading Graphs** For Lift A, how much force must be applied to lift a 12,000-N object?

3. **Interpreting Data** By how much is the applied force multiplied for each lift?

4. **Interpreting Data** What can you learn from the slope of the line for each lift?

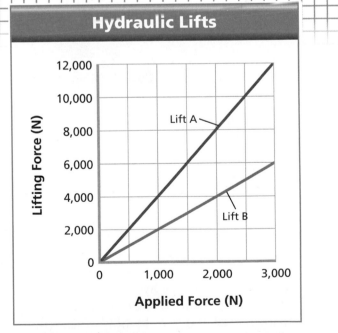

5. **Drawing Conclusions** Which lift would you choose if you wanted to produce the greater lifting force?

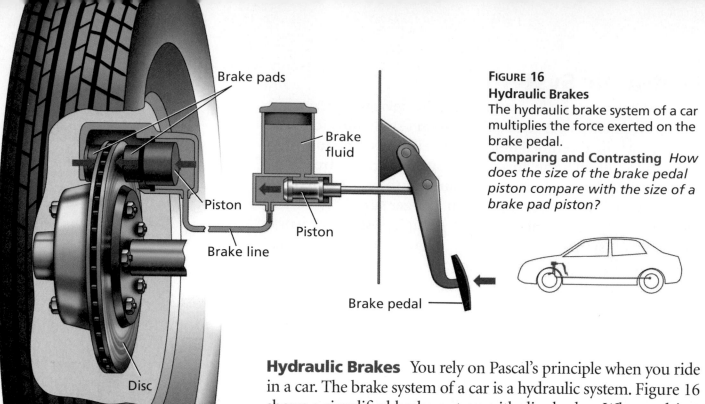

Brake pads

Brake fluid

Piston

Piston

Brake line

Brake pedal

Disc

Tire

FIGURE 16
Hydraulic Brakes
The hydraulic brake system of a car multiplies the force exerted on the brake pedal.
Comparing and Contrasting *How does the size of the brake pedal piston compare with the size of a brake pad piston?*

Hydraulic Brakes You rely on Pascal's principle when you ride in a car. The brake system of a car is a hydraulic system. Figure 16 shows a simplified brake system with disc brakes. When a driver pushes down on the brake pedal, he or she pushes a small piston. The piston exerts pressure on the brake fluid. The increased pressure is transmitted through the fluid in the brake lines to larger pistons within the wheels of the car. Each of these pistons pushes on a brake pad. The brake pads rub against the brake disc, and the wheel's motion is slowed down by the force of friction. Because the brake system multiplies force, a person can stop a large car with only a light push on the brake pedal.

Section 3 Assessment

Target Reading Skill **Asking Questions** Use the answers to the questions you wrote about the headings to help you answer the questions below.

Reviewing Key Concepts

1. a. **Reviewing** According to Pascal's principle, how is pressure transmitted in a fluid?
   b. **Relating Cause and Effect** How does a hydraulic device multiply force?
   c. **Calculating** Suppose you apply a 10-N force to a 10-cm² piston in a hydraulic device. If the force is transmitted to another piston with an area of 100 cm², by how much will the force be multiplied?
2. a. **Defining** What is a hydraulic system?
   b. **Explaining** How does a hydraulic system work?

   c. **Sequencing** Describe what happens in the brake system of a car from the time a driver steps on the brake pedal to the time the car stops.

Writing in Science

Cause-and-Effect Letter You are a mechanic who fixes hydraulic brakes. A customer asks you why his brakes do not work. When you examine the car, you notice a leak in the brake line and repair it. Write a letter to the customer explaining why a leak in the brake line caused his brakes to fail.

Bernoulli's Principle

Reading Preview

Key Concepts
- According to Bernoulli's principle, how is fluid pressure related to the motion of a fluid?
- What are some applications of Bernoulli's principle?

Key Terms
- Bernoulli's principle
- lift

Target Reading Skill
Identifying Main Ideas As you read the Applying Bernoulli's Principle section, write the main idea in a graphic organizer like the one below. Then write three supporting details that give examples of the main idea.

Main Idea

Bernoulli's principle is a factor that helps explain . . .

Detail	Detail	Detail

Lab zone Discover Activity

Does the Movement of Air Affect Pressure?

1. Use your thumb and forefinger to hold a sheet of paper by the corners.
2. Hold the paper just below your mouth, so that its edge is horizontal and the paper hangs down.
3. Blow across the top of the paper.
4. Repeat this several times, blowing harder each time.

Think It Over
Inferring On what side of the paper is the pressure lower? How do you know?

In December 1903, Wilbur and Orville Wright brought an odd-looking vehicle to a deserted beach in Kitty Hawk, North Carolina. People had flown in balloons for more than a hundred years, but the Wright brothers' goal was something no one had ever done before. They flew a plane that was heavier (denser) than air! They had spent years experimenting with different wing shapes and surfaces, and they had carefully studied the flight of birds. Their first flight at Kitty Hawk lasted just 12 seconds. The plane flew more than 36 meters and made history.

What did the Wright brothers know about flying that allowed them to construct the first airplane? And how can the principles they used explain how a jet can fly across the country? The answer has to do with fluid pressure and what happens when a fluid moves.

◀ On December 17, 1903, the Wright brothers' plane *Flyer* flew for the first time.

FIGURE 17
Making Air Move
Blowing air quickly between two cans lowers the air pressure between them. Higher pressure exerted by the still air to either side pushes the cans toward each other.
Relating Cause and Effect *How does the flowing air affect the air pressure around the two cans?*

Pressure and Moving Fluids

So far in this chapter, you have learned about fluids that are not moving. What makes a fluid flow? And what happens to fluid pressure when a fluid moves?

Fluid Motion A fluid naturally flows from an area of high pressure to an area of low pressure. This happens, for example, when you sip a drink from a straw. When you start to sip, you remove the air from the straw. This creates an area of low pressure in the straw. The higher air pressure pushing down on the surface of your drink forces the drink up into the straw.

What Is Bernoulli's Principle? In the 1700s, Swiss scientist Daniel Bernoulli (bur NOO lee) discovered that the pressure of a moving fluid is different than the pressure of a fluid at rest. **Bernoulli's principle** states that the faster a fluid moves, the less pressure the fluid exerts.

If you did the Discover Activity, you saw that air moving over the paper caused the paper to rise. Bernoulli's principle explains the behavior of the paper. **Bernoulli's principle states that as the speed of a moving fluid increases, the pressure within the fluid decreases.** The air above the paper moves, but the air below the paper does not. The moving air exerts less pressure than the still air. As a result, the still air exerts greater pressure on the bottom of the paper, pushing the paper up.

✓ **Reading Checkpoint** What is Bernoulli's principle?

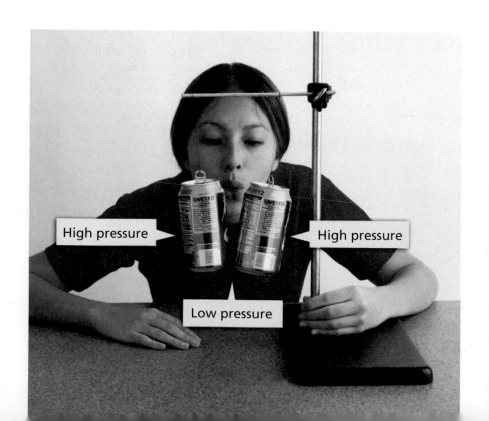

High pressure

High pressure

Low pressure

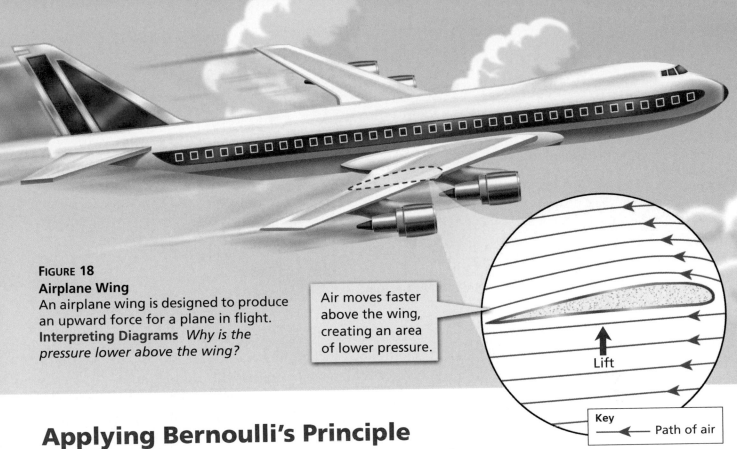

FIGURE 18
Airplane Wing
An airplane wing is designed to produce an upward force for a plane in flight. **Interpreting Diagrams** *Why is the pressure lower above the wing?*

Air moves faster above the wing, creating an area of lower pressure.

Lift

Key
⟵ Path of air

Applying Bernoulli's Principle

The Wright brothers understood Bernoulli's principle. They used it when they designed and built their plane. **Bernoulli's principle helps explain how planes fly. It also helps explain why smoke rises up a chimney, how an atomizer works, and how a flying disk glides through the air.**

Objects in Flight Bernoulli's principle is one factor that helps explain flight—from a small kite to a huge airplane. Objects can be designed so that their shapes cause air to move at different speeds above and below them. If the air moves faster above the object, fluid pressure pushes the object upward. If the air moves faster below the object, fluid pressure pushes it downward.

The wing of an airplane is designed to produce **lift**, or an upward force. Look at Figure 18 to see the design of a wing. Both the slant and the shape of the wing are sources of lift. Because the wing is slanted, the air that hits it is forced downward as the plane moves. The air exerts an equal and opposite force on the wing and pushes it upward. This upward force helps an airplane to take off.

The curved shape of a wing also gives an airplane lift. Because the top of the wing is curved, air moving over the top has a greater speed than air moving under the bottom. As a result, the air moving over the top exerts less pressure than the air below. The difference in air pressure above and below the wing creates lift.

Go Online
sciLINKS NSTA

For: Links on Bernoulli's principle
Visit: www.SciLinks.org
Web Code: scn-1334

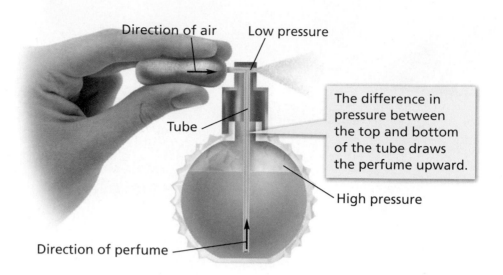

FIGURE 19
Perfume Atomizer
An atomizer is an application of Bernoulli's principle.
Applying Concepts *Why is the perfume pushed up and out of the flask?*

Direction of air   Low pressure

The difference in pressure between the top and bottom of the tube draws the perfume upward.

Tube

High pressure

Direction of perfume

Atomizers Bernoulli's principle can help you understand how the perfume atomizer shown in Figure 19 works. When you squeeze the rubber bulb, air moves quickly past the top of the tube. The moving air lowers the pressure at the top of the tube. The greater pressure in the flask pushes the liquid up into the tube. The air stream breaks the liquid into small drops, and the liquid comes out as a fine mist. In a similar way, pressure differences in the carburetors of older gasoline engines push gasoline up a tube. There, the gasoline combines with air to create the mixture of air and fuel that runs the engine.

Chimneys You can sit next to a fireplace enjoying a cozy fire thanks in part to Bernoulli's principle. Smoke rises up the chimney partly because hot air rises, and partly because it is pushed. Wind blowing across the top of a chimney lowers the air pressure there. The higher pressure at the bottom pushes air and smoke up the chimney. Smoke will rise faster in a chimney on a windy day than on a calm day.

 **Reading Checkpoint** **How does an atomizer work?**

Direction of wind

Lower pressure area

Direction of smoke

Wind blowing across the top of a chimney creates an area of low pressure.

The difference in air pressure between the top and bottom of the chimney helps keep air moving upward.

Higher pressure area

FIGURE 20
Chimney
Thanks in part to Bernoulli's principle, you can enjoy an evening by a warm fireplace without the room filling up with smoke.
Making Generalizations *Why does the smoke rise up the chimney?*

Flying Disks Did you ever wonder what allows a flying disk to glide through the air? The upper surface of a flying disk is curved like an airplane wing. Bernoulli's principle explains that the faster-moving air following the disk's curved upper surface exerts less pressure than the slower-moving air beneath it. A net force acts upward on the flying disk, creating lift. Tilting the disk slightly toward you as you throw it also helps to keep it in the air. A tilted disk pushes air down. The air exerts an equal and opposite force on the disk, pushing it up. The spinning motion of a flying disk keeps it stable as it flies.

FIGURE 21
Flying Disk
Like an airplane wing, a flying disk uses a curved upper surface to create lift. **Comparing and Contrasting** *How does a flying disk differ from an airplane wing?*

Key ◄—— Path of air

Section 4 Assessment

🎯 **Target Reading Skill** Identifying Main Ideas Use your graphic organizer to help you answer Question 1 below.

Reviewing Key Concepts

1. a. **Reviewing** What makes fluids flow?
   b. **Summarizing** What does Bernoulli's principle say about the pressure exerted by a moving fluid?
   c. **Applying Concepts** You are riding in a car on a highway when a large truck speeds by you. Explain why your car is pushed toward the truck.
2. a. **Listing** List four applications of Bernoulli's principle.
   b. **Explaining** Why does the air pressure above an airplane wing differ from the pressure below it? How is this pressure difference involved in flight?
   c. **Relating Cause and Effect** How could strong winds from a hurricane blow the roof off a house?

Lab zone **At-Home Activity**

Paper Chimney With a family member, see how a chimney works by using a paper cup and a hair dryer. Cut up several small pieces of tissue and place them in the bottom of a paper cup. Hold on to the paper cup with one hand. With your other hand, use the hair dryer to blow cool air across the top of the cup. Explain to your family member how Bernoulli's principle explains how the chimney works.

Helicopters

Most aircraft are like eagles—they take off majestically, glide among the clouds, and land with ease. But helicopters are the hummingbirds of aircraft. They can fly forward, backward, sideways, and up and down. They can stop abruptly and hover in midair. In fact, helicopters can fly circles around other types of aircraft.

Science in Action

On the top of a helicopter are large blades that turn rapidly. These blades are curved on top like the wings of an airplane. Air flowing over the curved blades helps cause lift— the upward force for the helicopter—just as air flowing over wings helps cause lift for most airplanes. Action and reaction forces as described by Newton's third law of motion also play a role in causing lift. As the tilted blades push down on the air, the air pushes up on the blade.

Main Rotor
The main rotor turns the blades and controls their angle.

Blades
Air flows over the curved, rotating blades. Along with action and reaction forces, this helps to give the helicopter lift.

As the main rotor spins, the reaction force pushes the helicopter's body in the opposite direction. If not for the tail rotor, the body would spin too.

Hand Controls and Foot Pedals
These controls are connected to the main rotor. The collective control guides the helicopter up or down. The cyclic control guides the helicopter forward, backward, or sideways. The foot pedals allow the helicopter to rotate in tight circles.

The Aircraft of Choice—Or Not?

Helicopters can hover and land nearly anywhere. So they are often the aircraft of choice in emergency situations. They are used in search and rescue missions, in fighting forest fires, and in speeding injured people to the hospital. Construction companies also use helicopters to raise heavy equipment.

Despite these benefits, there are constraints to using helicopters. Compared to an airplane, a helicopter must refuel more often and can remain in the air for less time. Another constraint is that a helicopter cannot transport heavy equipment over long distances or carry large numbers of people.

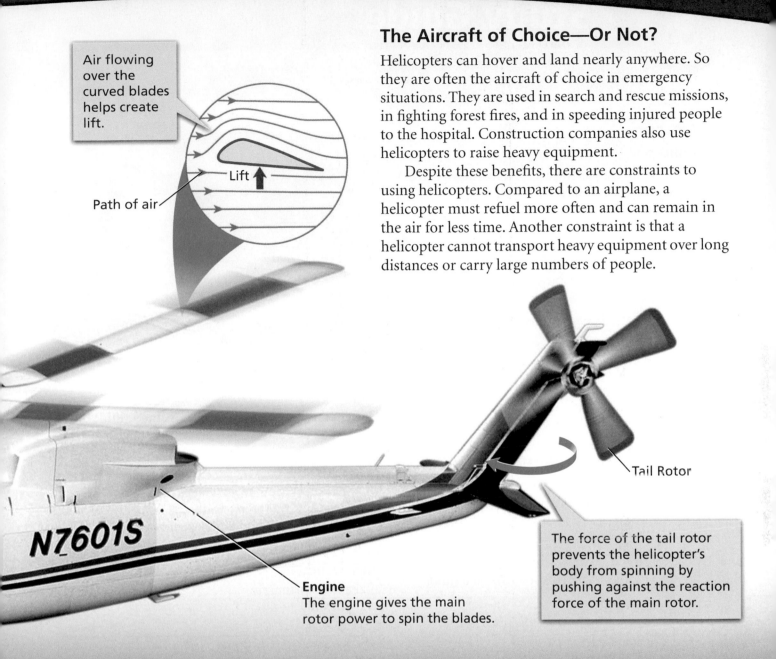

Air flowing over the curved blades helps create lift.

Lift

Path of air

N7601S

Engine
The engine gives the main rotor power to spin the blades.

Tail Rotor

The force of the tail rotor prevents the helicopter's body from spinning by pushing against the reaction force of the main rotor.

Weigh the Impact

1. Identify the Need
What advantages do helicopters have over airplanes?

2. Research
Using the Internet, research how helicopters are used in national parks, such as Yellowstone National Park. Choose one helicopter mission. Make notes on the mission's difficulty level, purpose, location, procedures, and outcome.

3. Write
Suppose you are a park ranger. Use your notes to write a report to your supervisor explaining why a helicopter was or was not the best technology to use for this mission.

Go Online
PHSchool.com

For: More on helicopters
Visit: PHSchool.com
Web Code: cgh-3030

The BIG Idea **Science and Technology** If an object is less dense than a fluid, it will float. If an object is denser than a fluid, it will sink.

① Pressure

Key Concepts

- Pressure decreases as the area over which a force is distributed increases.

- $\text{Pressure} = \dfrac{\text{Force}}{\text{Area}}$

- All of the forces exerted by the individual particles in a fluid combine to make up the pressure exerted by the fluid.

- As elevation increases, atmospheric pressure decreases.

- Water pressure increases as depth increases.

Key Terms

pressure   fluid
pascal   barometer

② Floating and Sinking

Key Concepts

- The buoyant force acts in the direction opposite to the force of gravity, so it makes an object feel lighter.

- By comparing densities, you can predict whether an object will float or sink in a fluid.

- $\text{Density} = \dfrac{\text{Mass}}{\text{Volume}}$

Key Terms

buoyant force
Archimedes' principle
density

③ Pascal's Principle

Key Concepts

- When force is applied to a confined fluid, the change in pressure is transmitted equally to all parts of the fluid.

- A hydraulic system multiplies force by applying the force to a small surface area. The increase in pressure is then transmitted to another part of the confined fluid, which pushes on a larger surface area.

Key Terms

Pascal's principle
hydraulic system

④ Bernoulli's Principle

Key Concepts

- Bernoulli's principle states that as the speed of a moving fluid increases, the pressure within the fluid decreases.

- Bernoulli's principle helps explain how planes fly. It also helps explain why smoke rises up a chimney, how an atomizer works, and how a flying disk glides through the air.

Key Terms

Bernoulli's principle
lift

Organizing Information

Sequencing Create a flowchart that shows how a hydraulic device multiplies force. (For more on Sequencing, see the Skills Handbook.)

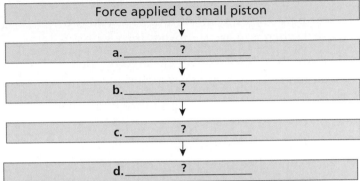

How a Hydraulic Device Works

Force applied to small piston

↓

a. _____ ?

↓

b. _____ ?

↓

c. _____ ?

↓

d. _____ ?

Reviewing Key Terms

Choose the letter of the best answer.

1. If you divide the force exerted on a surface by the total area of the surface, you will know
   a. density.　　**b.** pressure.
   c. lift.　　**d.** buoyant force.

2. If you know the weight of an object that floats, you know the
   a. object's density.
   b. object's mass.
   c. object's volume.
   d. buoyant force.

3. If you divide the mass of an object by its volume, you know the object's
   a. mass.　　**b.** weight.
   c. density.　　**d.** pressure.

4. The concept that an increase in pressure on a confined fluid is transmitted equally to all parts of the fluid is known as
   a. Pascal's principle.
   b. Bernoulli's principle.
   c. Archimedes' principle.
   d. Newton's third law.

5. The concept that the pressure in a fluid decreases as the speed of the fluid increases is known as
   a. Pascal's principle.
   b. Bernoulli's principle.
   c. Archimedes' principle.
   d. Newton's first law.

If the statement is true, write _true_. If it is false, change the underlined word or words to make the statement true.

6. Pressure is force per unit of <u>mass</u>.

7. A <u>fluid</u> is a material that can easily flow.

8. A factor that helps explain flight is <u>Archimedes' principle</u>.

9. A hydraulic system is designed to take advantage of <u>Pascal's principle</u>.

10. <u>Lift</u> is an upward force.

Writing in Science

News Report Suppose that you are a newspaper journalist on the day after the *Titanic* sank. Write a news report that tells what happened. Explain how the buoyancy of a ship is affected when it fills with water. Include information about the various fluid forces involved.

Discovery CHANNEL SCHOOL

Forces in Fluids

Video Preview
Video Field Trip
▶ Video Assessment

Review and Assessment

Checking Concepts

11. How does the amount of pressure you exert on the floor when you are lying down compare with the amount of pressure you exert when you are standing up?

12. Why aren't deep-sea fish crushed by the tremendous pressure they experience?

13. Why do you seem to weigh more in air than you do in water?

14. In a hydraulic system, why is the force exerted on a small piston multiplied when it acts on a larger piston?

15. Name two hydraulic systems that an auto mechanic would know well.

16. Why is air pressure at the top of a chimney less than air pressure at the bottom?

Thinking Critically

17. Making Generalizations How does the water pressure change at each level in the jug below? How can you tell?

18. Developing Hypotheses A sphere made of steel is put in water and, surprisingly, it floats. Develop a possible explanation for this observation.

19. Applying Concepts One method of raising a sunken ship to the surface is to inflate large bags or balloons inside its hull. Explain why this procedure could work.

20. Problem Solving You have two fluids of unknown density. Suggest a method to determine which is denser, without mixing the two fluids.

Math Practice

21. Area The cover of your textbook measures about 28 cm × 22 cm. Find its area.

22. Area A dollar bill measures about 15.9 cm × 6.7 cm. The Chinese yuan note measures 14.5 cm × 7.0 cm. Which currency uses a larger bill?

Applying Skills

The illustration shows an object supported by a spring scale, both in and out of water. Use the illustration to answer Questions 23–25.

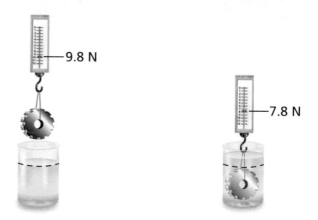

23. Inferring Why is there a difference between the weight of the object in air and its measured weight in water?

24. Calculating What is the buoyant force acting on the object?

25. Drawing Conclusions What can you conclude about the water above the dotted line?

Lab zone Chapter **Project**

Performance Assessment Test your boat to make sure it does not leak. Display the diagrams of different designs you tried and the observations and data you recorded for each design. Then demonstrate for the class how the boat floats. Point out to your classmates the features you used in your final design.

Standardized Test Prep

Choose the letter of the best answer.

1. The upward force that acts on an airplane's wing is called
   - **A** density.
   - **B** inertia.
   - **C** lift.
   - **D** pressure.

2. Which of the following is an example of a hydraulic system?
   - **F** a car's brakes
   - **G** a barometer
   - **H** an airplane's wing
   - **J** a submarine's flotation tanks

3. A boat that weighs 28,800 N is loaded with 7,200 N of cargo. After it is loaded, what is the buoyant force acting on the boat?
   - **A** 400 N
   - **B** 22,000 N
   - **C** 36,000 N
   - **D** 360,000 N

4. Why doesn't air pressure crush human beings standing at sea level?
   - **F** Air pressure at sea level is very low.
   - **G** Clothing on our bodies shields us from air pressure.
   - **H** Air is not as heavy as human beings.
   - **J** Pressure from the fluids inside our bodies balances the air pressure outside.

5. You observe that a chunk of tar sinks in puddles of rainwater but floats on the ocean. An experiment to explain the behavior of the tar should measure
   - **A** the difference between atmospheric pressure and water pressure.
   - **B** the densities of fresh water, salt water, and tar.
   - **C** the height from which the chunk of tar is dropped.
   - **D** the depth of each type of water.

Constructed Response

Use the diagram below and your knowledge of science to help you answer Question 6.

6. Use Bernoulli's principle to explain why the fabric of a domed tent bulges outward on a windy day.

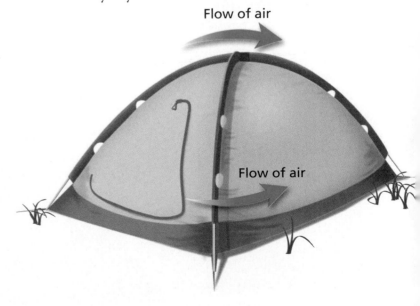

Flow of air

Flow of air

Chapter

4

Work and Machines

The BIG Idea
Work and Energy

Q How do simple machines make work easier?

Chapter Preview

❶ **What Is Work?**
Discover What Happens When You Pull at an Angle?
Try This Is Work Always the Same?

❷ **How Machines Do Work**
Discover Is It a Machine?
Try This Going Up
Analyzing Data Mechanical Advantage
Skills Lab Seesaw Science

❸ **Simple Machines**
Discover How Can You Increase Force?
Try This A Paper Screw
Skills Activity Communicating
Active Art Types of Pulleys
At-Home Activity Machines in the Kitchen
Skills Lab Angling for Access

A Maori woodcarver in New Zealand ▶
creates a traditional carving.

Work and Machines

▶ Video Preview
Video Field Trip
Video Assessment

Lab zone™ Chapter **Project**

The Nifty Lifting Machine

In this Chapter Project, you will design and build a lifting machine and then demonstrate it to the class.

Your Goal To design, build, and test a complex machine that can lift a 600-gram soup can 5 centimeters

Your machine must
- be made of materials that are approved by your teacher
- consist of at least two simple machines working in combination
- be able to lift the soup can to a height of at least 5 centimeters
- be built following the safety guidelines in Appendix A

Plan It! Preview the chapter to find out what simple machines you can use and how to use them. Determine the amount of work your machine must do. Brainstorm different machine designs and materials with your classmates. Analyze factors affecting efficiency and mechanical advantage, and then construct your machine. When your teacher has approved your design, build and test your machine.

What Is Work?

Reading Preview

Key Concepts
- When is work done on an object?
- How do you determine the work done on an object?
- What is power?

Key Terms
- work • joule • power

🎯 Target Reading Skill
Asking Questions Before you read, preview the red headings. In a graphic organizer like the one below, ask a *what* or *how* question for each heading. As you read, write the answers to your questions.

Question	Answer
What is work?	Work is . . .

Lab zone Discover **Activity**

What Happens When You Pull at an Angle?

1. Fill a mug half full with water.
2. Cut a medium-weight rubber band to make a strand of elastic. Thread the elastic through a mug handle. By pulling on the elastic, you can move the mug across a table.
3. You can hold the two halves of elastic parallel to each other or at an angle to each other, as shown. Predict which way will be more effective in moving the mug.
4. Pull on the elastic both ways. Describe any differences you observe.

Think It Over
Developing Hypotheses Which of the two pulls was more effective in moving the mug? Explain why.

This morning you probably woke up and went to school with your backpack of books. You lifted the backpack and then carried it with you. If you had a lot of books to bring home, carrying your backpack might have felt like a lot of work. But in the scientific definition of work, after you lifted the backpack, you did no work to carry it at all!

The Meaning of Work

In scientific terms, you do **work** when you exert a force on an object that causes the object to move some distance. **Work is done on an object when the object moves in the same direction in which the force is exerted.** If you push a child on a swing, for example, you are doing work on the child. If you pull your books out of your backpack, you do work on the books. If you lift a bag of groceries out of a shopping cart, you do work on the bag of groceries.

FIGURE 1
Doing Work
Lifting books out of a backpack is work, but carrying them to class is not.

No Work Without Motion To do work on an object, the object must move some distance as a result of your force. If the object does not move, no work is done, no matter how much force is exerted.

There are many situations in which you exert a force but don't do any work. Suppose, for example, you are pushing a car that is stuck in the snow. You certainly exert a force on the car, so it might seem as if you do work. But if the force you exert does not make the car move, you are not doing any work on it.

Force in the Same Direction So why didn't you do any work when you carried your books to school? To do work on an object, the force you exert must be in the same direction as the object's motion. When you carry an object at constant velocity, you exert an upward force to hold the object so that it doesn't fall to the ground. The motion of the object, however, is in the horizontal direction. Since the force is vertical and the motion is horizontal, you don't do any work on the object as you carry it.

How much work do you do when you pull a suitcase with wheels? When you pull a suitcase, you pull on the handle at an angle to the ground. As you can see in Figure 2, your force has both a horizontal part and a vertical part. When you pull this way, only part of your force does work—the part in the same direction as the motion of the suitcase. The rest of your force does not help pull the suitcase forward.

✔ **Reading Checkpoint** If you pull an object horizontally, what part of your force does work?

FIGURE 2
Force, Motion, and Work
Whether the girl does work on the suitcase depends on the direction of her force and the suitcase's motion. **Drawing Conclusions** *Why doesn't the girl do work when she carries her suitcase rather than pulling it?*

Direction of motion

A The lifting force is not in the direction of the suitcase's motion, so no work is done.

Force

Direction of motion

B The force acts in the same direction as the suitcase's motion, so the maximum work is done.

Part of the force that does no work

Force

Part of the force that does work

Direction of motion

C Only the horizontal part of the force does work to move the suitcase.

FIGURE 3
Amount of Work
When you lift a plant, you do work. You do more work when you lift a heavier plant the same distance.
Relating Cause and Effect
Why does it take more work to lift the heavier plant?

Calculating Work

Which do you think involves more work: lifting a 50-newton potted plant 0.5 meter off the ground onto a table, or lifting a 100-newton plant onto the same table? Your common sense may suggest that lifting a heavier object requires more work than lifting a lighter object. This is true. Is it more work to lift a plant onto a table or up to the top story of a building? As you might guess, moving an object a greater distance requires more work than moving the same object a shorter distance.

The amount of work you do depends on both the amount of force you exert and the distance the object moves. **The amount of work done on an object can be determined by multiplying force times distance.**

Work = Force × Distance

You can use the work formula to calculate the amount of work you do to lift a plant. When you lift an object, the upward force you exert must be at least equal to the object's weight. So, to lift the lighter plant, you would have to exert a force of 50 newtons. The distance you lift the plant is 0.5 meter. The amount of work you do on the plant can be calculated using the work formula.

Work = Force × Distance
Work = 50 N × 0.5 m = 25 N·m

To lift the heavier plant, you would have to exert a force of 100 newtons. So the amount of work you do would be 100 newtons × 0.5 meter, or 50 N·m. As you can see, you do more work to lift the heavier object.

Go Online
SCiLINKS™ NSTA

For: Links on work
Visit: www.SciLinks.org
Web Code: scn-1341

When force is measured in newtons and distance in meters, the SI unit of work is the newton × meter (N·m). This unit is also called a joule (JOOL) in honor of James Prescott Joule, a physicist who studied work in the mid-1800s. One **joule** (J) is the amount of work you do when you exert a force of 1 newton to move an object a distance of 1 meter. You would have to exert 25 joules of work to lift the lighter plant and 50 joules of work to lift the heavier plant.

Reading Checkpoint **What is the SI unit for work?**

Power

The amount of work you do on an object is not affected by the time it takes to do the work. For example, if you carry a backpack up a flight of stairs, the work you do is the weight of the backpack times the height of the stairs. Whether you walk or run up the stairs, you do the same amount of work because time is not part of the definition of work.

But time is important when you talk about power. **Power** is the rate at which work is done. **Power equals the amount of work done on an object in a unit of time.** You need more power to run up the stairs with your backpack than to walk because it takes you less time to do the same work.

You can think of power in another way. An object that has more power than another object does more work in the same time. It can also mean doing the same amount of work in less time.

For example, a car's engine does work to accelerate the car from its rest position. The greater a car engine's power, the faster the engine can accelerate the car.

Try This Activity

Is Work Always the Same?

1. Obtain a pinwheel along with a hair dryer that has at least two power settings.
2. Set the dryer on its lowest setting. Use it to blow the pinwheel. Observe the pinwheel's motion.
3. Set the dryer on its highest setting. Again, blow the pinwheel and observe its motion.

Inferring Explain why work is done on the pinwheel. How are the two situations different? Is the amount of work done greater for the high or low setting? Why?

FIGURE 4
Work and Power
Whether you use a rake or a blower, the same amount of work is done to gather leaves. However, the blower has more power.
Inferring *Will the blower or the rake do the same amount of work in less time?*

Calculating Power Whenever you know how fast work is done, you can calculate power. Power is calculated by dividing the amount of work done by the amount of time it takes to do the work. This can be written as the following formula.

$$\text{Power} = \frac{\text{Work}}{\text{Time}}$$

Since work is equal to force times distance, you can rewrite the equation for power as follows.

$$\text{Power} = \frac{\text{Force} \times \text{Distance}}{\text{Time}}$$

Math ➤ Sample Problem

Calculating Power

A tow truck exerts a force of 11,000 N to pull a car out of a ditch. It moves the car a distance of 5 m in 25 seconds. What is the power of the tow truck?

1 Read and Understand
What information are you given?
  Force of the tow truck (*F*) = 11,000 N
  Distance (*d*) = 5.0 m
  Time (*t*) = 25 s

2 Plan and Solve
What quantity are you trying to calculate?
  The power (*P*) of the tow truck = ■

What formula contains the given quantities and the unknown quantity?

$$\text{Power} = \frac{\text{Force} \times \text{Distance}}{\text{Time}}$$

Perform the calculation.

$$\text{Power} = \frac{11,000 \text{ N} \times 5.0 \text{ m}}{25 \text{ s}}$$

$$\text{Power} = \frac{55,000 \text{ N·m}}{25 \text{ s}} \text{ or } \frac{55,000 \text{ J}}{25 \text{ s}}$$

$$\text{Power} = 2,200 \text{ J/s} = 2,200 \text{ W}$$

3 Look Back and Check
Does your answer make sense?
  The answer tells you that the tow truck pulls the car with a power of 2,200 W. This value is about the same power of three horses, so the answer is reasonable.

Full Serve

Math ➤ Practice

1. **Calculating Power** A motor exerts a force of 12,000 N to lift an elevator 8.0 m in 6.0 seconds. What is the power of the motor?

2. **Calculating Power** A crane lifts an 8,000-N beam 75 m to the top of a building in 30 seconds. What is the crane's power?

Power Units When work is measured in joules and time in seconds, the SI unit of power is the joule per second (J/s). This unit is also known as the watt (W), in honor of James Watt, who made great improvements to the steam engine. One joule of work done in one second is one watt of power. In other words, 1 J/s = 1 W.

A watt is a relatively small unit of power. Because a watt is so small, power is often measured in larger units. One kilowatt (kW) equals 1,000 watts.

When people talk about engines for vehicles, they use another power unit instead of the watt. This unit is the horsepower. One horsepower equals 746 watts. (The horsepower is not an SI unit.)

FIGURE 5
Horsepower
James Watt used the word *horsepower* to advertise the advantages of his improved steam engine (next to the chimney) of 1769.

 **Reading Checkpoint** What is a kilowatt?

Section 1 Assessment

Target Reading Skill Asking Questions Use the answers to the questions you wrote about the headings to help you answer the questions below.

Reviewing Key Concepts

1. a. **Reviewing** What is work?
   b. **Describing** In order for work to be done on an object, what must happen to the object?
   c. **Applying Concepts** In which of the following situations is work being done: rolling a bowling ball, pushing on a tree for ten minutes, kicking a football?
2. a. **Identifying** What is a joule?
   b. **Explaining** How can you determine the amount of work done on an object?
   c. **Problem Solving** Is more work done when a force of 2 N moves an object 3 m or when a force of 3 N moves an object 2 m? Explain.

3. a. **Defining** What is power?
   b. **Summarizing** How are power and work related?

Math Practice

4. **Calculating Power** Your laundry basket weighs 22 N and your room is 3.0 m above you on the second floor. It takes you 6.0 seconds to carry the laundry basket up. What is your power?

5. **Calculating Power** If you take only 4.4 seconds to carry the basket upstairs, what is your power?

How Machines Do Work

Reading Preview

Key Concepts
- How do machines make work easier?
- What is a machine's mechanical advantage?
- How can you calculate the efficiency of a machine?

Key Terms
- machine • input force
- output force • input work
- output work
- mechanical advantage
- efficiency

Target Reading Skill

Identifying Main Ideas As you read the What Is a Machine? section, write the main idea in a graphic organizer like the one below. Then write three supporting details.

Main Idea

The mechanical advantage of a machine helps by . . .

Detail	Detail	Detail

Lab zone Discover Activity

Is It a Machine?

1. Examine the objects that your teacher gives you.
2. Sort the objects into those that are machines and those that are not machines.
3. Determine how each object that you classified as a machine functions. Explain each object to another student.

Think It Over
Forming Operational Definitions Why did you decide certain objects were machines while other objects were not?

A load of soil for your school garden has been dumped 10 meters from the garden. How can you move the soil easily and quickly? You could move the soil by handfuls, but that would take a long time. Using a shovel would make the job easier. If you had a wheelbarrow, that would make the job easier still! But be careful what you think. Using a machine may make work go faster, but it doesn't mean you do less work.

FIGURE 6
Using Machines
Shovels and rakes make the work of these students easier.

What Is a Machine?

Shovels and wheelbarrows are two examples of machines. A **machine** is a device that allows you to do work in a way that is easier. You may think of machines as complex gadgets with motors, but a machine can be quite simple. For example, think about using a shovel. A shovel makes the work of moving soil easier, so a shovel is a machine.

Moving a pile of soil will involve the same amount of work whether you use your hands or a shovel. What a shovel or any other machine does is change the way in which work is done. **A machine makes work easier by changing at least one of three factors. A machine may change the amount of force you exert, the distance over which you exert your force, or the direction in which you exert your force.** In other words, a machine makes work easier by changing either force, distance, or direction.

Input and Output Forces When you use a machine to do work, you exert a force over some distance. For example, you exert a force on the shovel when you use it to lift soil. The force you exert on the machine is called the **input force.** The input force moves the machine a certain distance, called the input distance. The machine does work by exerting a force over another distance, called the output distance. The force the machine exerts on an object is called the **output force.**

Input and Output Work The input force times the input distance is called the **input work.** The output force times the output distance is called the **output work.** When you use a machine, the amount of output work can never be greater than the amount of input work.

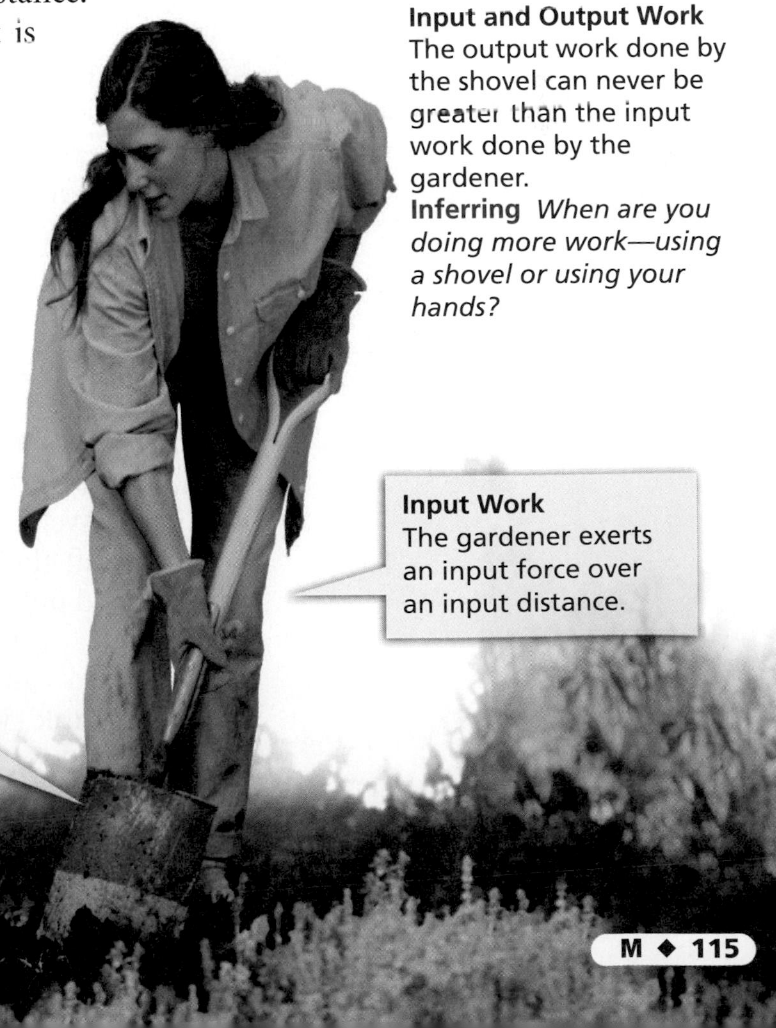

FIGURE 7
Input and Output Work
The output work done by the shovel can never be greater than the input work done by the gardener.
Inferring *When are you doing more work—using a shovel or using your hands?*

Input Work
The gardener exerts an input force over an input distance.

Output Work
The shovel exerts an output force over an output distance.

Lab zone Try This Activity

Going Up

Does a rope simply turn your force upside down? Find out!

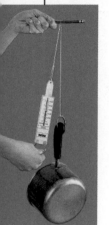

1. Tie a piece of string about 50 cm long to an object, such as an empty cooking pot. Make a small loop on the other end of the string.

2. Using a spring scale, slowly lift the pot 20 cm. Note the reading on the scale.

3. Now loop the string over a pencil and pull down on the spring scale to lift the pot 20 cm. Note the reading on the scale.

Developing Hypotheses
How did the readings on the spring scale compare? If the readings were different, suggest a reason why. What might be an advantage to using this system?

Changing Force In some machines, the output force is greater than the input force. How can this happen? Recall the formula for work: Work = Force × Distance. If the amount of work stays the same, a decrease in force must mean an increase in distance. So if a machine allows you to use less input force to do the same amount of work, you must apply that input force over a greater distance.

What kind of machine allows you to exert a smaller input force? Think about a ramp. Suppose you have to lift a heavy box onto a stage. Instead of lifting the box, you could push it up a ramp. Because the length of the ramp is greater than the height of the stage, you exert your input force over a greater distance. However, when you use the ramp, the work is easier because you can exert a smaller input force. The faucet knob in Figure 8 changes force in the same way.

Changing Distance In some machines, the output force is less than the input force. Why would you want to use a machine like this? This kind of machine allows you to exert your input force over a shorter distance. In order to apply a force over a shorter distance, you need to apply a greater input force.

When do you use this kind of machine? Think about taking a shot with a hockey stick. You move your hands a short distance, but the other end of the stick moves a greater distance to hit the puck. When you use chopsticks to eat your food, you move the hand holding the chopsticks a short distance. The other end of the chopsticks moves a greater distance, allowing you to pick up and eat food. When you ride a bicycle in high gear, you apply a force to the pedals over a short distance. The bicycle, meanwhile, travels a much longer distance.

Changing Direction Some machines don't change either force or distance. What could be the advantage of these machines? Well, think about a weight machine. You could stand and lift the weights. But it is much easier to sit on the machine and pull down than to lift up. By running a steel cable over a small wheel at the top of the machine, as shown in Figure 8, you can raise the weights by pulling down on the cable. This cable system is a machine that makes your job easier by changing the direction in which you exert your force.

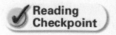 **Reading Checkpoint** How does the cable system on a weight machine make raising the weights easier?

FIGURE 8
Making Work Easier

A machine can make work easier
in one of three ways.

Input force

Output
force

When a machine increases force, you must exert the
input force over a greater distance.

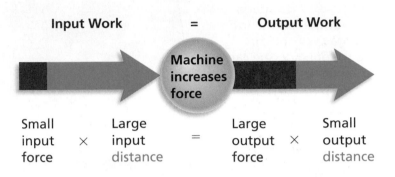

Input Work		=	Output Work	
Machine increases force				
Small input force	× Large input distance	=	Large output force	× Small output distance

When a machine increases distance, you must apply a
greater input force.

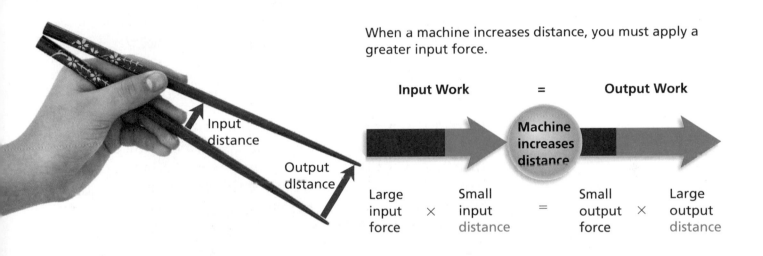

Input
distance

Output
distance

Input Work		=	Output Work	
Machine increases distance				
Large input force	× Small input distance	=	Small output force	× Large output distance

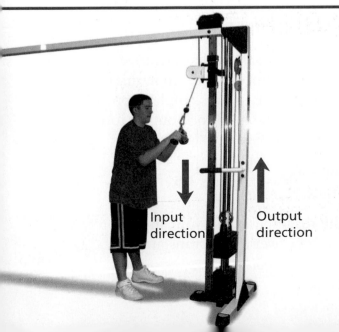

Input
direction

Output
direction

When a machine changes the direction of the input
force, the amount of force and the distance remain
the same.

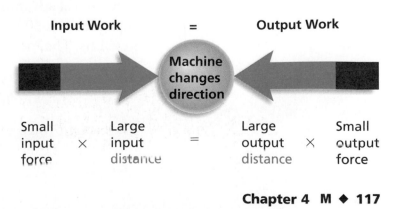

Input Work		=	Output Work	
Machine changes direction				
Small input force	× Large input distance	=	Large output distance	× Small output force

Mechanical Advantage

If you compare the input force to the output force, you can find the advantage of using a machine. **A machine's mechanical advantage is the number of times a machine increases a force exerted on it.** Finding the ratio of output force to input force gives you the **mechanical advantage** of a machine.

$$\text{Mechanical advantage} = \frac{\text{Output force}}{\text{Input force}}$$

Increasing Force When the output force is greater than the input force, the mechanical advantage of a machine is greater than 1. Suppose you exert an input force of 10 newtons on a hand-held can opener, and the opener exerts an output force of 30 newtons on a can. The mechanical advantage of the can opener is

$$\frac{\text{Output force}}{\text{Input force}} = \frac{30 \text{ N}}{10 \text{ N}} = 3$$

The can opener triples your input force!

Increasing Distance For a machine that increases distance, the output force is less than the input force. So in this case, the mechanical advantage is less than 1. For example, suppose your input force is 20 newtons and the machine's output force is 10 newtons. The mechanical advantage is

$$\frac{\text{Output force}}{\text{Input force}} = \frac{10 \text{ N}}{20 \text{ N}} = 0.5$$

The output force of the machine is half your input force, but the machine exerts that force over a longer distance.

Mechanical Advantage

The input force and output force for three different ramps are shown in the graph.

1. **Reading Graphs** What variable is plotted on the horizontal axis?

2. **Interpreting Data** If an 80-N input force is exerted on Ramp 2, what is the output force?

3. **Interpreting Data** Find the slope of the line for each ramp.

4. **Drawing Conclusions** Why does the slope represent each ramp's mechanical advantage? Which ramp has the greatest mechanical advantage?

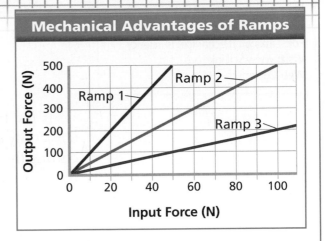

Mechanical Advantages of Ramps

Graph — vertical axis: Output Force (N), 0 to 500; horizontal axis: Input Force (N), 0 to 100. Three lines labeled Ramp 1, Ramp 2, and Ramp 3.

Changing Direction What can you predict about the mechanical advantage of a machine that changes the direction of the force? If only the direction changes, the input force will be the same as the output force. The mechanical advantage will always be 1.

Efficiency of Machines

So far, you have learned that the work you put into a machine is exactly equal to the work done by the machine. In an ideal situation, this equation is true. In real situations, however, the output work is always less than the input work.

Friction and Efficiency If you have ever tried to cut something with scissors that barely open and close, you know that a large part of your work is wasted overcoming the tightness, or friction, between the parts of the scissors.

In every machine, some work is wasted overcoming the force of friction. The less friction there is, the closer the output work is to the input work. The **efficiency** of a machine compares the output work to the input work. Efficiency is expressed as a percent. The higher the percent, the more efficient the machine is. If you know the input work and output work for a machine, you can calculate a machine's efficiency.

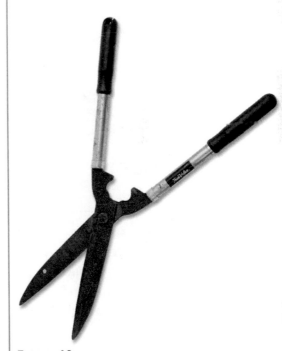

FIGURE 10
Efficiency
A rusty pair of shears is less efficient than a new pair of shears.
Applying Concepts *What force reduces the efficiency of the shears?*

Reading Checkpoint Why is output work always less than input work in real situations?

Go Online

SCLINKS NSTA

For: Links on mechanical efficiency
Visit: www.SciLinks.org
Web Code: scn-1342

Calculating Efficiency To calculate the efficiency of a machine, divide the output work by the input work and multiply the result by 100 percent. This is summarized by the following formula.

$$\text{Efficiency} = \frac{\text{Output work}}{\text{Input work}} \times 100\%$$

If the tight scissors described above have an efficiency of 60%, only a little more than half of the work you do goes into cutting the paper. The rest is wasted overcoming the friction in the scissors.

Math Sample Problem

Calculating Efficiency

You do 250,000 J of work to cut a lawn with a hand mower. If the work done by the mower is 200,000 J, what is the efficiency of the lawn mower?

1 **Read and Understand.**
What information are you given?

Input work (W_{input}) = 250,000 J

Output work (W_{output}) = 200,000 J

2 **Plan and Solve**
What quantity are you trying to calculate?

The efficiency of the lawn mower = ■

What formula contains the given quantities and the unknown quantity?

$$\text{Efficiency} = \frac{\text{Output work}}{\text{Input work}} \times 100\%$$

Perform the calculation.

$$\text{Efficiency} = \frac{200,000 \text{ J}}{250,000 \text{ J}} \times 100\%$$

$$\text{Efficiency} = 0.8 \times 100\% = 80\%$$

The efficiency of the lawn mower is 80%.

3 **Look Back and Check**
Does your answer make sense?

An efficiency of 80% means that 80 out of every 100 J of work went into cutting the lawn. This answer makes sense because most of the input work is converted to output work.

Math Practice

1. **Calculating Efficiency** You do 20 J of work while using a hammer. The hammer does 18 J of work on a nail. What is the efficiency of the hammer?

2. **Calculating Efficiency** Suppose you left your lawn mower outdoors all winter. Now it's rusty. Of your 250,000 J of work, only 100,000 J go to cutting the lawn. What is the efficiency of the lawn mower now?

FIGURE 11
An Ideal Machine?
The balls of this Newton's cradle may swing for a long time, but friction will eventually bring them to rest.

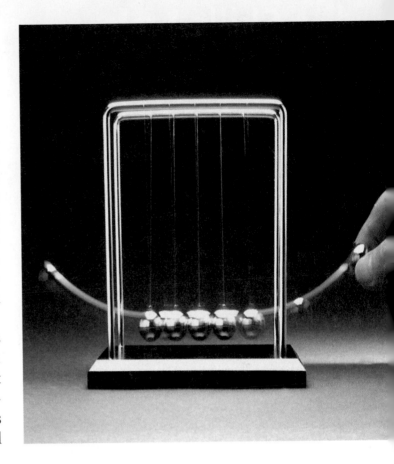

Real and Ideal Machines If you could find a machine with an efficiency of 100%, it would be an ideal machine. Unfortunately, such a machine does not exist. In all machines, some work is wasted due to friction. Even the balls in Figure 11 will eventually come to rest. All machines have an efficiency of less than 100%. The machines you use every day, such as scissors, screwdrivers, and rakes, lose some work due to friction.

A machine's ideal mechanical advantage is its mechanical advantage with 100% efficiency. However, if you measure a machine's input force and output force, you will find the efficiency is always less than 100%. A machine's measured mechanical advantage is called actual mechanical advantage.

 **Reading Checkpoint** What is a machine's ideal mechanical advantage?

Section 2 Assessment

Target Reading Skill

Identifying Main Ideas Use your graphic organizer to help you answer Question 1 below.

Reviewing Key Concepts

1. a. **Defining** What is a machine?
   b. **Describing** In what three ways can machines make work easier?
   c. **Applying Concepts** How does a screwdriver make work easier?

2. a. **Reviewing** What is the mechanical advantage of a machine?
   b. **Making Generalizations** What is the mechanical advantage of a machine that changes only the direction of the applied force?
   c. **Calculating** If a machine has an input force of 40 N and an output force of 80 N, what is its mechanical advantage?

3. a. **Reviewing** What must you know in order to calculate a machine's efficiency?
   b. **Explaining** What is an ideal machine?
   c. **Comparing and Contrasting** How is a real machine like an ideal machine, and how is it different?

Math Practice

4. **Calculating Efficiency** The input work you do on a can opener is 12 J. The output work the can opener does is 6 J. What is the efficiency of the can opener?

5. **Calculating Efficiency** Suppose the efficiency of a manual pencil sharpener is 58%. If the output work needed to sharpen a pencil is 4.8 J, how much input work must you do to sharpen the pencil?

Seesaw Science

Problem

What is the relationship between distance and weight for a balanced seesaw?

Skills Focus

controlling variables, interpreting data

Materials

- meter stick • masking tape
- 28 pennies, minted after 1982
- small object with a mass of about 50 g
- dowel or other cylindrical object for pivot point, about 10 cm long and 3 cm in diameter

Procedure

1. Begin by using the dowel and meter stick to build a seesaw. Tape the dowel firmly to the table so that it does not roll.

2. Choose the meter stick mark that will rest on the dowel from the following: 55 cm or 65 cm. Record your choice. Position your meter stick so that it is on your chosen pivot point with the 100-cm mark on your right.

3. Slide the 50-g mass along the shorter end of the meter stick until the meter stick is balanced, with both sides in the air. (This is called "zeroing" your meter stick.)

4. Copy the data table into your notebook.

5. Place a stack of 8 pennies exactly over the 80-cm mark. Determine the distance, in centimeters, from the pivot point to the pennies. Record this distance in the "Distance to Pivot" column for the right side of the seesaw.

6. Predict where you must place a stack of 5 pennies in order to balance the meter stick. Test your prediction and record the actual position in the "Position of Pennies" column for the left side of the seesaw.

Data Table

Your group's pivot point position: _____ cm

Trial Number	Side of Seesaw	Number of Pennies or Weight of Pennies (pw)	Position of Pennies (cm)	Distance to Pivot (cm)	Weight of Pennies × Distance
1	Right				
	Left				
2	Right				
	Left				
3	Right				

7. Determine the distance, in centimeters, from the pivot point to the left stack of pennies. Record this distance in the "Distance to Pivot" column for the left side of the seesaw.

8. If you use an imaginary unit of weight, the pennyweight (pw), then one penny weighs 1 pw. Multiply the weight of each stack of pennies by the distance to the pivot point. Record the result in the last column of the data table.

9. Predict how the position of the pennies in Step 6 would change if you used 7, 12, 16, and 20 pennies instead of 5 pennies. Test your predictions.

Analyze and Conclude

1. **Controlling Variables** In this experiment, what is the manipulated variable? The responding variable? How do you know which is which?

2. **Interpreting Data** As you increase the number of pennies on the left, what happens to the distance at which you must place the stack in order to balance the meter stick?

3. **Drawing Conclusions** What conclusion can you draw about the relationship between distances and weights needed to balance a seesaw?

4. **Controlling Variables** Why was it important to zero the meter stick with the 50-g mass?

5. **Interpreting Data** Compare your results with those of the other groups. How do different pivot point positions affect the results?

6. **Communicating** Write a dialogue that occurs when two friends try to balance themselves on opposite sides of a seesaw. One friend has a mass of 54 kg and the other friend has a mass of 42 kg.

Design an Experiment

Suppose you have a seesaw with a movable pivot. You want to use it with a younger friend who weighs half what you weigh. If you and your friend sit on the ends of the seesaw, where should you position the pivot point? Develop a hypothesis and then design an experiment to test it. *Obtain your teacher's permission before carrying out your investigation.*

Simple Machines

Reading Preview

Key Concepts
- What are the six kinds of simple machines, and how are they used?
- What is the ideal mechanical advantage of each simple machine?
- What is a compound machine?

Key Terms
- inclined plane • wedge
- screw • lever • fulcrum
- wheel and axle • pulley
- compound machine

🎯 Target Reading Skill
Previewing Visuals Before you read, preview Figure 17. Then write two questions that you have about the diagram in a graphic organizer like the one below. As you read, answer your questions.

Three Classes of Levers

Q.	What are the three classes of levers?
A.	
Q.	

Lab zone | Discover **Activity**

How Can You Increase Force?
1. Working with two partners, wrap a rope around two broomsticks as shown.
2. Your two partners should try to hold the brooms apart with the same amount of force throughout the activity. For safety, they should hold firmly, but not with all their strength.
3. Try to pull the two students together by pulling on the broomsticks. Can you do it?
4. Can you pull them together by pulling on the rope?

Think It Over
Predicting What do you think will be the effect of wrapping the rope around the broomsticks several more times?

Look at the objects shown on these pages. Which of them would you call machines? Would it surprise you to find out that each is made up of one or more simple machines? As you learned in the last section, a machine helps you do work by changing the amount or direction of the force you apply.

There are six basic kinds of simple machines: the inclined plane, the wedge, the screw, the lever, the wheel and axle, and the pulley. In this section, you will learn how the different types of simple machines help you do work.

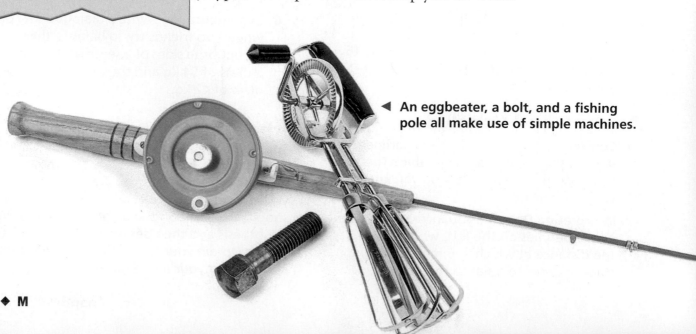

◀ An eggbeater, a bolt, and a fishing pole all make use of simple machines.

Input force

Output force

Input force

Output force

Inclined Plane

Have you ever had to lift something from a lower level to a higher level? The job is much easier if you have a ramp. For example, a ramp makes it much easier to push a grocery cart over a curb. A ramp is an example of a simple machine called an inclined plane. An **inclined plane** is a flat, sloped surface.

How It Works An inclined plane allows you to exert your input force over a longer distance. As a result, the input force needed is less than the output force. The input force that you use on an inclined plane is the force with which you push or pull an object. The output force is the force that you would need to lift the object without the inclined plane. Recall that this force is equal to the weight of the object.

Mechanical Advantage You can determine the ideal mechanical advantage of an inclined plane by dividing the length of the incline by its height.

$$\text{Ideal mechanical advantage} = \frac{\text{Length of incline}}{\text{Height of incline}}$$

For example, if you are loading a truck that is 1 meter high using a ramp that is 3 meters long, the ideal mechanical advantage of the ramp is 3 meters ÷ 1 meter, or 3. The inclined plane increases the force you exerted three times. If the height of the incline does not change, increasing the length of the incline will increase the mechanical advantage. The longer the incline, the less input force you need to push or pull an object.

FIGURE 12
Inclined Plane
Although the amount of work is the same whether you lift the boxes or push them up the ramp to the truck, you need less force when you use an inclined plane.
Relating Cause and Effect *When you use a ramp, what happens to the distance over which you exert your force?*

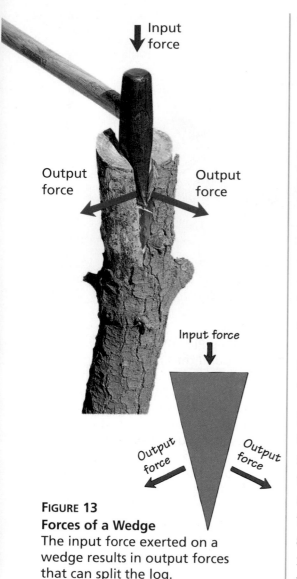

FIGURE 13
Forces of a Wedge
The input force exerted on a wedge results in output forces that can split the log.

Wedge

If you've ever sliced an apple with a knife, pulled up a zipper, or seen someone chop wood with an ax, you are familiar with another simple machine known as a wedge. A **wedge** is a device that is thick at one end and tapers to a thin edge at the other end. It might be helpful to think of a wedge, like the one shown in Figure 13, as an inclined plane (or sometimes two inclined planes back to back) that can move.

How It Works When you use a wedge, instead of moving an object along the inclined plane, you move the inclined plane itself. For example, when an ax is used to split wood, the ax handle exerts a force on the blade of the ax, which is the wedge. That force pushes the wedge down into the wood. The wedge in turn exerts an output force at a 90° angle to its slope, splitting the wood in two.

Wedges are a part of your everyday life. For example, a zipper depends on wedges to close and open. A pencil sharpener, a cheese grater, and a shovel all make use of wedges.

Mechanical Advantage The mechanical advantage of the wedge and the inclined plane are similar. **The ideal mechanical advantage of a wedge is determined by dividing the length of the wedge by its width.** The longer and thinner a wedge is, the greater its mechanical advantage. For example, the cutting edge of a steel carving knife is a wedge. When you sharpen a knife, you make the wedge thinner and increase its mechanical advantage. That is why sharp knives cut better than dull knives.

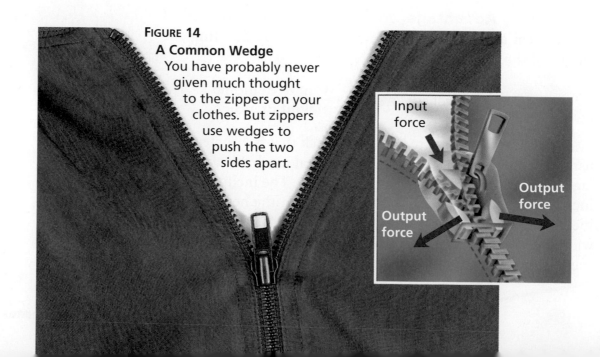

FIGURE 14
A Common Wedge
You have probably never given much thought to the zippers on your clothes. But zippers use wedges to push the two sides apart.

FIGURE 15
It's All in the Threads
Examples of the screw are found in jars and hardware fasteners.
Relating Cause and Effect *How does the distance between the threads of a screw affect its mechanical advantage?*

Screws

Like a wedge, a screw is a simple machine that is related to the inclined plane. A **screw** can be thought of as an inclined plane wrapped around a cylinder. This spiral inclined plane forms the threads of the screw.

How It Works When you twist a screw into a piece of wood, you exert an input force on the screw. The threads of a screw act like an inclined plane to increase the distance over which you exert the input force. As the threads of the screw turn, they exert an output force on the wood, pulling the screw into the wood. Friction between the screw and the wood holds the screw in place.

Many devices act like screws. Examples include bolts, light bulbs, and jar lids. Look at the jar lid in Figure 15. When you turn the lid, your small input force is greatly increased because of the screw threads on the lid. The threads on the lid are pulled against the matching threads on the jar with a strong enough force to make a tight seal.

Mechanical Advantage The closer together the threads of a screw are, the greater the mechanical advantage. This is because the closer the threads are, the more times you must turn the screw to fasten it into a piece of wood. Your input force is applied over a longer distance. The longer input distance results in an increased output force. Think of the length around the threads as the length of the inclined plane, and the length of the screw as the height of the inclined plane. **The ideal mechanical advantage of a screw is the length around the threads divided by the length of the screw.**

Reading Checkpoint How is a screw like an inclined plane?

Levers

Have you ever ridden on a seesaw or pried open a paint can with an opener? If so, then you are already familiar with another simple machine called a lever. A **lever** is a rigid bar that is free to pivot, or rotate, on a fixed point. The fixed point that a lever pivots around is called the **fulcrum.**

How It Works To understand how levers work, think about using a paint-can opener. The opener rests against the edge of the can, which acts as the fulcrum. The tip of the opener is under the lid of the can. When you push down, you exert an input force on the handle, and the opener pivots on the fulcrum. As a result, the tip of the opener pushes up, thereby exerting an output force on the lid.

Mechanical Advantage A lever like the paint-can opener helps you in two ways. It increases your input force and it changes the direction of your input force. When you use the paint-can opener, you push the handle a long distance down in order to move the lid a short distance up. However, you are able to apply a smaller force than you would have without the opener.

The ideal mechanical advantage of a lever is determined by dividing the distance from the fulcrum to the input force by the distance from the fulcrum to the output force.

$$\text{Ideal mechanical advantage} = \frac{\text{Distance from fulcrum to input force}}{\text{Distance from fulcrum to output force}}$$

In the case of the paint-can opener, the distance from the fulcrum to the input force is greater than the distance from the fulcrum to the output force. This means that the mechanical advantage is greater than 1.

Different Types of Levers When a paint-can opener is used as a lever, the fulcrum is located between the input and output forces. But this is not always the case. As shown in Figure 17, there are three different types of levers. Levers are classified according to the location of the fulcrum relative to the input and output forces.

 **Reading Checkpoint** What point on a lever does not move?

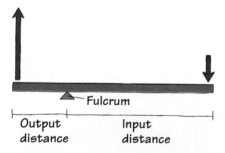

FIGURE 16
Mechanical Advantage of a Lever
A lever's input distance and output distance determine its ideal mechanical advantage.

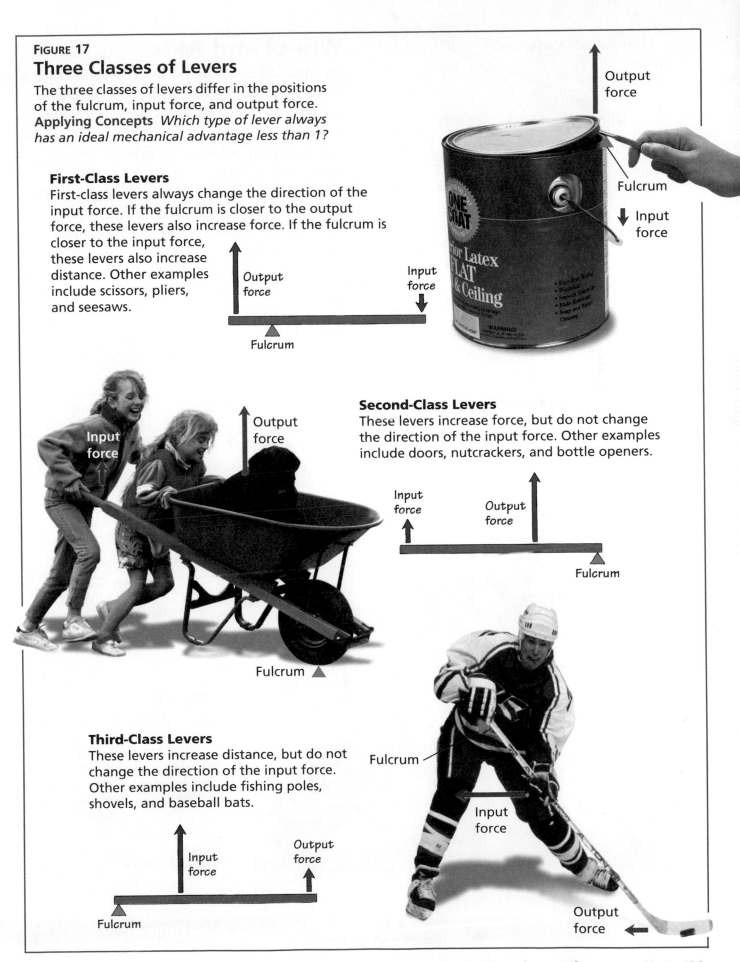

FIGURE 17

Three Classes of Levers

The three classes of levers differ in the positions of the fulcrum, input force, and output force. **Applying Concepts** *Which type of lever always has an ideal mechanical advantage less than 1?*

First-Class Levers

First-class levers always change the direction of the input force. If the fulcrum is closer to the output force, these levers also increase force. If the fulcrum is closer to the input force, these levers also increase distance. Other examples include scissors, pliers, and seesaws.

Output force

Input force

Fulcrum

Output force

Fulcrum

Input force

Second-Class Levers

These levers increase force, but do not change the direction of the input force. Other examples include doors, nutcrackers, and bottle openers.

Input force

Output force

Fulcrum

Input force

Output force

Fulcrum

Third-Class Levers

These levers increase distance, but do not change the direction of the input force. Other examples include fishing poles, shovels, and baseball bats.

Input force

Output force

Fulcrum

Fulcrum

Input force

Output force

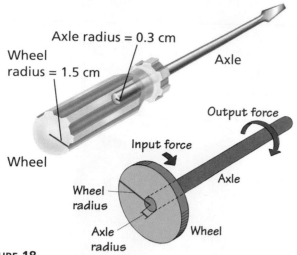

Axle radius = 0.3 cm

Wheel radius = 1.5 cm

Axle

Wheel

Output force

Input force

Wheel radius

Axle

Axle radius

Wheel

FIGURE 18

Wheel and Axle

A screwdriver increases force by exerting the output force over a shorter distance. **Observing** *Which has a larger radius, the wheel or the axle?*

Wheel and Axle

It's almost impossible to insert a screw into a piece of wood with your fingers. But with a screwdriver, you can turn the screw easily. A screwdriver makes use of a simple machine known as the **wheel and axle.** A wheel and axle is a simple machine made of two circular or cylindrical objects fastened together that rotate about a common axis. The object with the larger radius is called the wheel and the object with the smaller radius is called the axle. In a screwdriver, the handle is the wheel and the shaft is the axle. A doorknob and a car's steering wheel are also examples of a wheel and axle.

Science and **History**

Engineering Marvels

Simple machines have been used to create some of the most beautiful and useful structures in the world.

2550 B.C.
Great Pyramid, Giza, Egypt
Workers used wedges to cut 2.3 million blocks of stone to build the pyramid. At the quarry, the wedges were driven into cracks in the rock. The rock split into pieces. Workers hauled the massive blocks up inclined planes to the tops of pyramid walls.

500 B.C.
Theater at Epidaurus, Greece
Instead of ramps, the Greeks relied on a crane powered by pulleys to lift the stone blocks to build this theater. The crane was also used to lower actors to the stage during performances.

3000 B.C.   2000 B.C.   1000 B.C.

How It Works How does a screwdriver make use of a wheel and axle to do work? Look at Figure 18. When you use a screwdriver, you apply an input force to turn the handle, or wheel. Because the wheel is larger than the shaft, or axle, the axle rotates and exerts a large output force. The wheel and axle increases your force, but you must exert your force over a long distance.

What would happen if the input force were applied to the axle rather than the wheel? For the riverboat in Figure 19 on the next page, the force of the engine is applied to the axle of the large paddle wheel. The large paddle wheel in turn pushes against the water. In this case, the input force is exerted over a short distance. So when the input force is applied to the axle, a wheel and axle multiplies distance.

Writing in Science

Research and Write
Suppose that you are the person who first thought of using a simple machine at one of the construction sites in the timeline. Write out your proposal. You'll need to research the time and place. Explain to the people in charge why the simple machine you suggest will give workers a mechanical advantage.

A.D. 1000 Brihadeshwara Temple, India
The temple's tower at Thanjavur is more than 60 meters high. Workers dragged the dome-shaped capstone, a mass of 70,000 kilograms, to the top of the structure along an inclined plane several kilometers long.

A.D. 1056 Yingxian Pagoda, China
Slanted wooden beams called *ang* act as first-class levers to hold up the roof of this pagoda. The weight of the center of the roof presses down on one end of the beam. The other end of the beam swings up to support the outer edge of the roof.

A.D. 1994 The Chunnel, United Kingdom to France
Special drilling equipment was built to tunnel under the English Channel. Opened in May of 1994, the tunnel is 50 kilometers long. It carries only railway traffic.

0	A.D. 1000	A.D. 2000

Mechanical Advantage You can find the ideal mechanical advantage of a wheel and axle by dividing the radius of the wheel by the radius of the axle. (A radius is the distance from the outer edge of a circle to the circle's center.) The greater the ratio between the radius of the wheel and the radius of the axle, the greater the mechanical advantage.

$$\text{Mechanical advantage} = \frac{\text{Radius of wheel}}{\text{Radius of axle}}$$

Suppose the radius of a screwdriver's wheel is 1.5 cm and its axle radius is 0.3 cm. The screwdriver's ideal mechanical advantage would be 1.5 centimeters ÷ 0.3 centimeter, or 5.

Reading Checkpoint What is a radius?

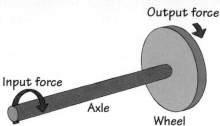

Output force

Input force

Axle

Wheel

FIGURE 19
Increasing Distance
In a riverboat paddle wheel, the axle turns the wheel. The output force is less than the input force, but it is exerted over a longer distance.

Lab zone Skills Activity

Communicating
Write a packaging label for a machine that uses a wheel and axle. On your label, describe the advantages of using this simple machine. Include a drawing of the forces that act on the machine.

Pulley

When you raise a flag on a flagpole or when you open and close window blinds, you are using a pulley. A **pulley** is a simple machine made of a grooved wheel with a rope or cable wrapped around it.

How It Works You use a pulley by pulling on one end of the rope. This is the input force. At the other end of the rope, the output force pulls up on the object you want to move. To move a heavy object over a distance, a pulley can make work easier in two ways. First, it can decrease the amount of input force needed to lift the object. Second, the pulley can change the direction of your input force. For example, you pull down on the flagpole rope, and the flag moves up.

Types of Pulleys There are two basic types of pulleys. A pulley that you attach to a structure is called a fixed pulley. Fixed pulleys are used at the tops of flagpoles. If you attach a pulley to the object you wish to move, you use a movable pulley. Construction cranes often use movable pulleys. By combining fixed and movable pulleys, you can make a pulley system called a block and tackle. **The ideal mechanical advantage of a pulley is equal to the number of sections of rope that support the object.**

Reading Checkpoint A pulley is attached to the object that is being moved. What kind of pulley is it?

FIGURE 20

Types of Pulleys

A fixed pulley and a movable pulley are the two basic types of pulleys. A block and tackle combines a fixed and movable pulley.
Comparing and Contrasting *Which type of pulley has the greatest mechanical advantage?*

Fixed Pulley

A fixed pulley does not change the amount of force applied. It does change the direction of the force.

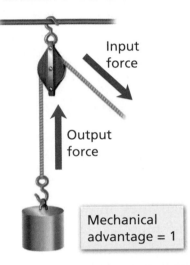

Input force

Output force

Mechanical advantage = 1

Movable Pulley

A movable pulley decreases the amount of input force needed. It does not change the direction of the force.

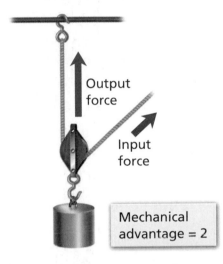

Output force

Input force

Mechanical advantage = 2

Block and Tackle

A block and tackle is a pulley system made up of fixed and movable pulleys.

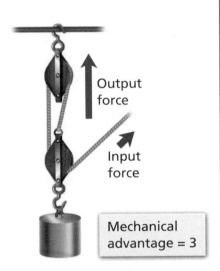

Output force

Input force

Mechanical advantage = 3

Cranes use block-and-tackle systems to lift heavy loads.

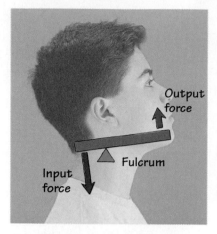 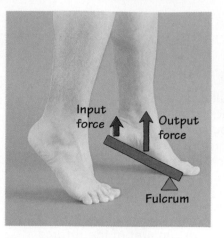 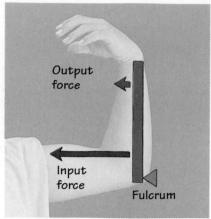

First-Class Lever The joint at the top of your neck is the fulcrum of a first-class lever. The muscles in the back of your neck provide the input force. The output force is used to tilt your head back.

Second-Class Lever The ball of your foot is the fulcrum of a second-class lever. The muscle in the calf of your leg provides the input force. The output force is used to raise your body.

Third-Class Lever Your elbow is the fulcrum of a third-class lever. Your biceps muscle provides the input force. The output force is used to lift your arm.

FIGURE 21
Levers in the Body
You don't need to look further than your own body to find simple machines. Three different types of levers are responsible for many of your movements.

Simple Machines in the Body

You probably don't think of the human body as being made up of machines. Believe it or not, machines are involved in much of the work that your body does.

Living Levers Most of the machines in your body are levers that consist of bones and muscles. Every time you move, you use a muscle. Your muscles are attached to your bones by connecting structures called tendons. Tendons and muscles pull on bones, making them work as levers. The joint, near where the tendon is attached to the bone, acts as the fulcrum. The muscles produce the input force. The output force is used for doing work, such as lifting your hand.

Working Wedges When you bite into an apple, you use your sharp front teeth, called incisors. Your incisors are shaped like wedges to enable you to bite off pieces of food. When you bite down on something, the wedge shape of your front teeth produces enough force to break it into pieces, just as an ax splits a log. The next time you take a bite of a crunchy apple, think about the machines in your mouth!

✓ **Reading Checkpoint** What type of simple machine do your front teeth resemble?

FIGURE 22
Wedges to Help You Eat
Your front teeth, known as incisors, are shaped like wedges.

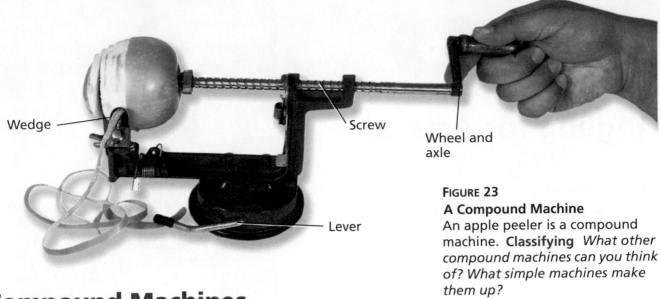

Wedge

Screw

Wheel and axle

Lever

FIGURE 23
A Compound Machine
An apple peeler is a compound machine. **Classifying** *What other compound machines can you think of? What simple machines make them up?*

Compound Machines

Many machines do not resemble the six simple machines you just read about. That's because many machines consist of combinations of simple machines.

A **compound machine** is a machine that utilizes two or more simple machines. **The ideal mechanical advantage of a compound machine is the product of the individual ideal mechanical advantages of the simple machines that make it up.**

An apple peeler like the one shown in Figure 23 is a compound machine. Four different simple machines make it up. The handle is a wheel and axle. The axle is also a screw that turns the apple. A wedge peels the apple's skin. To hold the machine in place, a lever can be switched to engage a suction cup.

Section 3 Assessment

Target Reading Skill Previewing Visuals Refer to your questions and answers about Figure 17 to help you answer Question 1 below.

Reviewing Key Concepts

1. a. **Listing** List the six kinds of simple machines.
   b. **Classifying** What type of simple machine is a door stopper? A rake? A windmill? A slide?
   c. **Developing Hypotheses** Can you consider your thumb to be a lever? Why or why not?
2. a. **Identifying** What is the ideal mechanical advantage of each type of simple machine?
   b. **Inferring** How can you increase a pulley's mechanical advantage?
   c. **Drawing Conclusions** How is calculating the ideal mechanical advantage of an inclined plane similar to calculating that of a screw?

3. a. **Reviewing** How many simple machines are needed to make a compound machine?
   b. **Describing** How do you find the mechanical advantage of a compound machine?

Lab zone At-Home **Activity**

Machines in the Kitchen Look around your kitchen with a family member. Identify at least five machines. Classify each as a simple machine or a compound machine. Explain to your family member how each machine makes work easier.

Angling for Access

Problem

How does the steepness of a wheelchair-access ramp affect its usefulness?

Skills Focus

making models, calculating

Materials

- 4 books, about 2 cm thick • metric ruler
- wooden block with eye-hook • marker
- board, at least 10 cm wide and 50 cm long
- spring scale, 0–10 N, or force sensor

Procedure

1. Preview the following steps that describe how you can construct and use a ramp. Then copy the data table into your notebook.

2. The output force with an inclined plane is equal to the weight of the object. Lift the block with the spring scale to measure its weight. Record this value in the data table. If you are using a force sensor, see your teacher for instructions.

3. Make a mark on the side of the board about 3 cm from one end. Measure the length from the other end of the board to the mark and record it in the data table.

4. Place one end of the board on top of a book. The mark you made on the board should be even with the edge of the book.

5. Measure the vertical distance in centimeters from the top of the table to where the underside of the incline touches the book. Record this value in the data table as "Height of Incline."

6. Lay the block on its largest side and use the spring scale to pull the block straight up the incline at a slow, steady speed. Be sure to hold the spring scale parallel to the incline, as shown in the photograph. Measure the force needed and record it in the data table.

7. Predict how your results will change if you repeat the investigation using two, three, and four books. Test your predictions.

8. For each trial, determine the ideal mechanical advantage and the actual mechanical advantage. Record the calculations in your data table.

Data Table						
Number of Books	Output Force (N)	Length of Incline (cm)	Height of Incline (cm)	Input Force (N)	Ideal Mechanical Advantage	Actual Mechanical Advantage
1						
2						
3						
4						

Analyze and Conclude

1. **Interpreting Data** How did the ideal mechanical advantage and the actual mechanical advantage compare each time you repeated the experiment? Explain your answer.

2. **Making Models** How did the model help you in determining the ramp's usefulness? What kind of limitations does your model have?

3. **Making Models** What happens to the actual mechanical advantage as the inclined plane gets steeper? On the basis of this fact alone, which of the four inclined planes models the best steepness for a wheelchair-access ramp? Explain your answer.

4. **Drawing Conclusions** What other factors, besides mechanical advantage, should you consider when deciding on the steepness of the ramp?

5. **Calculating** Suppose the door of the local public library is 2.0 m above the ground and the distance from the door to the parking lot is 15 m. What is the ideal mechanical advantage of a ramp built from the door to the parking lot?

6. **Communicating** Write a letter to a local business explaining how a ramp could help the employees and customers. Give some examples of work that could be made easier using a ramp. Explain how the steepness of a ramp affects its mechanical advantage.

More to Explore

Find actual ramps that provide access for people with disabilities. Measure the heights and lengths of these ramps and calculate their ideal mechanical advantages. Find out what the requirements are for access ramps in your area. Should your ramp be made of a particular material? Should it level off before it reaches the door? How wide should it be? How does it provide water drainage?

Science and Society

Automation in the Workplace— Lost Jobs or New Jobs?

In the 1800s, the first makers of baseball bats spent long days carving bats by hand. In a modern American factory, bat-making machines can produce a much larger number of bats in a shorter time. Since ancient times, people have invented machines to help with their work. Today, factories can use automated machines to perform jobs that are difficult, dangerous, or even just boring. Like science-fiction robots, these machines can do a whole series of different tasks.

But if a machine does work instead of a person, then someone loses a job. How can society use machines to make work easier and more productive without some people losing their chance to work?

The Issues

What Are the Effects of Automation?

New machines replace some jobs, but they also can create jobs. Suppose an automobile factory starts using machines instead of people to paint cars. At first, some workers may lose their jobs. But the factory may be able to produce more cars. Then it may need to hire more workers—to handle old tasks as well as some new ones. New jobs are created for people who are educated and skilled in operating and taking care of the new machines.

Still, some workers whose skills are no longer needed lose their jobs. Some may find work in different jobs for less money. Others may be unable to find new jobs. Can society provide people who are out of work with the skills they need to start a new career?

Carving a single bat with a lathe can take several hours.

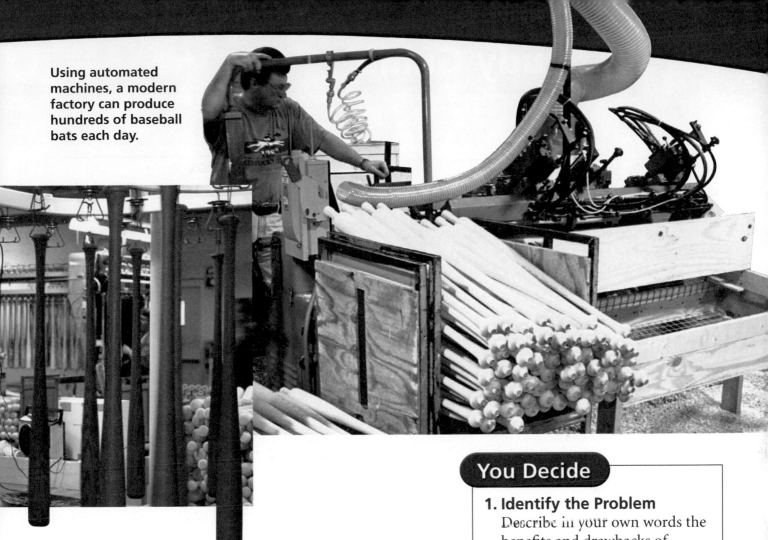

Using automated machines, a modern factory can produce hundreds of baseball bats each day.

What Can People Do?

Education programs can train young people for new jobs and teach older workers new skills. Those who learn how to use computers and other new technologies can take on new tasks. Learning how to sell or design a product can also prepare workers for new careers. Workers who have lost jobs can train for different types of work that cannot be done by machines. For example, a machine cannot replace human skill in day care or medical care.

Who Should Pay?

Teaching young people how to work in new kinds of jobs costs money. So do training programs for adult workers who have lost jobs. How could society pay for these costs? Businesses might share some of the costs. Some businesses give workers full pay until they are retrained or find new work. Also, the government might provide unemployment pay or training for jobless workers. Then all taxpayers would share the costs.

You Decide

1. Identify the Problem
Describe in your own words the benefits and drawbacks of workplace automation.

2. Analyze the Options
List ways society could deal with the effects of automation. For each plan, give the benefits and drawbacks and tell how it would be paid for.

3. Find a Solution
The owner of the pizza shop in your neighborhood has bought an automated pizza-making system. Make a plan for the shop to use the system without having to fire workers.

For: More on automation in the workplace
Visit: PHSchool.com
Web Code: cgh-3040

The BIG Idea **Work and Energy** Simple machines make work easier by changing the amount of force needed, the distance over which a force is exerted, or the direction in which a force is exerted.

1 What Is Work?

Key Concepts

- Work is done on an object when the object moves in the same direction in which the force is exerted.

- The amount of work done on an object can be determined by multiplying force times distance.

$$\text{Work} = \text{Force} \times \text{Distance}$$

- Power equals the amount of work done on an object in a unit of time.

$$\text{Power} = \frac{\text{Work}}{\text{Time}}$$

Key Terms

work   joule   power

2 How Machines Do Work

Key Concepts

- A machine makes work easier by changing at least one of three factors. A machine may change the amount of force you exert, the distance over which you exert your force, or the direction in which you exert your force.

- A machine's mechanical advantage is the number of times a machine increases a force exerted on it.

- Mechanical advantage $= \dfrac{\text{Output force}}{\text{Input force}}$

- To calculate the efficiency of a machine, divide the output work by the input work and multiply the result by 100 percent.

$$\text{Efficiency} = \frac{\text{Output work}}{\text{Input work}} \times 100\%$$

Key Terms

machine   output work
input force   mechanical advantage
output force   efficiency
input work

3 Simple Machines

Key Concepts

- There are six basic kinds of simple machines: the inclined plane, the wedge, the screw, the lever, the wheel and axle, and the pulley.

- You can determine the ideal mechanical advantage of an inclined plane by dividing the length of the incline by its height.

- The ideal mechanical advantage of a wedge is determined by dividing its length by its width.

- The ideal mechanical advantage of a screw is the length around the threads divided by the length of the screw.

- The ideal mechanical advantage of a lever is determined by dividing the distance from the fulcrum to the input force by the distance from the fulcrum to the output force.

- You can find the ideal mechanical advantage of a wheel and axle by dividing the radius of the wheel by the radius of the axle.

- The ideal mechanical advantage of a pulley is equal to the number of sections of rope that support the object.

- Most of the machines in your body are levers that consist of bones and muscles.

- The ideal mechanical advantage of a compound machine is the product of the individual ideal mechanical advantages of the simple machines that make it up.

Key Terms

• inclined plane • wedge • screw • lever
• fulcrum • wheel and axle • pulley
• compound machine

Review and Assessment

Organizing Information

Comparing and Contrasting Copy the compare/contrast table about simple machines onto a separate sheet of paper. Then complete it for each type of simple machine and add a title. (For more on Comparing and Contrasting, see the Skills Handbook.)

Simple Machine	Ideal Mechanical Advantage	Example
Inclined plane	Length of incline ÷ Height of incline	Ramp
a. ___?___	b. ___?___	c. ___?___

Reviewing Key Terms

Choose the letter of the best answer.

1. The amount of work done on an object is obtained by multiplying
   a. input force and output force.
   b. force and distance.
   c. time and force.
   d. efficiency and work.

2. The rate at which work is done is called
   a. output force.
   b. efficiency.
   c. power.
   d. mechanical advantage.

3. One way a machine can make work easier for you is by
   a. decreasing the amount of work you do.
   b. changing the direction of your force.
   c. increasing the amount of work required for a task.
   d. decreasing the friction you encounter.

4. The output force is greater than the input force for a
   a. pizza cutter.
   b. hockey stick.
   c. single fixed pulley.
   d. screw.

5. An example of a second-class lever is a
   a. seesaw.
   b. shovel.
   c. paddle.
   d. wheelbarrow.

If the statement is true, write *true*. **If it is false, change the underlined word or words to make the statement true.**

6. The SI unit of work is the <u>newton</u>.

7. The work you do on a machine is called the <u>input work</u>.

8. The ratio of output work to input work is <u>mechanical advantage</u>.

9. An <u>inclined plane</u> is a flat, sloped surface.

10. A <u>pulley</u> can be thought of as an inclined plane wrapped around a cylinder.

Writing in Science

Proposed Solution A community of people in Pennsylvania known as the Old Order Amish can build a wooden barn in a single day—without using electricity. Suppose you were faced with this task. Propose how you would use simple machines to help with the construction.

Discovery CHANNEL **SCHOOL**™

Work and Machines

Video Preview
Video Field Trip
▶ Video Assessment

Chapter 4 M ◆ 141

Review and Assessment

Checking Concepts

11. The mythical god Atlas was believed to hold the weight of the sky on his shoulders. Was Atlas performing any work? Explain.

12. The mechanical advantage of a machine is 3. If you exert an input force of 5 N, what output force is exerted by the machine?

13. Which has a greater mechanical advantage, a wedge that is 6 cm long and 3 cm wide, or a wedge that is 12 cm long and 4 cm wide? Explain your answer.

14. Why will decreasing the radius of the axle improve the mechanical advantage of a wheel and axle?

15. Describe a lever in your body. Locate the input force, output force, and fulcrum.

Thinking Critically

16. Relating Cause and Effect Describe the relationship between friction and the efficiency of a machine.

17. Classifying What type of simple machine would be used to lower an empty bucket into a well and then lift the bucket full of water?

18. Applying Concepts To open a door, you push on the part of the door that is farthest from the hinges. Why would it be harder to open the door if you pushed on the center of it?

19. Interpreting Diagrams Which ramp has the greater ideal mechanical advantage?

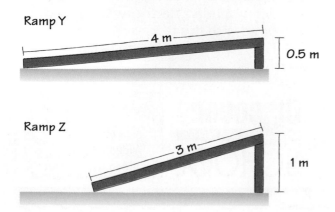

Ramp Y — 4 m — 0.5 m

Ramp Z — 3 m — 1 m

Math Practice

20. Calculating Power A bulldozer does 72,000 J of work in 48 seconds. How much power does the bulldozer use?

21. Calculating Efficiency A machine with 75% efficiency does 3,300 J of work. Using the machine, how much work did you do?

Applying Skills

Use the illustration to answer Questions 22–25.

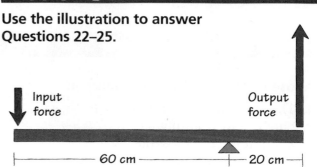

Input force — Output force — 60 cm — 20 cm

22. Calculating Use the input and output distances to calculate the ideal mechanical advantage of the lever.

23. Predicting What would the ideal mechanical advantage be if the distance from the fulcrum to the input force were 20 cm? 40 cm? 80 cm?

24. Graphing Use your answers to Questions 22 and 23 to graph the distance from the fulcrum to the input force on the x-axis and the ideal mechanical advantage on the y-axis.

25. Interpreting Data What does your graph show you about the relationship between the ideal mechanical advantage of a first-class lever and the distance between the fulcrum and the input force?

Lab zone Chapter Project

Performance Assessment Finalize your design and build your machine. Consider how you can improve the machine's efficiency. Check all measurements and calculations. Does it lift the soup can at least 5 cm? Is it made of two or more simple machines? When you show your machine to the class, explain why you built it as you did.

Standardized Test Prep

Choose the letter of the best answer.

1. What simple machine is used in *all* of the following jobs: moving a flag to the top of a flagpole, lifting equipment with a construction crane, and using a block and tackle to move a crate?

    A lever

    B pulley

    C wedge

    D wheel and axle

2. The table below shows the input work and output work for four different pulleys. Which pulley has the highest efficiency?

Work of Different Pulleys		
Pulley	**Input Work**	**Output Work**
Fixed pulley A	20,000 J	8,000 J
Fixed pulley B	20,000 J	10,000 J
Movable pulley	20,000 J	12,000 J
Block and tackle	20,000 J	16,000 J

    F Fixed pulley A   **H** Movable pulley

    G Fixed pulley B   **J** Block and tackle

3. Which is the *best* definition of a machine?

    A A machine is a time-saving device that uses motors and gears.

    B A machine changes the amount of input force.

    C A machine makes work easier by changing force, distance, or direction.

    D A machine can be either simple or compound.

4. Which of the following will increase the ideal mechanical advantage of a wheel and axle?

    F increasing the wheel's radius

    G decreasing the wheel's radius

    H increasing the axle's radius

    J increasing the wheel's radius and the axle's radius equally

5. Which activity describes work being done on an object?

    A walking a dog on a leash

    B lifting a bag of groceries

    C holding up an umbrella

    D pressing a stamp onto an envelope

Constructed Response

6. Explain why an engineer would design a road to wind around a mountain rather than go straight up the side. Show how this design would be better.

The BIG Idea

Energy Forms and Conservation

Q What is energy and how can it be transformed?

Chapter Preview

❶ **What Is Energy?**
Discover How High Does a Ball Bounce?
Math Skills Exponents

❷ **Forms of Energy**
Discover What Makes a Flashlight Shine?
Analyzing Data Calculating Mechanical Energy
Skills Lab Can You Feel the Power?

❸ **Energy Transformations and Conservation**
Discover What Would Make a Card Jump?
Skills Activity Classifying
Active Art Energy Transformations
Try This Pendulum Swing
At-Home Activity Hot Wire
Skills Lab Soaring Straws

❹ **Energy and Fossil Fuels**
Discover What Is a Fuel?
Skills Activity Graphing
At-Home Activity Burning Fossils

Cars powered by the sun's ▶ energy race in Suzuka, Japan.

Lab zone™ Chapter **Project**

Design and Build a Roller Coaster

In this chapter, you will learn about energy, the forms it takes, and how it is transformed and conserved. You will use what you learn to design and construct your own roller coaster.

Your Goal To design and construct a roller coaster that uses kinetic and potential energy to move

Your roller coaster must

- be no wider than 2 meters and be easily disassembled and reassembled
- have a first hill with a height of 1 meter and have at least two additional hills
- have an object that moves along the entire track without stopping
- follow the safety guidelines in Appendix A

Plan It! Brainstorm the characteristics of a fun roller coaster. Consider how fast a roller coaster moves and how its speed changes throughout the ride. Then choose materials for your roller coaster and sketch a design. When your teacher has approved your design, build your roller coaster. Experiment with different hill heights and inclines. Add turns and loops to determine their effect.

What Is Energy?

Reading Preview

Key Concepts
- How are energy, work, and power related?
- What are the two basic kinds of energy?

Key Terms
- energy • kinetic energy
- potential energy
- gravitational potential energy
- elastic potential energy

Target Reading Skill

Using Prior Knowledge Before you read, look at the section headings and visuals to see what this section is about. Then write what you know about energy in a graphic organizer like the one below. As you read, write what you learn.

What You Know
1. The joule is the unit of work.
2.

What You Learned
1.
2.

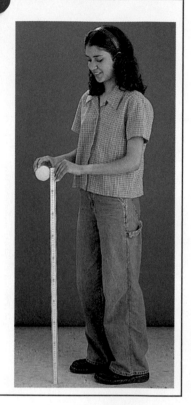

Lab zone Discover **Activity**

How High Does a Ball Bounce?

1. Hold a meter stick vertically, with the zero end on the ground.
2. Drop a tennis ball from the 50-cm mark and record the height to which it bounces.
3. Drop the tennis ball from the 100-cm mark and record the height to which it bounces.
4. Predict how high the ball will bounce if dropped from the 75-cm mark. Test your prediction.

Think It Over
Observing How does the height from which you drop the ball relate to the height to which the ball bounces?

Brilliant streaks of lightning flash across the night sky. The wind howls, and thunder cracks and rumbles. Then a sound like a runaway locomotive approaches, growing louder each second. Whirling winds rush through the town. Roofs are lifted off of buildings. Cars are thrown about like toys. Then, in minutes, the tornado is gone.

The next morning, a light breeze carries leaves past the debris. The wind that destroyed buildings hours before is now barely strong enough to move a leaf. Wind is just moving air, but it has energy.

When a breeze does work lifting leaves, it transfers energy to them. ▶

Energy, Work, and Power

When wind moves a house, or even a leaf, it causes a change. In this case, the change is in the position of the object. Recall that work is done when a force moves an object through a distance. The ability to do work or cause change is called **energy.** So the wind has energy.

Work and Energy When an object or living thing does work on another object, some of its energy is transferred to that object. You can think of work, then, as the transfer of energy. When energy is transferred, the object upon which the work is done gains energy. Energy is measured in joules—the same units as work.

Power and Energy You may recall that power is the rate at which work is done. **If the transfer of energy is work, then power is the rate at which energy is transferred, or the amount of energy transferred in a unit of time.**

$$\text{Power} = \frac{\text{Energy transferred}}{\text{Time}}$$

Power is involved whenever energy is being transferred. For example, a calm breeze's power is its rate of energy transfer to lift a leaf a certain distance. The tornado in Figure 1 transfers the same amount of energy when it lifts the leaf the same distance. However, the tornado has a greater power than the breeze because it transfers energy to the leaf in less time.

 **Reading Checkpoint** What is power in terms of energy?

FIGURE 1
Energy and Power
A tornado and a calm breeze each do the same amount of work if they transfer the same amount of energy to a leaf. However, the tornado has a greater power than the breeze because it transfers its energy in less time.
Drawing Conclusions *Why is the same amount of work done on the leaf?*

Kinetic Energy

Two basic kinds of energy are kinetic energy and potential energy. Whether energy is kinetic or potential depends on whether an object is moving or not.

A moving object, such as the wind, can do work when it strikes another object and moves it some distance. Because the moving object does work, it has energy. The energy an object has due to its motion is called **kinetic energy.** The word *kinetic* comes from the Greek word *kinetos*, which means "moving."

Exponents

An exponent tells how many times a number is used as a factor. For example, 3 × 3 can be written as 3^2. You read this number as "three squared." An exponent of 2 indicates that the number 3 is used as a factor two times. To find the value of a squared number, multiply the number by itself.

$$3^2 = 3 \times 3 = 9$$

Practice Problem What is the value of the number 8^2?

Factors Affecting Kinetic Energy The kinetic energy of an object depends on both its mass and its velocity. Kinetic energy increases as mass increases. For example, think about rolling a bowling ball and a golf ball down a bowling lane at the same velocity, as shown in Figure 2. The bowling ball has more mass than the golf ball. If both balls have the same velocity, the bowling ball is more likely to knock down the pins because it has more kinetic energy than the golf ball.

Kinetic energy also increases when velocity increases. For example, suppose you have two identical bowling balls and you roll one ball so it moves at a greater velocity than the other. You must throw the ball harder to give it the greater velocity. In other words, you transfer more energy to it. Therefore, the faster ball has more kinetic energy.

Calculating Kinetic Energy There is a mathematical relationship between kinetic energy, mass, and velocity.

$$\text{Kinetic energy} = \frac{1}{2} \times \text{Mass} \times \text{Velocity}^2$$

Do changes in velocity and mass have the same effect on kinetic energy? No—changing the velocity of an object will have a greater effect on its kinetic energy than changing its mass by the same factor. This is because velocity is squared in the kinetic energy equation. For instance, doubling the mass of an object will double its kinetic energy. But doubling its velocity will quadruple its kinetic energy.

 **Reading Checkpoint** Which has a greater effect on an object's kinetic energy—doubling its mass or doubling its velocity?

FIGURE 2
Kinetic Energy
Kinetic energy increases as mass and velocity increase.
Predicting *In each example, which object will transfer more energy to the pins? Why?*

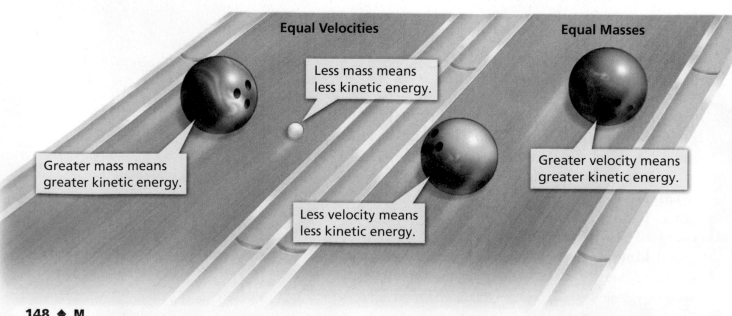

Equal Velocities

Less mass means less kinetic energy.

Greater mass means greater kinetic energy.

Less velocity means less kinetic energy.

Equal Masses

Greater velocity means greater kinetic energy.

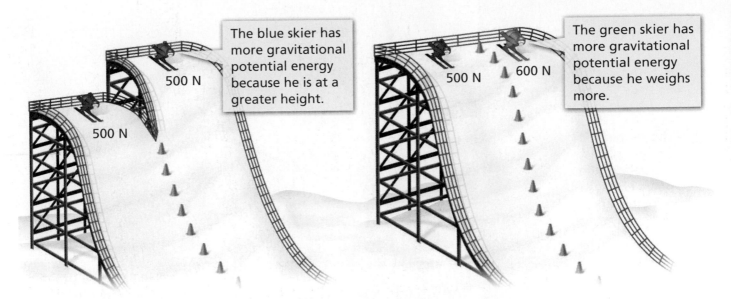

The blue skier has more gravitational potential energy because he is at a greater height.

500 N

500 N

The green skier has more gravitational potential energy because he weighs more.

500 N   600 N

Potential Energy

An object does not have to be moving to have energy. Some objects have stored energy as a result of their positions or shapes. When you lift a book up to your desk from the floor or compress a spring to wind a toy, you transfer energy to it. The energy you transfer is stored, or held in readiness. It might be used later when the book falls to the floor or the spring unwinds. Stored energy that results from the position or shape of an object is called **potential energy**. This type of energy has the potential to do work.

Gravitational Potential Energy Potential energy related to an object's height is called **gravitational potential energy.** The gravitational potential energy of an object is equal to the work done to lift it. Remember that Work = Force × Distance. The force you use to lift the object is equal to its weight. The distance you move the object is its height. You can calculate an object's gravitational potential energy using this formula.

> **Gravitational potential energy = Weight × Height**

For example, the red skier on the left in Figure 3 weighs 500 newtons. If the ski jump is 40 meters high, then the skier has 500 newtons × 40 meters, or 20,000 J, of gravitational potential energy.

The more an object weighs, or the greater the object's height, the greater its gravitational potential energy. At the same height, a 600-newton skier has more gravitational potential energy than a 500-newton skier. Similarly, a 500-newton skier has more gravitational potential energy on a high ski jump than on a low one.

FIGURE 3
Gravitational Potential Energy
Gravitational potential energy increases as weight and height increase.
Interpreting Diagrams *Does the red skier have more gravitational potential energy on the higher ski jump or the lower one? Why?*

For: Links on energy
Visit: www.SciLinks.org
Web Code: scn-1351

The farther the string is pulled, the greater the bow's elastic potential energy.

Pulling the string changes the bow's shape and stores elastic potential energy.

FIGURE 4
Elastic Potential Energy
The energy stored in a stretched object, such as a bow, is elastic potential energy. *Interpreting Photographs When the energy stored in the bow is released, how is it used?*

Elastic Potential Energy An object gains a different type of potential energy when it is stretched. The potential energy associated with objects that can be stretched or compressed is called **elastic potential energy.** For example, when an archer pulls back an arrow, the bow changes shape. The bow now has potential energy. When the archer releases the string, the stored energy sends the arrow flying to its target.

Reading Checkpoint What type of energy does a bow have when you pull back an arrow?

Section 1 Assessment

Target Reading Skill

Using Prior Knowledge Review your graphic organizer and revise it based on what you just learned in the section.

Reviewing Key Concepts

1. a. **Defining** What is energy?
   b. **Describing** How are energy, work, and power related?
   c. **Applying Concepts** If a handsaw does the same amount of work on a log as a chainsaw does, which has a greater power? Why?
2. a. **Identifying** What is kinetic energy? What is potential energy?
   b. **Explaining** What factors affect an object's kinetic energy?
   c. **Problem Solving** At a given height above Earth, how would you determine the potential energy of a sky diver? The kinetic energy of a sky diver?

Math Practice

3. **Exponents** What is the value of the number 10^2?

4. **Exponents** What number when squared gives you the value 36?

Forms of Energy

Reading Preview

Key Concepts
- How can you determine an object's mechanical energy?
- What are some forms of energy associated with the particles that make up objects?

Key Terms
- mechanical energy
- thermal energy
- electrical energy
- chemical energy
- nuclear energy
- electromagnetic energy

Target Reading Skill
Building Vocabulary After you read the section, reread the paragraphs that contain definitions of Key Terms. Use the information you have learned to write a definition of each Key Term in your own words.

Discover Activity

What Makes a Flashlight Shine?

1. Remove the batteries from a flashlight and examine them. Think about what type of energy is stored in the batteries.
2. Replace the batteries and turn on the flashlight. What type of energy do you observe?
3. After a few minutes, place your hand near the bulb of the flashlight. What type of energy do you feel?

Think It Over
Inferring Describe how you think a flashlight works in terms of energy. Where does the energy come from? Where does the energy go?

You are on the edge of your seat as the quarterback drops back, steps forward, and then launches a deep pass. The ball soars down the field and drops into the receiver's hands. The electronic scoreboard flashes TOUCH-DOWN. You jump to your feet and cheer!

As the crowd settles back down, you shiver. The sun is setting, and the afternoon is growing cool. A vendor hands you a hot dog, and its heat helps warm your hands. Suddenly, the stadium lights switch on. You can see the players more clearly as they line up for the next play.

The thrown football, the scoreboard, the sun, the hot dog, and the stadium lights all have energy. You have energy, too! Energy comes in many different forms.

Mechanical Energy

Think about the pass thrown by the quarterback. A football thrown by a quarterback has mechanical energy. So does a moving car or a trophy on a shelf. The form of energy associated with the position and motion of an object is called **mechanical energy.**

◀ A quarterback transfers mechanical energy to the football.

An object's mechanical energy is a combination of its potential energy and kinetic energy. **You can find an object's mechanical energy by adding the object's kinetic energy and potential energy.**

Mechanical Energy = Potential energy + Kinetic energy

For example, a football thrown by a quarterback has both potential energy and kinetic energy. The higher the football, the greater its potential energy. The faster the football moves, the greater its kinetic energy.

You can add the potential energy and kinetic energy of the football in Figure 5 to find its mechanical energy. The football has 32 joules of potential energy due to its position above the ground. It also has 45 joules of kinetic energy due to its motion. The total mechanical energy of the football is equal to 32 joules + 45 joules, or 77 joules.

An object with mechanical energy can do work on another object. In fact, you can think of mechanical energy as the ability to do work. The more mechanical energy an object has, the more work it can do.

✓ **Reading Checkpoint** What two forms of energy combine to make mechanical energy?

FIGURE 5
Mechanical Energy
To find the football's mechanical energy, add its kinetic energy to its potential energy. **Observing** *Why does the football have potential energy?*

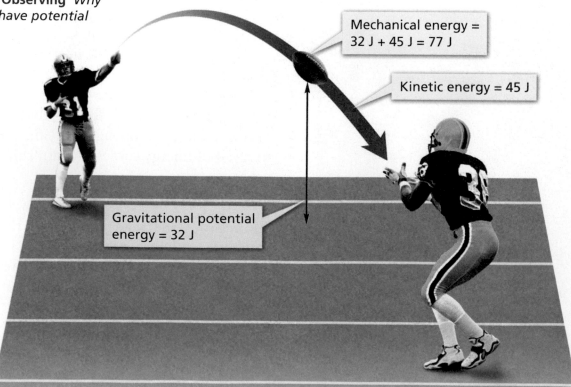

Mechanical energy = 32 J + 45 J = 77 J

Kinetic energy = 45 J

Gravitational potential energy = 32 J

Calculating Mechanical Energy

The kinetic energy of a 500-N diver during a dive from a 10-m platform was measured. These data are shown in the graph.

1. **Reading Graphs** According to the graph, how much kinetic energy does the diver have at 8 m?

2. **Calculating** Using the graph, find the kinetic energy of the diver at 6 m. Then calculate the diver's potential energy at that point.

3. **Inferring** The mechanical energy of the diver is the same at every height. What is the mechanical energy of the diver?

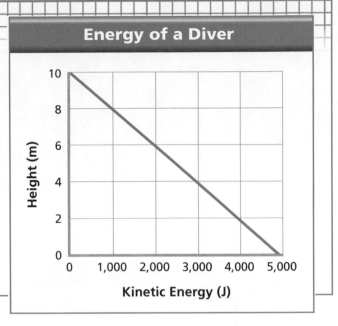

Energy of a Diver

(Graph: Height (m) vs. Kinetic Energy (J))

Other Forms of Energy

So far in this chapter, you have read about energy that involves the motion and position of an object. But an object can have other forms of kinetic and potential energy. Most of these other forms are associated with the particles that make up objects. These particles are far too small to see. **Forms of energy associated with the particles of objects include thermal energy, electrical energy, chemical energy, nuclear energy, and electromagnetic energy.**

Thermal Energy All objects are made up of particles called atoms and molecules. Because these particles are constantly in motion, they have kinetic energy. The faster the particles move, the more kinetic energy they have. These particles are arranged in specific ways in different objects. Therefore, they also have potential energy. The total potential and kinetic energy of the particles in an object is called **thermal energy.** Look at Figure 6. Even though the lava may be flowing slowly down the volcano, its particles are moving quickly. Because the particles have a large amount of kinetic energy, the lava has a large amount of thermal energy.

If you've ever eaten ice cream on a hot day, you've experienced thermal energy. Fast-moving particles in the warm air make the particles of ice cream move faster. As the kinetic energy of the particles increases, so does the thermal energy of the ice cream. Eventually, the ice cream melts.

FIGURE 6
Thermal Energy
The lava flowing from this volcano has a large amount of thermal energy. **Predicting** *Will the thermal energy of the lava increase or decrease as it flows away from the volcano?*

FIGURE 7
Electrical Energy
Electric charges in lightning
carry electrical energy.

Electrical Energy When you receive a shock from a metal doorknob, you are experiencing electrical energy. The energy of electric charges is **electrical energy.** Depending on whether the charges are moving or stored, electrical energy can be a form of kinetic or potential energy. The lightning in Figure 7 is a form of electrical energy. You rely on electrical energy from batteries or electrical lines to run devices such as flashlights, handheld games, and radios.

Chemical Energy Almost everything you see, touch, or taste is composed of chemical compounds. Chemical compounds are made up of atoms and molecules. Bonds between the atoms and molecules hold chemical compounds together. These bonds have chemical energy. **Chemical energy** is potential energy stored in the chemical bonds that hold chemical compounds together. Chemical energy is stored in the foods you eat, in the matches you can use to light a candle, and even in the cells of your body. When bonds in chemical compounds break, new chemical compounds may form. When this happens, chemical energy may be released.

FIGURE 8
Chemical Energy
The particles in these grapes contain chemical energy. Your body can use this energy after you eat them.

Nuclear Energy A type of potential energy called **nuclear energy** is stored in the nucleus of an atom. Nuclear energy is released during a nuclear reaction. One kind of nuclear reaction, known as nuclear fission, occurs when a nucleus splits. Nuclear power plants use fission reactions to produce electricity. Another kind of reaction, known as nuclear fusion, occurs when the nuclei of atoms fuse, or join together. Nuclear fusion reactions occur continuously in the sun, releasing tremendous amounts of energy.

Electromagnetic Energy The sunlight that you see each day is a form of **electromagnetic energy.** Electromagnetic energy travels in waves. These waves have some electrical properties and some magnetic properties.

The microwaves you use to cook your food and the X-rays doctors use to examine patients are types of electromagnetic energy. Other forms of electromagnetic energy include ultraviolet radiation, infrared radiation, and radio waves.

 **Reading Checkpoint** What form of energy are microwaves?

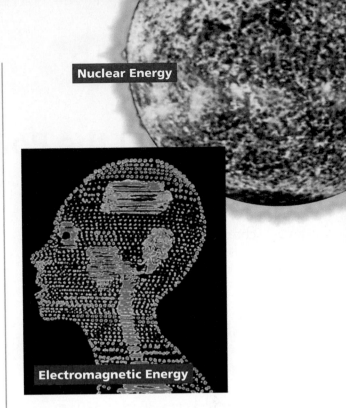

Nuclear Energy

Electromagnetic Energy

FIGURE 9
Nuclear and Electromagnetic Energy
The sun is a source of nuclear energy. Doctors use X-rays, a form of electromagnetic energy, when taking a CT scan to look for brain disorders. **Observing** *What other forms of energy from the sun can you observe?*

Section 2 Assessment

Target Reading Skill Building Vocabulary Use your definitions to help answer the questions.

Reviewing Key Concepts

1. a. **Defining** What is mechanical energy?
   b. **Drawing Conclusions** If an object's mechanical energy is equal to its potential energy, how much kinetic energy does the object have? How do you know?
   c. **Calculating** If the kinetic energy of a falling apple is 5.2 J and its potential energy is 3.5 J, what is its mechanical energy?
2. a. **Listing** List the five forms of energy associated with the particles that make up objects.
   b. **Explaining** Why do the particles of objects have both kinetic and potential energy?
   c. **Classifying** What kind of energy do you experience when you eat a peanut butter and jelly sandwich?

Writing in Science

Detailed Observation In terms of energy, think about what happens when you eat a hot meal. Describe all the different forms of energy that you experience. For example, if you are eating under a lamp, its electromagnetic energy helps you see the food. Explain the source of each form of energy.

Can You Feel the Power?

Problem

Can you change your power while exercising?

Skills Focus

calculating, interpreting data

Materials

- calculator
- meter stick
- stopwatch or clock with a second hand
- board, about 2.5 cm × 30 cm × 120 cm
- 18–20 books, each about 2 cm thick

Procedure 🖾

1. Construct a step by making two identical stacks of books. Each stack should be about 20 cm high. Place a board securely on top of the stacks of books so that the ends of the board are even with the outside edges of the books. **CAUTION:** *Be sure to have your partners hold the board steady and level throughout the procedure.*

2. Copy the data table into your notebook.

3. You gain gravitational potential energy every time you step up. Gaining energy requires work.

   Work = Weight × Height =
                  Gravitational potential energy

   a. Assume your weight is 400 N and your partners' weights are 425 N and 450 N.

   b. Measure the vertical distance in centimeters from the floor to the top of the board. Convert to meters by dividing by 100 and record this height in the data table.

4. Calculate the work you do in stepping up onto the board once. Then calculate the work you do stepping up onto the board 20 times. Record both answers in your data table.

5. Step up onto the board with both feet and then step backwards off the board onto the floor. This up and down motion is one repetition. Make sure you are comfortable with the motion.

6. Have one partner time how long it takes you to do 20 repetitions performed at a constant speed. Count out loud to help the timer keep track of the number of repetitions. Record the time in your data table.

7. Calculate the power over 20 repetitions. (Power = Energy transferred ÷ Time.) Predict how your results will change if you step up and down at different speeds.

8. Repeat Steps 6 and 7, but climb the step more slowly than you did the first time. Record the new data in the Trial 2 row of your data table.

9. Switch roles with your partners and repeat Steps 3 through 8 with a different weight from Step 3(a).

Data Table						
Trial	Weight (N)	Height of Board (m)	Time for 20 Repetitions (s)	Work for 1 Repetition (J)	Work for 20 Repetitions (J)	Power (W)
Student 1, Trial 1						
Student 1, Trial 2						

Analyze and Conclude

1. **Calculating** What is the gravitational potential energy gained from stepping up onto the board? How does this compare to the amount of work required to step up onto the board?

2. **Interpreting Data** Compare the amount of work you did during your first and second trials.

3. **Interpreting Data** Compare the power during your first and second trials.

4. **Drawing Conclusions** Did you and your partners all do the same amount of work? Did you all do work at the same rate? Explain your answers.

5. **Communicating** Often, a physical therapist will want to increase a patient's power. Write a letter to a physical therapist suggesting how he or she could use music to change a patient's power.

Design an Experiment

Design an experiment to test two other ways a physical therapist could change the power output of her patients. *Obtain your teacher's permission before carrying out your investigation.*

Energy Transformations and Conservation

Reading Preview

Key Concepts
- How are different forms of energy related?
- What is a common energy transformation?
- What is the law of conservation of energy?

Key Terms
- energy transformation
- law of conservation of energy
- matter

Target Reading Skill
Asking Questions Before you read, preview the red headings and ask a *what* or *how* question for each heading. As you read, write the answers to your questions.

Energy Transformations

Question	Answer
What is an energy transformation?	An energy transformation is . . .

▼ Niagara Falls is more than 50 meters high.

Lab zone — Discover Activity

What Would Make a Card Jump?
1. Fold an index card in half.
2. In the edge opposite the fold, cut two slits that are about 2 cm long and 2 cm apart.
3. Keep the card folded and loop a rubber band through the slits. With the fold toward you, gently open the card like a tent and flatten it against your desk.
4. Predict what will happen to the card if you let go. Then test your prediction.

Think It Over
Drawing Conclusions Describe what happened to the card. Based on your observations, what is the relationship between potential and kinetic energy?

The spray bounces off your raincoat as you look up at the millions of liters of water plunging toward you. The roar of the water is deafening. Are you doomed? Fortunately not—you are on a sightseeing boat at the foot of the mighty Niagara Falls. The waterfall carries the huge amount of water that drains from the upper Great Lakes. It lies on the border between Canada and the United States.

What many visitors don't know, however, is that Niagara Falls serves as much more than just a spectacular view. The Niagara Falls area is the center of a network of electrical power lines. Water that is diverted above the falls is used to generate electricity for much of the surrounding region.

Energy Transformations

What does flowing water have to do with electricity? You may already know that the mechanical energy of moving water can be transformed into electrical energy. **Most forms of energy can be transformed into other forms.** A change from one form of energy to another is called an **energy transformation.** Some energy changes involve single transformations, while others involve many transformations.

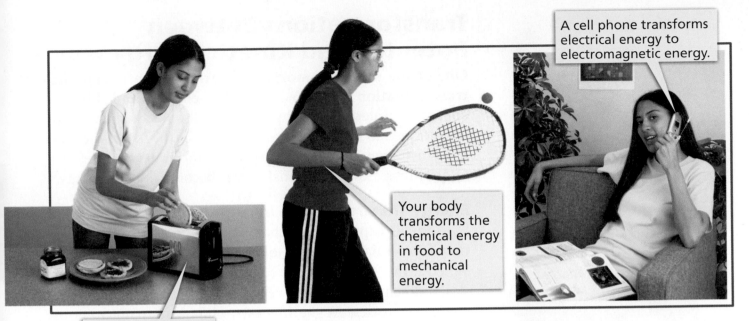

A cell phone transforms electrical energy to electromagnetic energy.

Your body transforms the chemical energy in food to mechanical energy.

A toaster transforms electrical energy to thermal energy.

FIGURE 10
Common Energy Transformations
Every day, energy transformations are all around you. Some of these transformations happen inside you! **Observing** *What other energy transformations do you observe every day?*

Single Transformations Sometimes, one form of energy needs to be transformed into another to get work done. You are already familiar with many such energy transformations. For example, a toaster transforms electrical energy to thermal energy to toast your bread. A cell phone transforms electrical energy to electromagnetic energy that travels to other phones.

Your body transforms the chemical energy in your food to mechanical energy you need to move your muscles. Chemical energy in food is also transformed to the thermal energy your body uses to maintain its temperature.

Multiple Transformations Often, a series of energy transformations is needed to do work. For example, the mechanical energy used to strike a match is transformed first to thermal energy. The thermal energy causes the particles in the match to release stored chemical energy, which is transformed to thermal energy and the electromagnetic energy you see as light.

In a car engine, another series of energy conversions occurs. Electrical energy produces a spark. The thermal energy of the spark releases chemical energy in the fuel. The fuel's chemical energy in turn becomes thermal energy. Thermal energy is converted to mechanical energy used to move the car, and to electrical energy to produce more sparks.

Reading Checkpoint What is an example of a multiple transformation of energy?

Lab zone Skills Activity

Classifying
Many common devices transform electrical energy into other forms. Think about the following devices in terms of energy transformations.

- steam iron • ceiling fan
- digital clock • dryer

For each device, describe which form or forms of energy the electrical energy becomes. Do these devices produce single or multiple transformations of energy?

Transformations Between Potential and Kinetic Energy

One of the most common energy transformations is the transformation between potential energy and kinetic energy. In waterfalls such as Niagara Falls, potential energy is transformed to kinetic energy. The water at the top of the falls has gravitational potential energy. As the water plunges, its velocity increases. Its potential energy becomes kinetic energy.

Energy Transformation in Juggling Any object that rises or falls experiences a change in its kinetic and gravitational potential energy. Look at the orange in Figure 11. When it moves, the orange has kinetic energy. As it rises, it slows down. Its potential energy increases as its kinetic energy decreases. At the highest point in its path, it stops moving. Since there is no motion, the orange no longer has kinetic energy. But it does have potential energy. As the orange falls, the energy transformation is reversed. Kinetic energy increases while potential energy decreases.

Energy Transformation in a Pendulum In a pendulum, a continuous transformation between kinetic and potential energy takes place. At the highest point in its swing, the pendulum in Figure 12 has no movement, so it only has gravitational potential energy. As it swings downward, it speeds up. Its potential energy is transformed to kinetic energy. The pendulum is at its greatest speed at the bottom of its swing. There, all its energy is kinetic energy.

FIGURE 11

Juggling The kinetic energy of an orange thrown into the air becomes gravitational potential energy. Its potential energy becomes kinetic energy as it falls.

Go Online
active art

For: Energy Transformations activity
Visit: PHSchool.com
Web Code: cgp-3053

FIGURE 12
Pendulum
A pendulum continuously transforms energy from kinetic to potential energy and back.
Interpreting Diagrams *At what two points is the pendulum's potential energy greatest?*

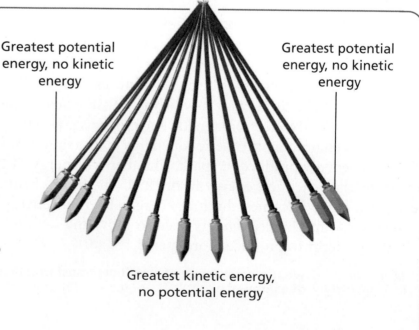

Greatest potential energy, no kinetic energy

Greatest potential energy, no kinetic energy

Greatest kinetic energy, no potential energy

FIGURE 13
Pole Vault
Energy transformations enable this athlete to vault more than six meters into the air.

As the pendulum swings to the other side, its height increases. The pendulum regains gravitational potential energy and loses kinetic energy. At the top of its swing, it comes to a stop again. And so the pattern of energy transformation continues.

Energy Transformation in a Pole Vault A pole-vaulter transforms kinetic energy to elastic potential energy, which then becomes gravitational potential energy. The pole-vaulter you see in Figure 13 has kinetic energy as he runs forward. When the pole-vaulter plants the pole to jump, his velocity decreases and the pole bends. His kinetic energy is transformed to elastic potential energy in the pole. As the pole straightens out, the pole-vaulter is lifted high into the air. The elastic potential energy of the pole is transformed to the gravitational potential energy of the pole-vaulter. Once he is over the bar, the pole-vaulter's gravitational potential energy is transformed back into kinetic energy as he falls toward the safety cushion.

Energy

Video Preview
▶ Video Field Trip
Video Assessment

 **Reading Checkpoint** What kind of energy lifts a pole-vaulter over the bar?

Pendulum Swing

1. Set up a pendulum using washers or a rubber stopper, string, a ring stand, and a clamp.

2. Pull the pendulum back so that it makes a 45° angle with the vertical. Measure the height of the stopper. Release it and observe how high it swings.

3. Use a second clamp to reduce the length of the pendulum as shown. The pendulum will run into the second clamp at the bottom of its swing.

4. Pull the pendulum back to the same height as you did the first time. Predict how high the pendulum will swing. Then set it in motion and observe.

Observing How high did the pendulum swing in each case? Explain your observations.

Conservation of Energy

If you set a spinning top in motion, will the top remain in motion forever? No, it will not. Then what happens to its energy? Is the energy destroyed? Again, the answer is no. The **law of conservation of energy** states that when one form of energy is transformed to another, no energy is destroyed in the process. **According to the law of conservation of energy, energy cannot be created or destroyed.** So the total amount of energy is the same before and after any transformation. If you add up all the new forms of energy after a transformation, all of the original energy will be accounted for.

Energy and Friction So what happens to the energy of the top in Figure 14? As the top spins, it encounters friction with the floor and friction from the air. Whenever a moving object experiences friction, some of its kinetic energy is transformed into thermal energy. So, the mechanical energy of the spinning top is transformed to thermal energy. The top slows and eventually falls on its side, but its energy is not destroyed—it is transformed.

The fact that friction transforms mechanical energy to thermal energy should not surprise you. After all, you take advantage of such thermal energy when you rub your cold hands together to warm them up. The fact that friction transforms mechanical energy to thermal energy explains why no machine is 100 percent efficient. You may recall that the output work of any real machine is always less than the input work. This reduced efficiency occurs because some mechanical energy is always transformed into thermal energy due to friction.

FIGURE 14

Conservation of Energy
A spinning top's kinetic energy is not lost. It is transformed into thermal energy through friction.
Applying Concepts *How much of the top's kinetic energy becomes thermal energy?*

Energy and Matter You might have heard of Albert Einstein's theory of relativity. His theory stated that energy *can* sometimes be created—by destroying matter! **Matter** is anything that has mass and takes up space. All objects are made up of matter.

Just as one form of energy can be transformed to other forms, Einstein discovered that matter can be transformed to energy. In fact, destroying just a small amount of matter releases a huge amount of energy.

Einstein's discovery meant that the law of conservation of energy had to be adjusted. In some situations, energy alone is not conserved. However, since matter can be transformed to energy, scientists say matter and energy together are always conserved.

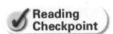 **Reading Checkpoint** How can energy be created?

FIGURE 15
Albert Einstein
Einstein published his theory of special relativity in 1905.

Section 3 Assessment

Target Reading Skill Asking Questions Use the answers to the questions you wrote about the headings to help you answer the questions below.

Reviewing Key Concepts

1. a. Reviewing What is the relationship between different forms of energy?
  b. Relating Cause and Effect When you turn a toaster on, what happens to the electrical energy?
  c. Sequencing Describe the energy transformations that happen when you strike a match. List them in the order in which they occur.
2. a. Identifying What common energy transformation allows you to send a rubber band flying across the room?
  b. Describing Describe the energy transformations that occur when you bounce a ball.
  c. Interpreting Diagrams Describe the energy transformations that occur in the pendulum in Figure 12.

3. a. Summarizing State the law of conservation of energy in your own words.
  b. Explaining Thermal energy is produced when a firefighter slides down a pole. Where does it come from?
  c. Making Generalizations Based on the theory of relativity, what must always be conserved?

Lab zone At-Home Activity

Hot Wire Straighten a wire hanger. Have a family member feel the wire and observe whether it feels cool or warm. Then hold the ends of the wire and bend it back and forth several times. **CAUTION:** *If the wire breaks, it can be sharp.* Do not bend it more than a few times. After bending the wire, have your family member feel it again. Explain how energy transformations can produce a change in temperature.

Soaring Straws

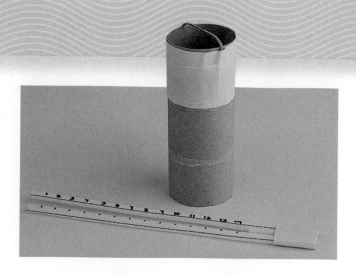

Problem

How does the gravitational potential energy of a straw rocket depend on the elastic potential energy of a rubber band launcher?

Skills Focus

controlling variables, graphing

Materials

- scissors
- rubber band
- 3 plastic straws
- meter stick
- marker
- metric ruler
- balance
- masking tape
- empty toilet paper tube

Procedure

1. Construct the rocket and launcher following the instructions in the box above. Use a balance to find the mass of the rocket in grams. Record the mass.

2. Hold the launcher in one hand with your fingers over the ends of the rubber band. Load the launcher by placing the straw rocket on the rubber band and pulling down from the other end as shown in the photograph. Let go and launch the rocket straight up. **CAUTION:** *Be sure to aim the straw rocket into the air, not at classmates.*

3. In your notebook, make a data table similar to the one on the next page.

4. Have your partner hold a meter stick, or tape it to the wall, so that its zero end is even with the top of the rocket launcher. Measure the height, in meters, to which the rocket rises. If the rocket goes higher than a single meter stick, use two meter sticks.

Making A Rocket and Launcher

A Cut a rubber band and tape it across the open end of a hollow cylinder, such as a toilet paper tube. The rubber band should be taut, but stretched only a tiny amount. This is the launcher.

B Cut about 3 cm off a plastic straw.

C Lay 2 full-length straws side by side on a flat surface with the 3-cm piece of straw between them. Arrange the straws so that their ends are even.

D Tape the straws together side by side. Starting from the untaped end, make marks every centimeter on one of the long straws. This is the rocket.

5. You can measure the amount of stretch of the rubber band by noting where the markings on the rocket line up with the bottom of the launching cylinder. Launch the rocket using five different amounts of stretch. Record your measurements.

6. For each amount of stretch, find the average height to which the rocket rises. Record the height in your data table.

7. Find the gravitational potential energy for each amount of stretch:

Gravitational potential energy =
    Mass × Gravitational acceleration × Height

You have measured the mass in grams. So the unit of energy is the millijoule (mJ), which is one thousandth of a joule. Record the results in your data table.

Data Table					
Amount of Stretch (cm)	Height Trial 1 (m)	Height Trial 2 (m)	Height Trial 3 (m)	Average Height (m)	Gravitational Potential Energy (mJ)

Analyze and Conclude

1. **Controlling Variables** Which variable in your data table is the manipulated variable? The responding variable? How do you know?

2. **Graphing** Graph your results. Show gravitational potential energy on the vertical axis and amount of stretch on the horizontal axis.

3. **Measuring** In this experiment, what measurement is related to elastic potential energy?

4. **Drawing Conclusions** Look at the shape of the graph. What conclusions can you reach about the relationship between the gravitational potential energy of the rocket and the elastic potential energy of the rubber band?

5. **Inferring** When you release the rocket, what kind of energy does the rocket have just after takeoff? What are the elastic potential energy and the gravitational potential energy at this point?

6. **Developing Hypotheses** Make an additional column on the right side of your data table labeled Kinetic Energy (mJ). For each row, write down what you think the rocket's kinetic energy is right after takeoff.

7. **Communicating** Write an advertisement for your rocket launcher. Include a diagram explaining how the rocket gains potential energy, how its potential energy is transformed to kinetic energy, and how its kinetic energy is transformed back into potential energy.

Design an Experiment

How would the height and distance the rocket travels be affected by the angle of launch? Design an experiment to measure the height and distance resulting from different launch angles. Keep the amount of stretch constant. *Obtain your teacher's permission before carrying out your investigation.*

Energy and Fossil Fuels

Reading Preview

Key Concepts
- What is the source of the energy stored in fossil fuels?
- How is energy transformed when fossil fuels are used?

Key Terms
- fossil fuel
- combustion

Target Reading Skill
Previewing Visuals When you preview, you look ahead at the material to be read. Preview Figure 18. Then write two questions that you have about the diagram in a graphic organizer like the one below. As you read, answer your questions.

Using Fossil Fuel Energy

Q.	What energy transformation occurs in the sun?
A.	
Q.	

Lab zone Discover **Activity**

What Is a Fuel?
1. Put on your goggles. Attach a flask to a ring stand with a clamp. Then place a thermometer in the flask.
2. Add enough water to the flask to cover the thermometer bulb. Record the temperature of the water. Remove the thermometer.
3. Fold a wooden coffee stirrer in three places to look like a W. Stand it in a small aluminum pan so that the W is upright. Position the pan 4–5 cm directly below the flask.
4. Ignite the coffee stirrer at its center. **CAUTION:** *Be careful when using matches.*
5. When the coffee stirrer has stopped burning, read the temperature of the water again. Allow the flask to cool before cleaning up.

Think It Over
Forming Operational Definitions Gasoline in a car, kerosene in a lantern, and a piece of wood are all fuels. Based on your observations, what is a fuel?

Imagine a lush, green, swampy forest. Ferns as tall as trees block the view. Enormous dragonflies buzz through the warm, moist air. Huge cockroaches, some longer than your finger, crawl across the ground. Where is this place? Actually, a better question to ask would be, *when* is it? The time is more than 400 million years ago. That's even before the dinosaurs lived! But what does this ancient forest have to do with you?

Formation of Fossil Fuels

The plants of vast forests that once covered Earth provide the energy stored in fuels. A fuel is a material that contains stored potential energy. The gasoline used in vehicles and the propane used in a gas grill are examples of fuels. Some of the fuels used today were made from materials that formed hundreds of millions of years ago. These fuels, which include coal, petroleum, and natural gas, are known as **fossil fuels.**

The vast, ancient forests were the source of coal. When plants and animals died, their remains piled up in thick layers in swamps and marshes. Clay and sand sediments covered their remains. The resulting pressure and high temperature turned the remains into coal.

Energy From the Sun Remember that energy is conserved. That means that fuels do not create energy. So if fossil fuels store energy, they must have gotten energy from somewhere else. But where did it come from? **Fossil fuels contain energy that came from the sun.** In fact, the sun is the source of energy for most of Earth's processes. Within the dense core of the sun, during the process of nuclear fusion, nuclear energy is transformed to electromagnetic energy as well as other forms. Some of this electromagnetic energy reaches Earth in the form of light.

FIGURE 16
Fossil Fuels
Offshore oil rigs drill for the fossil fuel petroleum under the ocean floor.

 **Reading Checkpoint** What is the source of the energy stored in fossil fuels?

FIGURE 17
Mining for Coal
Miners use heavy machinery to dig for coal. **Developing Hypotheses** *Why is coal usually found underground?*

① The sun transforms nuclear energy to electromagnetic energy.

FIGURE 18
Using Fossil Fuel Energy

The chemical energy in fossil fuels comes from the sun. Millions of years later, power plants transform that chemical energy to the electrical energy that powers your hair dryer.
Interpreting Diagrams *What does a turbine do?*

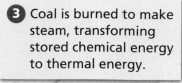

③ Coal is burned to make steam, transforming stored chemical energy to thermal energy.

② Ancient plants and animals transform electromagnetic energy from the sun to stored chemical energy. Their remains become coal.

Lab zone **Skills Activity**

Graphing
The following list shows what percent of power used in the United States in a recent year came from each energy source: coal, 23%; nuclear, 8%; oil, 39%; natural gas, 24%; water, 3%; and biofuels, 3%. Prepare a circle graph that presents these data. (See the Skills Handbook for more on circle graphs.)

What power source does the United States rely on most? What percent of the country's total energy needs is met by coal, oil, and natural gas combined?

The Sun's Energy on Earth When the sun's energy reaches Earth, certain living things—plants, algae, and certain bacteria—transform some of it to chemical energy. Some of the energy in the chemical compounds they make is used for their daily energy needs. The rest is stored. Animals that eat plants store some of the plant's chemical energy in their own cells. When ancient animals and plants died, the chemical energy they had stored was trapped within them. This trapped energy is the chemical energy found in coal.

Use of Fossil Fuels

Fossil fuels can be burned to release the chemical energy stored millions of years ago. The process of burning fuels is known as **combustion.** During combustion, the fuel's chemical energy is transformed to thermal energy. This thermal energy can be used to heat water until the water boils and produces steam. In modern, coal-fired power plants, the steam is raised to a very high temperature in a boiler. When it leaves the boiler it has enough pressure to turn a turbine.

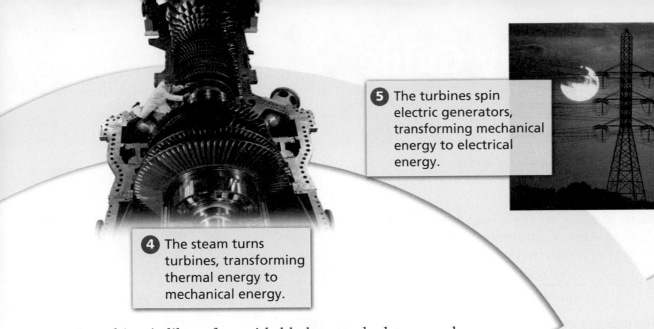

5 The turbines spin electric generators, transforming mechanical energy to electrical energy.

4 The steam turns turbines, transforming thermal energy to mechanical energy.

A turbine is like a fan, with blades attached to an axle. The pressure of the steam on the blades causes the turbine to spin very fast. In this process, the thermal energy of the steam is transformed to the mechanical energy of the moving turbine.

The turbines are connected to generators. When turbines spin them, generators produce electricity. As you can see in Figure 18, a power plant transforms chemical energy to thermal energy to mechanical energy to electrical energy. This electrical energy is then used to light your home and run other devices, such as a hair dryer.

6 Your hair dryer transforms electrical energy to thermal energy.

✓ **Reading Checkpoint** What energy transformations take place in a power plant?

Section 4 Assessment

 **Target Reading Skill** Previewing Visuals Refer to your questions and answers about Figure 18 to help you answer Question 2 below.

Reviewing Key Concepts

1. **a. Defining** What are fossil fuels?
   b. Explaining What role did the sun play in making fossil fuels?
   c. Drawing Conclusions How did ancient animals receive stored energy from the sun?
2. **a. Reviewing** How is the chemical energy stored in coal released?
   b. Sequencing Describe the steps in which a power plant transforms the energy in fossil fuels to electrical energy.
   c. Inferring Which steps in the power plant process rely on potential energy? Which steps rely on kinetic energy? Why?

Lab zone **At-Home Activity**

Burning Fossils Some appliances in your home, such as ovens, grills, and water heaters, may use fossil fuels as an energy source. With a family member, search your home for appliances that use fossil fuels such as petroleum, coal, or natural gas as a source of energy. Explain to your family member what fossil fuels are and how they form.

The BIG Idea **Energy Forms and Conservation** Energy is the ability to do work or cause change. Energy can be transformed from one form into another, but it cannot be created or destroyed.

① What Is Energy?

Key Concepts

- If the transfer of energy is work, then power is the rate at which energy is transferred, or the amount of energy transferred in a unit of time.

- Power $= \dfrac{\text{Energy transferred}}{\text{Time}}$

- Two basic kinds of energy are kinetic energy and potential energy.

- Kinetic energy $= \frac{1}{2} \times \text{Mass} \times \text{Velocity}^2$

- Gravitational potential energy $=$ Weight $\times$ Height

Key Terms

energy
kinetic energy
potential energy
gravitational potential energy
elastic potential energy

② Forms of Energy

Key Concepts

- You can find an object's mechanical energy by adding the object's kinetic energy and potential energy.

 Mechanical energy $=$ Kinetic energy $+$ Potential energy

- Forms of energy associated with the particles of objects include thermal energy, electrical energy, chemical energy, nuclear energy, and electromagnetic energy.

Key Terms

mechanical energy
thermal energy
electrical energy
chemical energy
nuclear energy
electromagnetic energy

③ Energy Transformations and Conservation

Key Concepts

- Most forms of energy can be transformed into other forms.

- One of the most common energy transformations is the transformation between potential energy and kinetic energy.

- According to the law of conservation of energy, energy cannot be created or destroyed.

Key Terms

energy transformation
law of conservation of energy
matter

④ Energy and Fossil Fuels

Key Concepts

- Fossil fuels contain energy that came from the sun.

- Fossil fuels can be burned to release the chemical energy stored millions of years ago.

Key Terms

fossil fuel
combustion

Review and Assessment

Go Online
PHSchool.com
For: Self-Assessment
Visit: PHSchool.com
Web Code: cga-3050

Organizing Information

Concept Mapping Copy the concept map about energy onto a separate sheet of paper. Then complete it and add a title. (For more on Concept Mapping, see the Skills Handbook.)

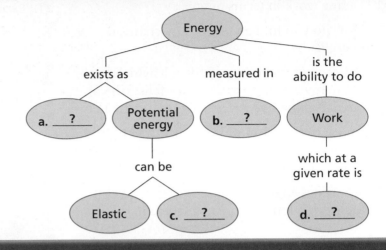

Reviewing Key Terms

Choose the letter of the best answer.

1. Energy of motion is called
   a. kinetic energy.
   b. elastic potential energy.
   c. gravitational potential energy.
   d. chemical energy.

2. When you stretch a rubber band, you give it
   a. kinetic energy.
   b. elastic potential energy.
   c. gravitational potential energy.
   d. electrical energy.

3. The energy associated with the position and motion of an object is called
   a. potential energy.
   b. nuclear energy.
   c. mechanical energy.
   d. thermal energy.

4. The energy stored in the nucleus of an atom is called
   a. electromagnetic energy.
   b. electrical energy.
   c. chemical energy.
   d. nuclear energy.

5. Fossil fuels store energy from the sun as
   a. chemical energy.
   b. thermal energy.
   c. electromagnetic energy.
   d. electrical energy.

If the statement is true, write *true*. If it is false, change the underlined word or words to make the statement true.

6. <u>Kinetic energy</u> is related to an object's height.

7. <u>Electrical energy</u> is the total kinetic and potential energy of the particles in an object.

8. The <u>law of conservation of energy</u> states that when one form of energy is transformed to another, no energy is destroyed.

9. <u>Energy</u> is anything that has mass and takes up space.

10. <u>Combustion</u> is the process of burning fuels.

Writing in Science

Interview You are preparing to interview an Olympic skier for a children's science magazine. Prepare a list of questions that you would ask the skier about the energy transformations that occur while skiing.

Discovery CHANNEL SCHOOL

Energy
Video Preview
Video Field Trip
▶ Video Assessment

Review and Assessment

Checking Concepts

11. Define work in terms of energy.

12. How do you find an object's mechanical energy?

13. For each of the following, decide which forms of energy are present: a walnut falls from a tree; a candle burns; a spring is stretched.

14. An eagle flies from its perch in a tree to the ground to capture and eat its prey. Describe its energy transformations.

15. How does energy become stored in a fossil fuel? What kind of energy is stored?

Thinking Critically

16. **Calculating** Find the power of a machine that transfers 450 J of energy in 9 s.

17. **Calculating** A 1,350-kg car travels at 12 m/s. What is its kinetic energy?

18. **Comparing and Contrasting** In the illustration below, which vehicle has the least kinetic energy? The greatest kinetic energy? Explain your answers.

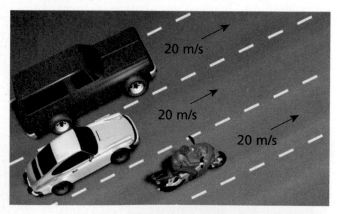

19. **Problem Solving** A 380-N girl walks down a flight of stairs so that she is 2.5 m below her starting level. What is the change in the girl's gravitational potential energy?

20. **Applying Concepts** One chef places a pie in the oven at a low setting so that it is baked in one hour. Another chef places a pie in the oven at a high setting so that the pie bakes in 30 minutes. Is the amount of energy the same in each case? Is the power the same?

Math Practice

21. **Exponents** What is the value of 12^2?

22. **Exponents** What is the value of $2^2 \times 3^2$?

Applying Skills

Use the photo to answer Questions 23–25.

The golfer in the photo is taking a swing. The golf club starts at Point A and ends at Point E.

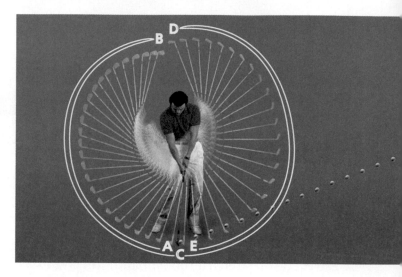

23. **Inferring** At which point(s) does the golf club have the greatest potential energy? At which point(s) does it have the greatest kinetic energy?

24. **Interpreting Diagrams** Describe the energy transformations from Point A to Point E.

25. **Drawing Conclusions** The kinetic energy of the club at Point C is more than the potential energy of the club at Point B. Does this mean that the law of conservation of energy is violated? Why or why not?

Lab zone Chapter **Project**

Performance Assessment Present your roller coaster to the class. Explain how you selected your materials, as well as the effect of hill height, incline, turns, and loops on the motion of the roller coaster. You should also explain how energy is transformed as the roller coaster moves along the tracks.

Standardized Test Prep

Choose the letter of the best answer.

1. Wind has energy because
   A it can change direction.
   B it can do work.
   C it has mass.
   D it is electrically charged.

Use the table below and your knowledge of science to answer Questions 2 and 3.

Summer Classic Diving Competition		
Name	Weight (N)	Height of Dive (m)
Clark	620	3
Simmons	640	3
Delgado	610	10
Chen	590	10

2. When standing on the diving board, which diver has the least gravitational potential energy?
   F Clark
   G Simmons
   H Delgado
   J Chen

3. In SI, which unit is used to express the divers' gravitational potential energy?
   A newton
   B kilowatt
   C horsepower
   D joule

4. A pendulum will eventually slow and stop because of
   F friction.
   G weight.
   H kinetic energy.
   J potential energy.

5. What energy transformation takes place when wood is burned?
   A nuclear energy to thermal energy
   B thermal energy to electrical energy
   C chemical energy to thermal energy
   D mechanical energy to thermal energy

Constructed Response

6. Explain the energy transformations involved in how fossil fuels formed and how they are used.

The BIG Idea
Transfer of Energy

How can heat be transferred from place to place?

Chapter Preview

❶ **Temperature, Thermal Energy, and Heat**
Discover How Cold Is the Water?
Math Skills Converting Units
Analyzing Data Specific Heat
Technology Lab Build Your Own Thermometer

❷ **The Transfer of Heat**
Discover What Does It Mean to Heat Up?
Try This Feel the Warmth
Skills Activity Inferring
Skills Lab Just Add Water

❸ **Thermal Energy and States of Matter**
Discover What Happens to Heated Metal?
Skills Activity Observing
At-Home Activity Frosty Balloons

❹ **Uses of Heat**
Discover What Happens at the Pump?
Try This Shake It Up
Active Art Four-Stroke Engine

Sparks fly as a welder melts
metal with intense heat. ▶

Discovery
CHANNEL
SCHOOL™

Thermal Energy and Heat

▶ Video Preview
Video Field Trip
Video Assessment

Lab zone™ Chapter **Project**

In Hot Water

In this chapter, you will find out what heat is and how it relates to thermal energy and temperature. As you read the chapter, you will use what you learn to construct a device that will insulate a container of hot water.

Your Goal To build a container for a 355-mL aluminum can that keeps water hot

Your container must

- minimize the loss of thermal energy from the hot water
- be built from materials approved by your teacher
- have insulation no thicker than 3 cm
- not use electricity or heating chemicals
- follow the safety guidelines in Appendix A

Plan It! With a group of classmates, brainstorm different materials that prevent heat loss. Write a plan for how you will test these materials. Include a list of the variables you will control when doing your tests. Perform your tests to determine the best insulating materials. Keep a log of your results. Then build and test the device.

Temperature, Thermal Energy, and Heat

Reading Preview

Key Concepts
• What are the three common temperature scales?
• How is thermal energy related to temperature and heat?
• What does having a high specific heat mean?

Key Terms
• temperature
• Fahrenheit scale
• Celsius scale
• Kelvin scale
• absolute zero
• heat
• specific heat

Target Reading Skill
Comparing and Contrasting
As you read, compare and contrast temperature, thermal energy, and heat by completing a table like the one below.

	Energy Measured	Units
Temp.	Average kinetic energy of particles	
Thermal energy		
Heat		

Discover **Activity**

How Cold Is the Water?

1. Fill a plastic bowl with cold water, another with warm water, and a third with water at room temperature. Label each bowl and line them up.

2. Place your right hand in the cold water and your left hand in the warm water.

3. After about a minute, place both your hands in the third bowl at the same time.

Think It Over
Observing How did the water in the third bowl feel when you touched it? Did the water feel the same on both hands? If not, explain why.

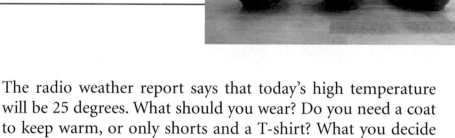

The radio weather report says that today's high temperature will be 25 degrees. What should you wear? Do you need a coat to keep warm, or only shorts and a T-shirt? What you decide depends on what "25 degrees" means.

Temperature

You don't need a science book to tell you that the word *hot* means higher temperatures or the word *cold* means lower temperatures. When scientists think about high and low temperatures, however, they do not think about "hot" and "cold." Instead, they think about particles of matter in motion.

Recall that all matter is made up of tiny particles. These particles are always moving even if the matter they make up is stationary. Recall that the energy of motion is called kinetic energy. So all particles of matter have kinetic energy. The faster particles move, the more kinetic energy they have. **Temperature** is a measure of the average kinetic energy of the individual particles in matter.

High-temperature particles have a high average kinetic energy.

Low-temperature particles have a low average kinetic energy.

FIGURE 1
Temperature
The particles of hot cocoa move faster than those of cold chocolate milk.
Applying Concepts *Which drink has particles with greater average kinetic energy?*

In Figure 1, the hot cocoa has a higher temperature than the cold chocolate milk. The cocoa's particles are moving faster, so they have greater average kinetic energy. If the milk is heated, its particles will move faster, so their kinetic energy will increase. The temperature of the milk will rise.

Measuring Temperature To measure the temperature of the heated milk, you would probably use a thermometer like the one shown in Figure 2. A thermometer usually consists of a liquid such as alcohol sealed inside a narrow glass tube. When the tube is heated, the particles of the liquid speed up and spread out so the particles take up more space, or volume. You see the level of the liquid move up the tube. The reverse happens when the tube is cooled. The particles of the liquid slow down and move closer, taking up less volume. You see the level of the liquid move down in the tube.

A thermometer has numbers and units, or a scale, on it. When you read the scale on a thermometer, you read the temperature of the surrounding matter. Thermometers can have different scales. The temperature reading you see depends on the thermometer's scale.

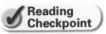 **Reading Checkpoint** What happens to the liquid particles inside a thermometer when it is heated?

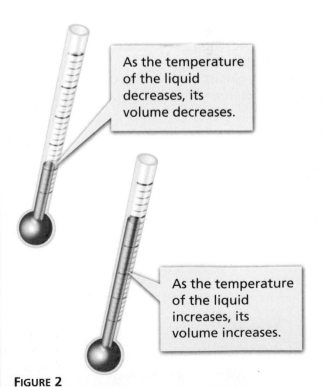

As the temperature of the liquid decreases, its volume decreases.

As the temperature of the liquid increases, its volume increases.

FIGURE 2
How a Thermometer Works
Temperature changes cause the level of the liquid inside a thermometer to rise and fall.

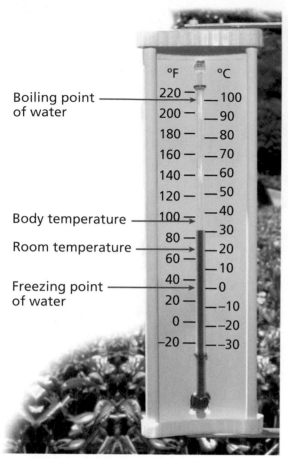

Boiling point of water

Body temperature

Room temperature

Freezing point of water

FIGURE 3
Temperature Scales
Many thermometers have both Celsius and Fahrenheit temperature scales.
Interpreting Photographs *What is the boiling point of water on the Celsius scale? On the Fahrenheit scale?*

Go Online
SciLINKS
NSTA

For: Links on temperature and heat
Visit: www.SciLinks.org
Web Code: scn-1361

Temperature Scales The three common scales for measuring temperature are the Fahrenheit, Celsius, and Kelvin scales. Each of these scales is divided into regular intervals.

The temperature scale you are probably most familiar with is the Fahrenheit scale. In the United States, the **Fahrenheit scale** is the most common temperature scale. The scale is divided into degrees Fahrenheit (°F). On this scale, the freezing point of water is 32°F and the boiling point is 212°F.

In nearly all other countries, however, the most common temperature scale is the **Celsius scale.** The Celsius scale is divided into degrees Celsius (°C), which are larger units than degrees Fahrenheit. On the Celsius scale, the freezing point of water is 0°C and the boiling point is 100°C.

The temperature scale commonly used in physical science is the **Kelvin scale.** Units on the Kelvin scale, called kelvins (K), are the same size as degrees on the Celsius scale. So, an increase of 1 K equals an increase of 1°C. The freezing point of water on the Kelvin scale is 273 K, and the boiling point is 373 K. The number 273 is special. Scientists have concluded from experiments that −273°C is the lowest temperature possible. No more thermal energy can be removed from matter at −273°C. Zero on the Kelvin scale represents −273°C and is called **absolute zero.**

Thermal Energy and Heat

Different objects at the same temperature can have different energies. To understand this, you need to know about thermal energy and about heat. You may be used to thinking about thermal energy as heat, but they are not the same thing. Temperature, thermal energy, and heat are closely related, but they are all different.

Thermal Energy You may recall that the total energy of all of the particles in an object is called thermal energy, or sometimes internal energy. The thermal energy of an object depends on the number of particles in the object, the temperature of the object, and the arrangement of the object's particles. You will learn about how the arrangement of particles affects thermal energy in Section 3.

The more particles an object has at a given temperature, the more thermal energy it has. For example, a 1-liter pot of hot cocoa at 75°C has more thermal energy than a 0.2-liter mug of hot cocoa at 75°C because the pot contains more cocoa particles. On the other hand, the higher the temperature of an object, the more thermal energy the object has. Therefore, if two 1-liter pots of hot cocoa have different temperatures, the pot with the higher temperature has more thermal energy. In Section 3, you will learn about how thermal energies differ for solids, liquids, and gases.

Heat Thermal energy that is transferred from matter at a higher temperature to matter at a lower temperature is called **heat.** The scientific definition of heat is different from its everyday use. In a conversation, you might say that an object contains heat. However, objects contain thermal energy, not heat. Only when thermal energy is transferred is it called heat. **Heat is thermal energy moving from a warmer object to a cooler object.** For example, when you hold an ice cube in your hand, as shown in Figure 4, the ice cube melts because thermal energy is transferred from your hand to the ice cube.

Recall that work also involves the transfer of energy. Since work and heat are both energy transfers, they are both measured in the same unit—joules.

 **Reading Checkpoint** Why does an ice cube melt in your hand?

Math Skills

Converting Units

To convert a Fahrenheit temperature to a Celsius temperature, use the following formula.

$$°C = \frac{5}{9}(°F - 32)$$

For example, if the temperature in your classroom is 68°F, what is the temperature in degrees Celsius?

$$°C = \frac{5}{9}(68 - 32)$$

$$°C = \frac{5}{9} \times 36$$

$$°C = 20$$

The temperature of your classroom is 20°C.

Practice Problem While at the beach, you measure the ocean temperature as 77°F. What is the temperature of the ocean in degrees Celsius?

FIGURE 4
Heat Your hand transfers thermal energy to the ice cube. Even though your hand is cold, this transfer is called heat. Your hand feels cold because it is losing thermal energy.

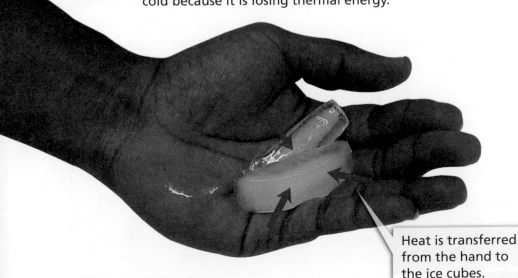

Heat is transferred from the hand to the ice cubes.

FIGURE 5
Specific Heat of Sand and Water
The specific heat of water is greater than the specific heat of sand. On a sunny day the water feels cooler than the sand.

Specific Heat

Imagine running across hot sand toward the ocean. You run to the water's edge, but you don't go any farther—the water is too cold. How can the sand be so hot and the water so cold? After all, the sun heats both of them. The answer is that water requires more heat to raise its temperature than sand does.

When an object is heated, its temperature rises. But the temperature does not rise at the same rate for all objects. The amount of heat required to raise the temperature of an object depends on the object's chemical makeup. To change the temperature of different objects by the same amount, different amounts of heat are required.

Scientists have defined a quantity to measure the relationship between heat and temperature change. The amount of energy required to raise the temperature of 1 kilogram of a material by 1 kelvin is called its **specific heat.** The unit of measure for specific heat is joules per kilogram-kelvin, or J/(kg·K).

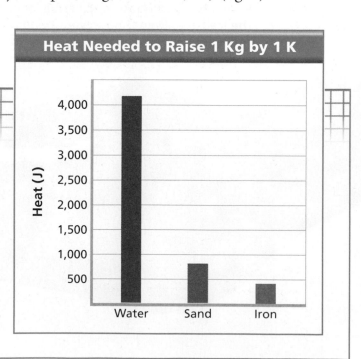

Math Analyzing Data

Specific Heat
The specific heat of three different materials was measured. These data are shown in the graph.

1. **Reading Graphs** What three materials are compared in the graph?

2. **Interpreting Data** About how much heat is required to raise 1 kg of water by 1 K?

3. **Drawing Conclusions** According to the graph, which material requires more heat to raise its temperature by 1 K, iron or sand?

Heat Needed to Raise 1 Kg by 1 K

Look at the specific heats of the materials listed in Figure 6. Notice that the specific heat of water is quite high. One kilogram of water requires 4,180 joules of energy to raise its temperature 1 kelvin.

A material with a high specific heat can absorb a great deal of thermal energy without a great change in temperature. On the other hand, a material with a low specific heat would have a large temperature change after absorbing the same amount of thermal energy.

The energy gained or lost by a material is related to its mass, change in temperature, and specific heat. You can calculate thermal energy changes with the following formula.

Change in energy =
Mass × Specific heat × Change in temperature

How much heat is required to raise the temperature of 5 kilograms of water by 10 kelvins?

Change in energy = 5 kg × 4,180 J/(kg·K) × 10 K
= 209,000 J

You need to transfer 209,000 joules to the water to increase its temperature by 10 kelvins.

 **Reading Checkpoint** What formula allows you to determine an object's change in thermal energy?

Specific Heat of Common Materials	
Material	**Specific Heat (J/(kg·K))**
Aluminum	903
Copper	385
Glass	837
Ice	2,060
Iron	450
Sand	800
Silver	235
Water	4,180

FIGURE 6
This table lists the specific heats of several common materials.
Interpreting Tables *How much more energy is required to raise the temperature of 1 kg of iron by 1 K than to raise the temperature of 1 kg of copper by 1 K?*

Section 1 Assessment

🎯 **Target Reading Skill Comparing and Contrasting** Use the information in your table to help you answer Questions 1 and 2 below.

Reviewing Key Concepts

1. a. Identifying What is temperature?
   b. Describing How do thermometers measure temperature?
   c. Comparing and Contrasting How are the three temperature scales alike? How are they different?
2. a. Defining What is heat?
   b. Explaining What is the relationship between thermal energy and temperature? Between thermal energy and heat?
   c. Relating Cause and Effect What happens to the motion of an object's particles as the object's thermal energy increases? What happens to the temperature of the object?

3. a. Reviewing Why do some materials get hot more quickly than others?
   b. Calculating You stir your hot cocoa with a silver spoon that has a mass of 0.032 kg. The spoon's temperature increases from 20 K to 60 K. What is the change in the spoon's thermal energy? (*Hint:* Use the table in Figure 6 to find the specific heat of silver.)

Math ➤ Practice

4. Converting Units Convert 5.0°F to degrees Celsius.

5. Converting Units The surface temperature on the planet Venus can reach 860°F. Convert this temperature to degrees Celsius.

Technology Lab

· Tech & Design ·

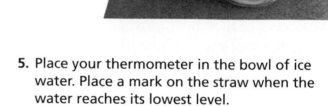

Build Your Own Thermometer

Problem

Can you build a thermometer out of simple materials?

Design Skills

evaluating the design, measuring, making models

Materials

- bowl of hot water   • bowl of ice water
- water of unknown temperature
- tap water   • 500-mL beaker
- clear glass juice or soda bottle, 20–25 cm
- clear plastic straw, 18–20 cm   • food coloring
- plastic dropper   • cooking oil
- modeling clay
- metric ruler
- fine-point marker

Procedure

1. You can use simple materials to build a model of an alcohol thermometer. First, mix food coloring into a beaker of tap water. Then fill a glass bottle with the colored water.

2. Place a straw in the bottle. Use modeling clay to position the straw so that it extends at least 10 cm above the bottle mouth. Do not let the straw touch the bottom. The clay should completely seal off the bottle mouth. Make sure there is no air in the bottle.

3. Using a dropper, add colored water into the straw to a level 5 cm above the bottle. Place a drop of cooking oil in the straw to prevent evaporation.

4. Place your thermometer into a bowl of hot water. When the colored water reaches its highest level, place a mark on the straw.

5. Place your thermometer in the bowl of ice water. Place a mark on the straw when the water reaches its lowest level.

6. Create a scale for your model thermometer. Divide the distance between the two marks into 5-mm intervals. Starting with the lowest point, label the intervals on the straw 0, 1, 2, 3, and so on.

7. Measure the temperature of two unknown samples with your thermometer. Record both temperatures.

Analyze and Conclude

1. **Evaluating the Design** Do you think your model accurately represents an alcohol thermometer? How is it like a real thermometer? How is it different?

2. **Inferring** How can you use the concepts of matter and the kinetic energy of particles to explain the way your model works?

3. **Measuring** Approximately what Celsius temperatures do you think your model measures? Explain your estimate.

4. **Making Models** Examine the structure and materials used in your model. Propose a change that would improve the model. Explain your choice.

Communicate

Create a poster to show how an alcohol thermometer works. Explain how the Celsius and Fahrenheit scales compare. For example, does 0° have the same meaning on both scales? Use a diagram with labels and captions to communicate your ideas.

The Transfer of Heat

Reading Preview

Key Concepts
- What are the three forms of heat transfer?
- In what direction does heat move?
- How are conductors and insulators different?

Key Terms
- conduction • convection
- convection current • radiation
- conductor • insulator

Target Reading Skill
Identifying Main Ideas As you read the How Is Heat Transferred? section, write the main idea in a graphic organizer like the one below. Then write three supporting details that give examples of the main idea.

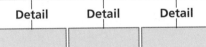

Main Idea

Heat can be transferred in three ways . . .

Detail	Detail	Detail

Lab zone Discover **Activity**

What Does It Mean to Heat Up?

1. Obtain several utensils made of different materials, such as silver, stainless steel, plastic, and wood.
2. Stand the utensils in a beaker so that they do not touch each other.
3. Press a small gob of frozen butter on the handle of each utensil. Make sure that when the utensils stand on end, the butter is at the same height on each one.
4. Pour hot water into the beaker until it is about 6 cm below the butter. Watch the butter on the utensils for several minutes. What happens?
5. Wash the utensils in soapy water when you finish.

Think It Over
Observing What happened to the butter? Did the same thing happen on every utensil? How can you account for your observations?

Blacksmithing is hot work. A piece of iron held in the fire of the forge becomes warmer and begins to glow. At the same time, the blacksmith feels hot air rising from the forge, and his face and arms begin to feel warmer. Each of these movements of energy is a transfer of heat.

A blacksmith at work ▶

Feel the Warmth

How is heat transferred from a light bulb?

1. Turn on a lamp without the shade. Wait about a minute.

2. Hold the palm of your hand about 10 cm from the side of the bulb for about 15 seconds. **CAUTION:** *Do not touch the bulb. Remove your hand sooner if it gets too warm.*

3. Now hold the palm of your hand about 10 cm above the top of the bulb for about 15 seconds.

Drawing Conclusions
In which location did your hand feel warmer? Explain your observations in terms of heat transfer.

How Is Heat Transferred?

There are three ways that heat can move. **Heat is transferred by conduction, convection, and radiation.** The blacksmith experiences all three.

Conduction In the process of **conduction,** heat is transferred from one particle of matter to another without the movement of the matter. Think of a metal spoon in a pot of water on an electric stove. The fast-moving particles in the hot electric coil collide with the slow-moving particles in the cool pot. The transfer of heat causes the pot's particles to move faster. Then the pot's particles collide with the water's particles, which in turn collide with the particles in the spoon. As the particles move faster, the metal spoon becomes hotter.

If you were to touch the spoon, heat would be transferred to your fingers. Too much heat transferred this way can cause a burn!

In Figure 7, heat from the fire is transferred to the stone beneath it. Then it is transferred from the stone to the metal tools. This transfer of heat from the fire to the tools is due to conduction.

Convection If you watch a pot of hot water on a stove, you will see the water moving. This movement transfers heat within the water. In **convection,** heat is transferred by the movement of currents within a fluid.

When the water at the bottom of the pot is heated, its particles move faster. The particles also move farther apart. As a result, the heated water becomes less dense. You may remember that a less dense fluid will float on top of a denser one. So the heated water rises. The surrounding, cooler water flows into its place. This flow creates a circular motion known as a **convection current.**

Convection currents can transfer heated air. As the air above the fire in Figure 7 is heated, it becomes less dense and rises up the chimney. When the warm air rises, cool air flows into its place.

Radiation **Radiation** is the transfer of energy by electromagnetic waves. You can feel the radiation from a fire in a fireplace all the way across the room. Unlike conduction and convection, radiation does not require matter to transfer thermal energy. All of the sun's energy that reaches Earth travels through millions of kilometers of empty space.

 **Reading Checkpoint** How does radiation transfer thermal energy?

FIGURE 7

Methods of Heat Transfer

Heat can be transferred by conduction, convection, or radiation. Heat from a fire is transferred by all three methods.
Interpreting Diagrams *Which of these methods requires the movement of currents with a fluid?*

Convection
When the air around the fire is heated, it becomes less dense than the cooler air nearby. The warm air rises up the chimney, and cool air flows in to take its place.

Radiation
The fire transforms chemical energy in the wood to electro-magnetic energy, which radiates heat across the room.

Conduction
Fast-moving particles in the fire transfer heat as they collide with slow-moving particles in the stone hearth. Eventually the heat conducts through the stones to the metal tools.

FIGURE 8
Heat Transfer From Food
The soup's heat is transferred to the bowl, the spoon, and the air.
Predicting *If the soup is not eaten, what will happen to its temperature?*

Heat Moves One Way

If two objects have different temperatures, heat will flow from the warmer object to the colder one. When heat flows into matter, the thermal energy of the matter increases. As the thermal energy increases, the temperature increases. At the same time, the temperature of the matter losing the heat decreases. Heat will flow from one object to the other until the two objects have the same temperature. You have probably seen this happen to your food. The bowl of hot soup shown in Figure 8, for example, cools to room temperature if you don't eat it quickly.

What happens when something becomes cold, such as when ice cream is made? The ingredients used to make it, such as milk and sugar, are not nearly as cold as the finished ice cream. In an ice cream maker, the ingredients are put into a metal can that is packed in ice. You might think that the ice transfers cold to the ingredients in the can. But this is not the case. There is no such thing as "coldness." Instead, the ingredients grow colder as thermal energy flows from them to the ice. Heat transfer occurs in only one direction.

 **Reading Checkpoint** Can heat flow from one object to a warmer object? Why or why not?

Conductors and Insulators

Have you ever stepped from a rug to a tile floor on a cold morning? The tile floor feels colder than the rug. Yet if you measured their temperatures, they would be the same—room temperature. The difference between them has to do with how materials conduct heat. A material can be either a conductor or an insulator. **A conductor transfers thermal energy well. An insulator does not transfer thermal energy well.**

Lab zone Skills **Activity**

Inferring
You pull some clothes out of the dryer as soon as they are dry. You grab your shirt without a problem, but when you pull out your jeans, you quickly drop them. The metal zipper is too hot to touch! What can you infer about which material in your jeans conducts thermal energy better? Explain.

Conductors A material that conducts heat well is called a **conductor.** Metals such as silver and stainless steel are good conductors. A metal spoon conducts heat better than a wooden spoon. Some materials are good conductors because of the particles they contain and how those particles are arranged. A good conductor, such as a tile floor, feels cool to the touch because it easily transfers heat away from your skin.

Insulators A material that does not conduct heat well is called an **insulator.** Wood, wool, straw, and paper are good insulators. So are the gases in air. Clothes and blankets are insulators that slow the transfer of heat out of your body.

A well-insulated building is comfortable inside whether it is hot or cold outdoors. Insulation prevents heat from entering the building in hot weather and from escaping in cold weather. Much of the heat transfer in a building occurs through the windows. For this reason, insulating windows have two panes of glass with a thin space of air between them. The trapped air does not transfer heat well.

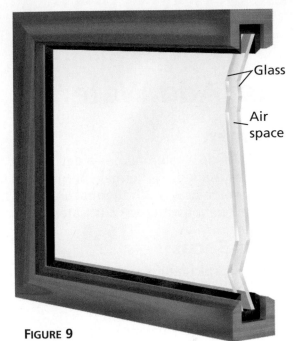

FIGURE 9
Insulating Windows
Air between the panes of this window acts as an insulator to slow the transfer of heat.

 **Reading Checkpoint** **Is air better as an insulator or as a conductor?**

Section 2 Assessment

Target Reading Skill
Identifying Main Ideas Use your graphic organizer to help you answer Question 1 below.

Reviewing Key Concepts

1. **a. Describing** What are conduction, convection, and radiation?
   b. Classifying Identify each example of heat transfer as conduction, convection, or radiation: opening the windows in a hot room; a lizard basking in the sun; putting ice on a sprained ankle.
   c. Inferring How can heat be transferred across empty space?

2. **a. Reviewing** In what direction will heat flow between two objects with different temperatures?
   b. Applying Concepts How does a glass of lemonade become cold when you put ice in it?

3. **a. Identifying** What kind of substance conducts thermal energy well?
   b. Making Judgments Would a copper pipe work better as a conductor or an insulator? Why do you think so?
   c. Interpreting Diagrams Why are two panes of glass used in the window in Figure 9?

Writing in Science

Explanation Suppose you are camping on a mountain, and the air temperature is very cold. How would you keep warm? Would you build a fire or set up a tent? Write an explanation for each action you would take. Tell whether conduction, convection, or radiation is involved with each heat transfer.

Just Add Water

Problem

Can you build a calorimeter—a device that measures changes in thermal energy—and use it to determine how much thermal energy is transferred from hot water to cold water?

Skills Focus

observing, calculating, interpreting data

Materials

- hot tap water • balance • scissors
- pencil • 4 plastic foam cups
- 2 thermometers or temperature probes
- beaker of water kept in an ice bath

Procedure

1. Predict how the amount of thermal energy lost by hot water will be related to the amount of thermal energy gained by cold water.

2. Copy the data table into your notebook.

3. Follow the instructions in the box to make two calorimeters. Find the mass of each empty calorimeter (including the cover) on a balance and record each mass in your data table.

4. From a beaker of water that has been sitting in an ice bath, add water (no ice cubes) to the cold-water calorimeter. Fill it about one-third full. Put the cover on, find the total mass, and record the mass in your data table.

5. Add hot tap water to the hot-water calorimeter. **CAUTION:** *Hot tap water can cause burns.* Fill the calorimeter about one-third full. Put the cover on, find the total mass, and record the mass in your data table.

6. Calculate the mass of the water in each calorimeter. Record the results in your data table.

7. Put thermometers through the holes in the covers of both calorimeters. Wait a minute or two and then record the temperatures. If you are using temperature probes, see your teacher for instructions.

MAKING A CALORIMETER

A Label a plastic foam cup with the letter C, which stands for cold water.

B Cut 2 to 3 cm from the top of a second plastic foam cup. Invert the second cup inside the first. Label the cover with a C also. The cup and cover are your cold-water calorimeter.

C Using a pencil, poke a hole in the cover large enough for a thermometer to fit into snugly.

D Repeat Steps A, B, and C with two other plastic foam cups. This time, label both cup and cover with an H. This is your hot-water calorimeter.

Data Table						
Calorimeter	Mass of Empty Cup (g)	Mass of Cup and Water (g)	Mass of Water (g)	Starting Temp. (°C)	Final Temp. (°C)	Change in Temp. (°C)
Cold Water						
Hot Water						

8. Remove both thermometers and covers. Pour the water from the cold-water calorimeter into the hot-water calorimeter. Put the cover back on the hot-water calorimeter, and insert a thermometer. Record the final temperature as the final temperature for both calorimeters.

Analyze and Conclude

1. **Observing** What is the temperature change of the cold water? Record your answer in the data table.

2. **Observing** What is the temperature change of the hot water? Record your answer in the data table.

3. **Calculating** Calculate the amount of thermal energy that enters the cold water by using the formula for the transfer of thermal energy. The specific heat of water is 4.18 J/(g·K).
Thermal energy transferred =
     4.18 J/(g·K) × Mass of cold water ×
     Temperature change of cold water
Remember that a change of 1°C is equal to a change of 1 K.

4. **Calculating** Now use the same formula to calculate the amount of thermal energy leaving the hot water.

5. **Calculating** What unit should you use for your results for Questions 3 and 4?

6. **Interpreting Data** Was your prediction from Step 1 confirmed? How do you know?

7. **Communicating** What sources of error might have affected your results? Write a paragraph explaining how the lab could be redesigned in order to reduce the errors.

Design an Experiment

How would your results be affected if you started with much more hot water than cold? If you used more cold water than hot? Make a prediction. Then design a procedure to test your prediction. *Obtain your teacher's permission before carrying out your investigation.*

Thermal Energy and States of Matter

Reading Preview

Key Concepts
- What are three states of matter?
- What causes matter to change state?
- What happens to a substance as its thermal energy increases?

Key Terms
- state • change of state
- melting • freezing
- evaporation • boiling
- condensation
- thermal expansion

Target Reading Skill

Building Vocabulary Using a word in a sentence helps you think about how best to explain the word. After you read the section, reread the paragraphs that contain definitions of Key Terms. Use all the information you have learned to write a meaningful sentence for each Key Term.

Lab zone Discover **Activity**

What Happens to Heated Metal?

1. Wrap one end of a one-meter-long metal wire around a clamp on a ring stand.
2. Tie the other end through several washers. Adjust the clamp so that the washers swing freely, but nearly touch the floor.
3. Light a candle. Hold the candle with an oven mitt, and heat the wire. **CAUTION:** *Be careful near the flame, and avoid dripping hot wax on yourself.* Predict how heat from the candle will affect the wire.
4. With your hand in the oven mitt, swing the wire. Observe any changes in the motion of the washers.
5. Blow out the candle and allow the wire to cool. After several minutes, swing the wire again and observe its motion.

Think It Over
Inferring Based on your observations, what can you conclude about the effect of heating a solid?

Throughout the day, the temperature at an orange grove drops steadily. The anxious farmer awaits the updated weather forecast. The news is not good. The temperature is expected to fall even further during the night. Low temperatures could wipe out the entire crop. He considers picking the crop early, but the oranges are not yet ripe.

Instead, the farmer tells his workers to haul in hoses and spray the orange trees with water. As the temperature drops, the water begins to freeze. The ice keeps the oranges warm!

How can ice possibly keep anything warm? The answer has to do with how thermal energy is transferred as water becomes ice.

◀ Oranges at 0°C sprayed with water

States of Matter

What happens when you hold an ice cube in your hand? It melts. The solid and the liquid are both the same material— water. Water can exist in three different **states,** or forms. **In fact, most matter on Earth can exist in three states—solid, liquid, and gas.** Although the chemical composition of matter remains the same, the arrangement of the particles that make up the matter differs from one state to another.

Solids The particles that make up a solid are packed together in relatively fixed positions. Particles of a solid cannot move out of their positions. They can only vibrate back and forth. This is why solids retain a fixed shape and volume. Because the shape and volume of the plastic helmets shown in Figure 10 do not change, the plastic is a solid.

Liquids The particles that make up a liquid are close together, but they are not held together as tightly as those of a solid. Because liquid particles can move around, liquids don't have a definite shape. But liquids do have a definite volume. In Figure 10, notice how the river water changes shape.

Gases In gases, the particles are moving so fast that they don't even stay close together. Gases expand to fill all the space available. They don't have a fixed shape or volume. Because air is a gas, it can expand to fill the raft in Figure 10 and also take the raft's shape.

Go Online
SciLINKS

For: Links on changes of state
Visit: www.SciLinks.org
Web Code: scn-1363

FIGURE 10
Three States of Matter
The plastic helmets, the water in the river, and the air that fills the raft are examples of three states of matter—solid, liquid, and gas.
Classifying *Which state of matter is represented by the plastic oars?*

Solid: plastic helmet

Liquid: river water

Gas: air inside raft

FIGURE 11
Melted Chocolate
Though normally a solid at room temperature, this chocolate has absorbed enough thermal energy to become a liquid.

Changes of State

The physical change from one state of matter to another is called a **change of state.** The state of matter depends on the amount of thermal energy it has. The more thermal energy matter has, the faster its particles move. Since a gas has more thermal energy than a liquid, the particles of a gas move faster than the particles of the same matter in the liquid state.

Matter can change from one state to another when thermal energy is absorbed or released. The graph in Figure 12 shows that as thermal energy increases, matter changes from a solid to a liquid and then to a gas. A gas changes to a liquid and then to a solid as thermal energy is removed from it.

The flat regions of the graph show conditions under which thermal energy is changing but temperature remains the same. Under these conditions, matter is changing from one state to another. During a change of state, the addition or loss of thermal energy changes the arrangement of the particles. However, the average kinetic energy of those particles does not change. Since temperature is a measure of average kinetic energy, temperature does not change as the state of matter changes.

Solid–Liquid Changes of State The change of state from a solid to a liquid is called **melting.** Melting occurs when a solid absorbs thermal energy. As the thermal energy of the solid increases, the structure of its particles breaks down. The particles become freer to move around. The temperature at which a solid changes to a liquid is called the melting point.

The change of state from a liquid to a solid is called **freezing.** Freezing occurs when matter releases thermal energy. The temperature at which matter changes from a liquid to a solid is called its freezing point.

FIGURE 12
During a change in state, the thermal energy of matter increases while its temperature remains the same.

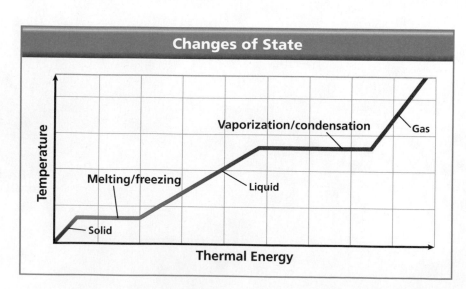

Changes of State

Temperature

Vaporization/condensation · Gas

Melting/freezing · Liquid

Solid

Thermal Energy

For a given type of matter, the freezing point and melting point are the same. The difference between the two is whether the matter is gaining or releasing thermal energy. The farmer had his workers spray the orange trees with water because the freezing water releases thermal energy into the oranges.

Liquid–Gas Changes of State The process by which matter changes from the liquid to the gas state is called vaporization. During this process, particles in a liquid absorb thermal energy and move faster. Eventually they move fast enough to escape the liquid as gas particles. If vaporization takes place at the surface of a liquid, it is called **evaporation.** At higher temperatures, vaporization can occur below the surface of a liquid as well. This process is called **boiling.** When a liquid boils, gas bubbles that form within the liquid rise to the surface. The temperature at which a liquid boils is called its boiling point.

When a gas loses a certain amount of thermal energy, it will change into a liquid. A change from the gas state to the liquid state is called **condensation.** You have probably seen beads of water appear on the outside of a cold drinking glass. This occurs because water vapor that is present in the air loses thermal energy when it comes in contact with the cold glass.

 **Reading Checkpoint** What change of state occurs in evaporation?

Lab zone **Skills Activity**

Observing
Put a teakettle on a stove or a lab burner and bring the water to a boil. Look carefully at the white vapor coming out of the spout. **CAUTION:** *Steam and boiling water can cause serious burns.* In what state of matter is the white vapor that you see? What is present, but not visible, in the small space between the white vapor and the spout?

FIGURE 13
Condensation
Under certain weather conditions, water vapor in the air can condense into fog. **Applying Concepts** *As it condenses, does water absorb or release thermal energy?*

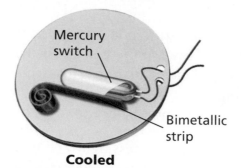

Mercury
switch

Bimetallic
strip

Cooled

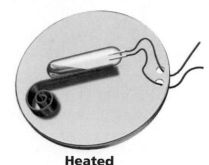

Wires to
heating
system

Heated

FIGURE 14
Thermostat
A bimetallic strip controls many thermostats. When it cools, the strip curls up and lowers the switch, allowing mercury to flow over the wires. When the strip warms up, it uncurls and raises the switch.

Thermal Expansion

Have you ever loosened a tight jar lid by holding it under a stream of hot water? This works because the metal lid expands a little. Do you know why? **As the thermal energy of matter increases, its particles spread out and the substance expands.** With a few exceptions, this is true for all matter, even when the matter is not changing state. The expanding of matter when it is heated is known as **thermal expansion.**

When matter is cooled, thermal energy is released. The motion of the particles slows down and the particles move closer together. In nearly all cases, as matter is cooled, it contracts, or decreases in volume.

Heat-regulating devices called thermostats use thermal expansion to work. Many thermostats contain bimetallic strips, which are strips of two different metals joined together. Different metals expand at different rates. When the bimetallic strip is heated, one side expands more than the other. This causes the strip to uncurl. The movement of the strip operates a switch, which can turn a heating system on or off.

Section 3 Assessment

Target Reading Skill Building Vocabulary Use your sentences to help answer the questions.

Reviewing Key Concepts

1. **a. Identifying** Name three states of matter.
   b. Comparing and Contrasting How are the three states of matter different from each other? How are they the same?
2. **a. Reviewing** What causes a change in state?
   b. Describing Why does the temperature of matter remain the same while the matter changes state?
   c. Relating Cause and Effect What causes a solid to melt?
3. **a. Defining** How can a liquid expand without changing state?

   b. Applying Concepts Why should you poke holes in a potato before baking it?
   c. Interpreting Diagrams How does a thermostat make use of thermal expansion?

Lab zone At-Home **Activity**

Frosty Balloons Blow up two balloons so that they are the same size. Have a family member use a measuring tape to measure the circumference of the balloons. Place one of the balloons in the freezer for 15 to 20 minutes. Then measure both balloons again. Explain how changes in thermal energy cause the change in size.

Uses of Heat

Reading Preview

Key Concepts
- How do heat engines use thermal energy?
- How do refrigerators keep things cold?

Key Terms
- heat engine
- external combustion engine
- internal combustion engine
- refrigerant

Target Reading Skill

Sequencing A sequence is the order in which the steps in a process occur. As you read, make a cycle diagram that shows how refrigerators work. Write each phase of the cooling system's cycle in a separate circle.

How Refrigerators Work

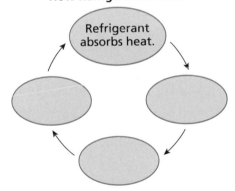

Refrigerant absorbs heat.

Lab zone · Discover **Activity**

What Happens at the Pump?
1. Obtain a bicycle pump and a deflated basketball or soccer ball.
2. Feel the pump with your hand. Note whether it feels cool or warm to the touch.
3. Use the pump to inflate the ball to the recommended pressure.
4. As soon as you stop pumping, feel the pump again. Observe any changes in temperature.

Think It Over
Developing Hypotheses Propose an explanation for any changes that you observed.

For more than 100 years, the steam locomotive was a symbol of power and speed. It first came into use in the 1830s, and was soon hauling hundreds of tons of freight faster than a horse could gallop. Today, many trains are pulled by diesel locomotives that are far more efficient than steam locomotives.

Heat Engines

To power a coal-burning steam locomotive, coal is shoveled into a roaring fire. Heat is then transferred from the fire to water in the boiler. But how can heat move a train?

The thermal energy of the coal fire must be transformed to the mechanical energy, or energy of motion, of the moving train. You already know about the reverse process, the transformation of mechanical energy to thermal energy. It happens when you rub your hands together to make them warm.

The transformation of thermal energy to mechanical energy requires a device called a **heat engine.** Heat engines usually make use of combustion. You may recall that combustion is the process of burning a fuel, such as coal or gasoline. During combustion, chemical energy that is stored in fuel is transformed to thermal energy. **Heat engines transform thermal energy to mechanical energy.** Heat engines are classified according to whether combustion takes place outside the engine or inside the engine.

FIGURE 15
External Combustion Engine

In a steam-powered external combustion engine, expanding steam pushes a piston back and forth inside a cylinder. The steam's thermal energy is transformed to mechanical energy.

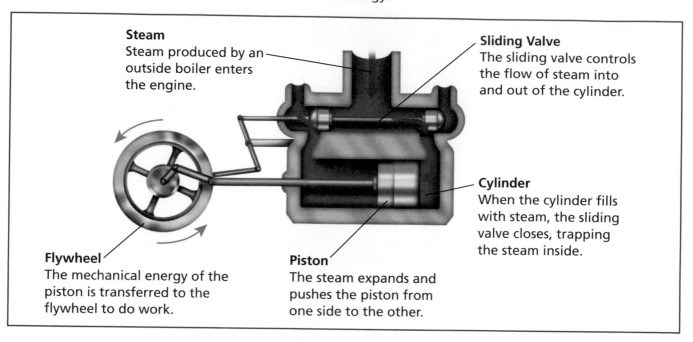

Steam
Steam produced by an outside boiler enters the engine.

Sliding Valve
The sliding valve controls the flow of steam into and out of the cylinder.

Cylinder
When the cylinder fills with steam, the sliding valve closes, trapping the steam inside.

Flywheel
The mechanical energy of the piston is transferred to the flywheel to do work.

Piston
The steam expands and pushes the piston from one side to the other.

Lab zone Try This Activity

Shake It Up
How does work relate to temperature?

1. Place a handful of dry sand in a metal container that has a cover.
2. Measure the temperature of the sand with a thermometer.
3. Cover the can and shake it vigorously for a minute or two.
4. Predict any change in the temperature of the sand. Was your prediction correct?

Classifying Identify any energy transformations and use them to explain your observations.

External Combustion Engines Engines that burn fuel outside the engine in a boiler are called **external combustion engines.** A steam engine, like the one shown in Figure 15, is an example of an external combustion engine. The combustion of wood, coal, or oil heats water in a boiler. As its thermal energy increases, the liquid water turns to water vapor, or steam. The steam is then passed through a sliding valve into the engine, where it pushes against a metal plunger called a piston. Work is done on the piston as it moves back and forth in a tube called a cylinder. The piston's motion turns a flywheel.

Internal Combustion Engines Engines that burn fuel in cylinders inside the engine are called **internal combustion engines.** Diesel and gasoline engines, which power most automobiles, are internal combustion engines. A piston inside a cylinder moves up and down, turning a crankshaft. The motion of the crankshaft is transferred to the wheels of the car.

Each up or down movement by a piston is called a stroke. Most diesel and gasoline engines are four-stroke engines, as shown in Figure 16. Automobile engines usually have four, six, or eight cylinders. The four-stroke process occurs in each cylinder, and is repeated many times each second.

Reading Checkpoint How many cylinders do automobiles usually have?

Air-fuel
mixture

Piston

Cylinder

Crankshaft

1 **Intake Stroke**
A mixture of fuel and
air is drawn into the
cylinder as the piston
moves down.

2 **Compression Stroke**
The mixture is compressed
into a smaller space as the
piston moves back up.

Spark plug

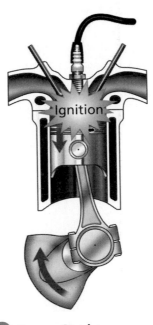

Ignition

3 **Power Stroke**
A spark plug ignites the
mixture. The heated gas
expands and pushes the
piston down. The piston
moves the crankshaft.

FIGURE 16
Four-Stroke Engine
Most automobiles use four-stroke
engines. These four strokes occur
repeatedly in each of the engine's
cylinders.
Interpreting Diagrams *During which
stroke is thermal energy transformed
to mechanical energy?*

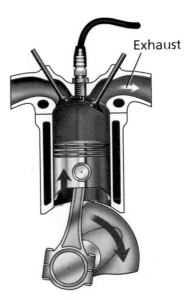

Exhaust

4 **Exhaust Stroke**
The piston moves back
up, pushing the heated
gas out. This makes
room for new fuel and
air, so that the cycle
can be repeated.

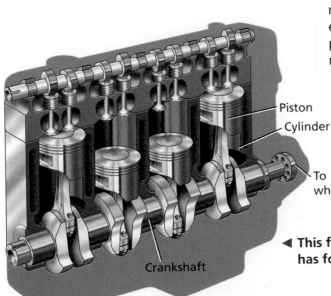

Piston

Cylinder

To
wheels

Crankshaft

◄ **This four-stroke engine
has four cylinders.**

Go Online
active art

For: Four-Stroke Engine activity
Visit: PHSchool.com
Web Code: cgp-3064

Cooling Systems

The transfer of heat can sometimes be used to keep things cool. Are you surprised? After all, heat naturally flows from a warm area to a cold area—not the other way around. But some devices, such as refrigerators, can transfer heat from cold areas to warm areas.

Refrigerators A refrigerator is cold inside. So where does the heat in the warm air rising from the back of a refrigerator come from? You may be surprised to learn that part of the heat actually comes from food in the refrigerator! **A refrigerator is a device that transfers thermal energy from inside the refrigerator to the room outside.** In doing so, the refrigerator transfers thermal energy from a cool area to a warm area.

FIGURE 17
Refrigerator

Inside a refrigerator, refrigerant moves through a system of pipes, transferring thermal energy from inside the refrigerator to the surrounding air. **Inferring** *Why must the temperature of the refrigerant be lower than that of the food to absorb the food's thermal energy?*

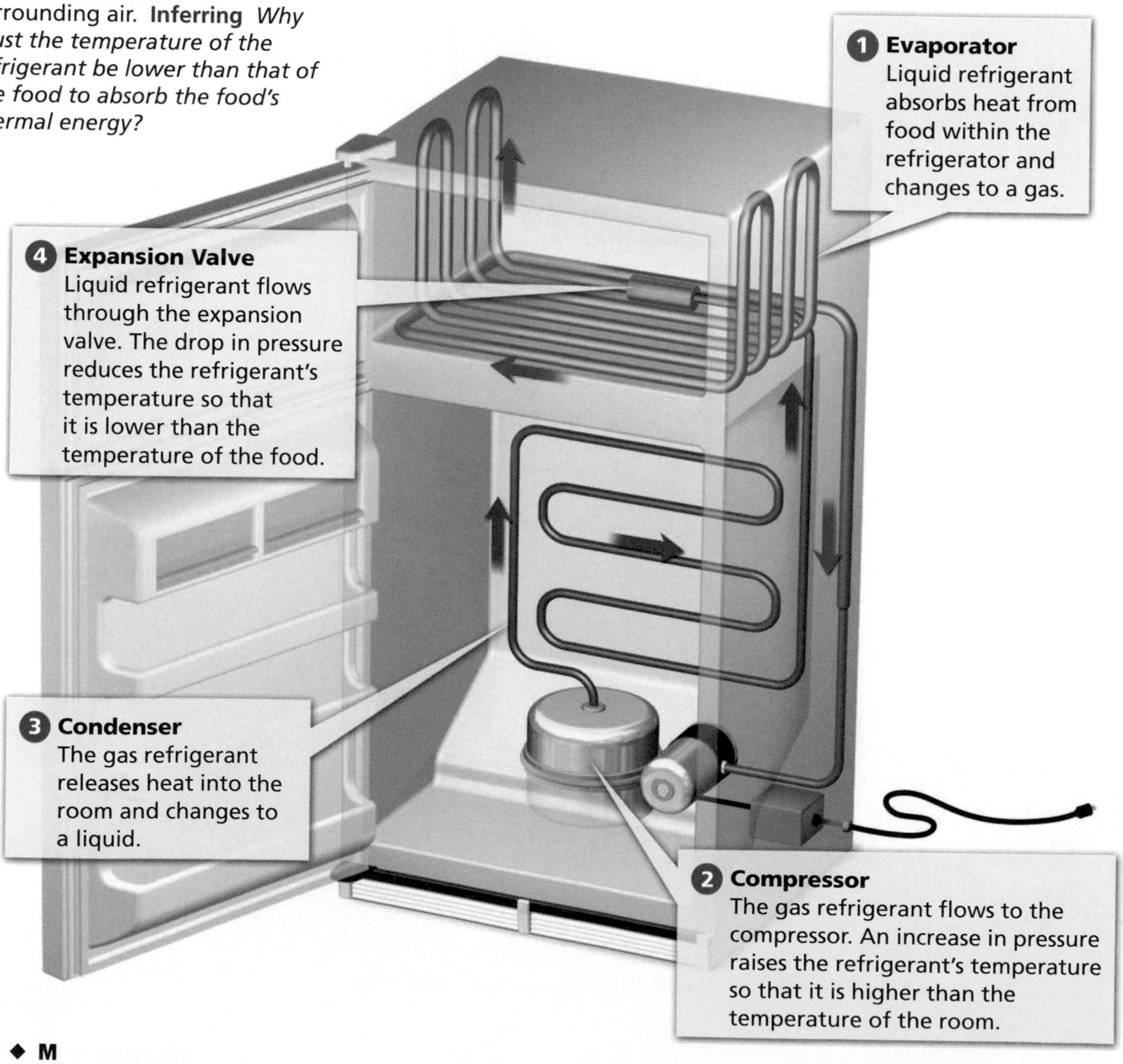

1 Evaporator
Liquid refrigerant absorbs heat from food within the refrigerator and changes to a gas.

4 Expansion Valve
Liquid refrigerant flows through the expansion valve. The drop in pressure reduces the refrigerant's temperature so that it is lower than the temperature of the food.

3 Condenser
The gas refrigerant releases heat into the room and changes to a liquid.

2 Compressor
The gas refrigerant flows to the compressor. An increase in pressure raises the refrigerant's temperature so that it is higher than the temperature of the room.

A substance called a **refrigerant** absorbs and releases heat in a refrigerator. As shown in Figure 17, the refrigerant moves through a closed system of pipes. These pipes run along the back of the refrigerator and inside where food is stored. The coiled pipes inside make up the evaporator. As the refrigerant enters the evaporator, it is a liquid. Because it is colder than the food, it absorbs the thermal energy of the food. The food's thermal energy raises the refrigerant's temperature, causing it to evaporate. Then, the gas refrigerant enters an electric pump called a compressor. The compressor increases the refrigerant's pressure, further raising its temperature.

From the compressor, the gas refrigerant flows to the coiled pipes at the back of the refrigerator that make up the condenser. When it enters the condenser, the refrigerant is warmer than the air in the room. It releases heat into the air and its temperature drops, causing the refrigerant to condense. The pressure of the liquid refrigerant is decreased as it flows into a narrow opening called an expansion valve. The decreased pressure lowers the refrigerant's temperature further. The refrigerant recycles as it flows back to the evaporator.

Air Conditioners The air conditioners used in homes, schools, and cars cool air in the same way that a refrigerator cools food. Refrigerant in a system of pipes changes from a liquid to a gas and back again to transfer heat. Unlike a refrigerator, however, an air conditioner absorbs heat from the air inside a room or car and transfers it to the outdoors.

 **Reading Checkpoint** How are air conditioners and refrigerators similar?

Section 4 Assessment

Target Reading Skill Sequencing Refer to your cycle diagram about cooling systems as you answer Question 2.

Reviewing Key Concepts

1. a. **Describing** What does a heat engine do?
   b. **Comparing and Contrasting** How are internal combustion engines different from external combustion engines? How are they similar?
   c. **Making Generalizations** Why do you think modern cars use internal rather than external combustion engines?
2. a. **Identifying** What changes of state occur in the refrigerant of a refrigerator?
   b. **Explaining** Where do the changes of state occur?
   c. **Predicting** If the compressor in a refrigerator stopped working, how would its failure affect the heat transfer cycle?

Writing in Science

Cause-and-Effect Paragraph The invention of the heat engine and refrigerator both had a great impact on society. Write about how daily life might be different if either system had not been invented.

Study Guide

① Temperature, Thermal Energy, and Heat

Key Concepts

- The three common scales for measuring temperature are the Fahrenheit, Celsius, and Kelvin scales.
- Heat is thermal energy moving from a warmer object to a cooler object.
- A material with a high specific heat can absorb a great deal of thermal energy without a great change in temperature.
- Change in energy = Mass × Specific heat × Change in temperature

Key Terms

temperature
Fahrenheit scale
Celsius scale
Kelvin scale
absolute zero
heat
specific heat

② The Transfer of Heat

Key Concepts

- Heat is transferred by conduction, convection, and radiation.
- If two objects have different temperatures, heat will flow from the warmer object to the colder one.
- A conductor transfers thermal energy well. An insulator does not transfer thermal energy well.

Key Terms

conduction
convection
convection current
radiation
conductor
insulator

③ Thermal Energy and States of Matter

Key Concepts

- Most matter on Earth can exist in three states— solid, liquid, and gas.
- Matter can change from one state to another when thermal energy is absorbed or released.
- As the thermal energy of matter increases, its particles spread out and the substance expands.

Key Terms

state
change of state
melting
freezing
evaporation
boiling
condensation
thermal expansion

④ Uses of Heat

Key Concepts

- Heat engines transform thermal energy to mechanical energy.
- A refrigerator is a device that transfers thermal energy from inside the refrigerator to the room outside.

Key Terms

heat engine
external combustion engine
internal combustion engine
refrigerant

Review and Assessment

Go Online
PHSchool.com

For: Self-Assessment
Visit: PHSchool.com
Web Code: cga-3060

Organizing Information

Concept Mapping Copy the concept map about heat onto a separate sheet of paper. Then complete it and add a title. (For more on Concept Mapping, see the Skills Handbook.)

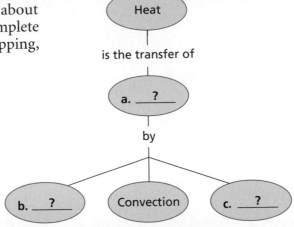

Heat

is the transfer of

a. _____?_____

by

b. _____?_____   Convection   c. _____?_____

Reviewing Key Terms

Choose the letter of the best answer.

1. A measure of the average kinetic energy of the particles of an object is its
   a. heat.
   b. temperature.
   c. specific heat.
   d. thermal energy.

2. If you want to know the amount of heat needed to raise the temperature of 2 kg of steel by 10°C, you need to know steel's
   a. temperature.   b. thermal energy.
   c. state.   d. specific heat.

3. The process by which heat moves from one particle of matter to another without the movement of matter itself is called
   a. convection.
   b. conduction.
   c. radiation.
   d. thermal expansion.

4. Vaporization that occurs below the surface of a liquid is called
   a. evaporation.   b. melting.
   c. boiling.   d. freezing.

5. The process of burning a fuel is called
   a. combustion.
   b. thermal expansion.
   c. radiation.
   d. boiling.

If the statement is true, write *true*. If it is false, change the underlined word or words to make the statement true.

6. A temperature reading of zero on the <u>Celsius scale</u> is equal to absolute zero.

7. A <u>convection current</u> is the circular motion of a fluid caused by the rising of heated fluid.

8. An <u>insulator</u> conducts heat well.

9. When a substance is <u>freezing</u>, the thermal energy of the substance decreases.

10. In an <u>external combustion engine</u>, the fuel is burned inside the engine.

Writing in Science

Proposed Solution You have been asked to design a bridge for an area that is quite hot in the summer and cold in the winter. Propose a design plan for the bridge. Include in your plan how expansion joints will help the bridge react in hot and cold temperatures.

Discovery CHANNEL SCHOOL

Thermal Energy and Heat
Video Preview
Video Field Trip
▶ Video Assessment

Review and Assessment

Checking Concepts

11. What happens to the particles of a solid as the thermal energy of the solid increases?

12. During a summer night, the air temperature drops by 10°C. Will the temperature of the water in a nearby lake change by the same amount? Explain why or why not.

13. When you heat a pot of water on the stove, a convection current is formed. Explain how this happens.

14. How can you add thermal energy to a substance without increasing its temperature?

15. When molten steel becomes solid, is energy absorbed or released by the steel? Explain.

16. Describe how a thermostat controls the temperature in a building.

Thinking Critically

17. **Relating Cause and Effect** Why is the air pressure in a car's tires different before and after the car has been driven for an hour?

18. **Applying Concepts** When they are hung, telephone lines are allowed to sag. Can you think of a reason why?

19. **Interpreting Diagrams** The three illustrations below represent the molecules in three different materials. Which is a solid? A liquid? A gas?

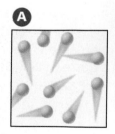 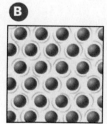 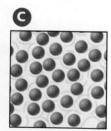

20. **Developing Hypotheses** A refrigerator is running in a small room. The refrigerator door is open, but the room does not grow any cooler. Use the law of conservation of energy to explain why the temperature does not drop.

Math Practice

21. **Converting Units** A recipe says to preheat your oven to 275°F. What is this temperature in degrees Celsius?

22. **Converting Units** The temperature in a greenhouse is 86°F. Convert this temperature to degrees Celsius.

Applying Skills

Use the illustration of three containers of water to answer Questions 23–25.

23. **Interpreting Data** Compare the average motion of the molecules in the three containers. Explain your answer.

24. **Drawing Conclusions** Compare the total amount of thermal energy in the three containers. Explain your answer.

25. **Calculating** Which container would need the least amount of thermal energy to raise its temperature by 1 K? The specific heat of water is 4,180 J/(kg·K).

Lab zone Chapter **Project**

Performance Assessment Talk with your classmates about their container designs. When you've had a chance to look them over, predict the final water temperature for each container. Record the starting temperature for each one, including your own. Record the final temperatures at the end of each demonstration. Which insulating materials seemed to work the best? Describe how you could improve your container, based on what you learned.

Standardized Test Prep

Choose the letter of the best answer.

1. When cold, dry air passes over a much warmer body of water, a type of fog called sea smoke is produced. Which process explains why this occurs?
   A melting
   B condensation
   C boiling
   D freezing

2. The table below shows the specific heat of four metals. If 1,540 J of heat is transferred to 4 kg of each metal, which metal will increase in temperature by 1 K?

Specific Heat of Metals	
Metal	**Specific Heat (J/(kg·K))**
Silver	235
Iron	450
Copper	385
Aluminum	903

   F Silver
   G Copper
   H Iron
   J Aluminum

3. A student wants to measure the temperature at which several different liquids freeze. In the student's experiment, temperature is the
   A hypothesis.
   B responding variable.
   C manipulated variable.
   D operational definition.

4. Two solid metal blocks are placed in a container. If there is a transfer of heat between the blocks, then they must have different
   F boiling points.
   G melting points.
   H specific heats.
   J temperatures.

5. A thermometer measures
   A temperature.
   B thermal energy.
   C heat.
   D specific heat.

Constructed Response

6. Explain how heat is transferred by conduction, convection, and radiation. Give an example of each.

Bridges—
From Vines to Steel

Have you ever

- balanced on a branch or log to cross a brook?
- jumped from rock to rock in a streambed?
- swung on a vine or rope over a river?

Vine Footbridge
A girl crosses over the Hunza River in northern Pakistan.

Then you have used the same ways that early people used to get over obstacles. Fallen trees, twisted vines, and natural stones formed the first bridges.

Bridges provide easy ways of getting over difficult obstacles. For thousands of years, bridges have also served as forts for defense, scenes of great battles, and homes for shops and churches. They have also been sites of mystery, love, and intrigue. They span history—linking cities, nations, and empires and encouraging trade and travel.

But bridges have not always been as elaborate as they are today. The earliest ones were made of materials that were free and plentiful. In deep forests, people used beams made from small trees. In tropical regions where vegetation was thick, people wove together vines and grasses, then hung them to make walkways over rivers and gorges.

No matter what the structures or materials, bridges reflect the people who built them. The ancient civilizations of China, Egypt, Greece, and Rome all designed strong, graceful bridges to connect and control their empires.

Roman Arch Bridge
Ponte Sant'Angelo is in Rome.

The Balance of Forces

What keeps a bridge from falling down? How does it support its own weight and the weight of people and traffic on it? Builders found the answers by considering the various forces that act on a bridge.

The weight of the bridge and the traffic on it are called the *load*. When a heavy truck crosses a beam bridge, the weight of the load forces the beam to curve downward. This creates tension forces that stretch the bottom of the beam. At the same time, the load also creates compression forces at the top of the beam.

Since the bridge doesn't collapse under the load, there must be upward forces to balance the downward forces. In simple beam bridges, builders anchor the beam to the ground or to end supports called abutments. To cross longer spans or distances, they construct piers under the middle span. Piers and abutments are structures that act as upward forces—reaction forces.

Another type of bridge, the arch bridge, supports its load by compression. A heavy load on a stone arch bridge squeezes or pushes the stones together, creating compression throughout the structure. Weight on the arch bridge pushes down to the ends of the arch. The side walls and abutments act as reaction forces.

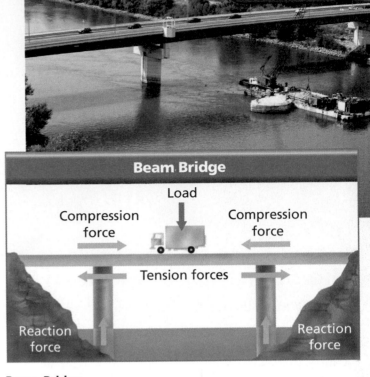

Beam Bridge
A beam bridge spans the Rhone River in France (top).

Early engineers discovered that arch bridges made of stone could span wider distances than simple beam bridges. Arch bridges are also stronger and more durable. Although the Romans were not the first to build arch bridges, they perfected the form in their massive, elegant structures. Early Roman arch bridges were built without mortar, or "glue." The arch held together because the stones were skillfully shaped to work in compression. After nearly 2,000 years, some of these Roman arch bridges are still standing.

The Structure of Modern Bridges

By the 1800s in the United States, bridge builders began to use cast iron instead of stone and wood. By the late 1800s, they were using steel, which was strong and relatively lightweight. The use of new building materials was not the only change. Engineers began designing different types of bridges as well. They found that they could build longer, larger bridges by using a suspension structure.

Suspension bridges are modern versions of long, narrow, woven bridges found in tropical regions. These simple, woven suspension bridges can span long distances. Crossing one of these natural structures is like walking a tightrope. The weight of people and animals traveling over the bridge pushes down on the ropes, stretching them and creating tension forces.

Modern suspension bridges follow the same principles of tension as do woven bridges. A suspension bridge is strong in tension. In suspension bridges, parallel cables are stretched the entire length of the bridge—over giant towers. The cables are anchored at each end of the bridge. The roadway hangs from the cables, attached by wire suspenders. The weight of the bridge and the load on it act to pull apart or stretch the cables. This pulling apart creates tension forces.

The towers of a suspension bridge act as supports for the bridge cables. The abutments that anchor the cables exert reaction forces as well. So forces in balance keep a suspension bridge from collapsing.

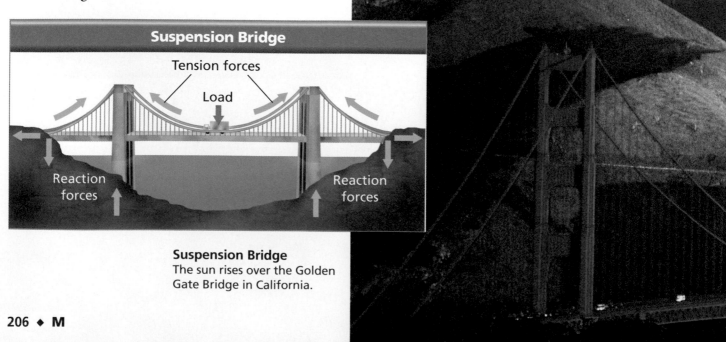

Suspension Bridge
The sun rises over the Golden Gate Bridge in California.

Cable-Stayed Bridge
The Sunshine Skyway Bridge spans a broad section of Tampa Bay in Florida. The cables, attached to the center of the roadway, enable travelers to have a clear view.

When the Brooklyn Bridge opened in New York City in 1883, it was the longest suspension bridge in the world. The Golden Gate Bridge in San Francisco, which was opened in 1937, was another great engineering feat.

Recently, engineers have developed a new bridge design called the cable-stayed bridge. It looks similar to a suspension bridge because both are built with towers and cables. But the two bridges are quite different. The cables on the cable-stayed bridge attach to the towers, so the towers bear the weight of the bridge and the load on it. In contrast, the cables on a suspension bridge ride over the towers and anchor at the abutments. So on a suspension bridge, both the towers and abutments bear the load.

Science Activity

Work in groups to make a suspension bridge, using two chairs, a wooden plank, rope, and some books.

- Place two chairs back-to-back and stretch 2 ropes over the backs of the chairs. Hold the ropes at both ends.
- Tie three pieces of rope to the longer ropes. Place the plank through the loops.
- With a partner, hold the ropes tightly at each end. Load books on top of the plank to see how much it will hold.

Why is it important to anchor the ropes tightly at each end?

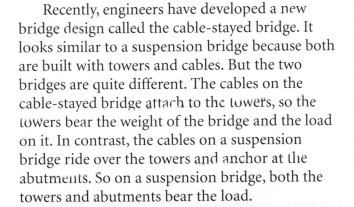

Brooklyn Bridge
This bridge connects Brooklyn and Manhattan (above).
It took 14 years for workers to complete the bridge (left).

Against All Odds

When John Roebling was hired in 1868 to build the Brooklyn Bridge, he was already a skilled suspension bridge engineer. He had been working on plans for the bridge since 1855.

But before bridge construction even began in 1869, John Roebling died in a construction accident. Fortunately, he had worked out his bridge design to the last detail. His son, Colonel Washington Roebling, who was also a skilled engineer, dedicated himself to carrying out his father's plans.

The construction dragged on for 14 years and cost nearly 30 lives. Colonel Roebling himself became so disabled that he was forced to direct construction from his home. Using a telescope, Colonel Roebling followed every detail. His remarkable, energetic wife, Emily Warren Roebling, learned enough engineering principles to deliver and explain his orders to the workers.

As soon as the giant towers were up, workers unrolled the steel wire back and forth across the towers to weave the cables. The next step was to twist the wires together. But the workmen were terrified of hanging so high on the bridge and refused to work.

Finally, Frank Farrington, the chief mechanic, crossed the river on a small chair dangling from a wheel that ran across an overhead line. Farrington completed his journey to the roar of the crowd. Somewhat reassured, the builders returned to work. But it took two more years to string the cables. The bridge was one of the greatest engineering achievements of its time.

In the end, the Brooklyn Bridge project succeeded only because of the determination and sacrifices of the Roebling family. It became the model for hundreds of other suspension bridges.

Social Studies Activity

How do you think the Brooklyn Bridge changed the lives of New Yorkers? In groups, research the history of another famous bridge. Present your findings to your class along with drawings and photos. Find out

- when and why the bridge was built
- what type of bridge it is
- what effects the bridge has on people's lives—on trade, travel, and population
- how landforms affected the bridge building
- about events connected to the bridge

TWO GREAT CITIES UNITED

MAY 25, 1883—The Brooklyn Bridge was successfully opened yesterday. The pleasant weather brought visitors by the thousands from all around. Spectators were packed in masses through which it was almost impossible to pass, and those who had tickets to attend the ceremonies had hard work to reach the bridge. Every available house-top and window was filled, and an adventurous party occupied a tall telegraph pole. It required the utmost efforts of the police to keep clear the necessary space.

After the exercises at the bridge were completed the Brooklyn procession was immediately re-formed and the march was taken up to Col. Roebling's residence. From the back study on the second floor of his house Col. Roebling had watched through his telescope the procession as it proceeded along from the New York side until the Brooklyn tower was reached. Mrs. Roebling received at her husband's side and accepted her share of the honors of the bridge.

For blocks and blocks on either side of the bridge there was scarcely a foot of room to spare. Many persons crossed and re-crossed the river on the ferry boats, and in that way watched the display. Almost every ship along the river front was converted into a grand stand.

The final ceremonies of the opening of the great bridge began at eight o'clock, when the first rocket was sent from the center of the great structure, and ended at nine o'clock, when a flight of 500 rockets illuminated the sky. The river-front was one blaze of light, and on the yachts and smaller vessels blue fires were burning and illuminating dark waters around them.

————Excerpted from
The New York Times

Brooklyn Bridge
This historic painting shows fireworks at the opening of the bridge in 1883.

Language Arts Activity

A reporter's goal is to inform and entertain the reader. Using a catchy opening line draws interest. Then the reader wants to know the facts—who, what, where, when, why, and how (5 W's and H).

You are a school reporter. Write about the opening of a bridge in your area. It could be a highway overpass or a bridge over water, a valley, or railroad tracks.

- Include some of the 5 W's and H.
- Add interesting details and descriptions.

THE GRAND DISPLAY OF FIREWORKS AND ILLUMINATIONS

Mathematics

Bridge Geometry

As railroad traffic increased in the late 1800s, truss bridges became popular. Designed with thin vertical and diagonal supports to add strength, truss bridges were actually reinforced beam bridge structures. Many of the early wood truss bridges couldn't support the trains that rumbled over them. Cast iron and steel trusses soon replaced wood trusses.

Using basic triangular structures, engineers went to work on more scientific truss bridge designs. The accuracy of the design is crucial to handling the stress from heavy train loads and constant vibrations. As in all bridge structures, each steel piece has to be measured and fitted accurately—including widths, lengths, angles, and points of intersection and attachment.

Geometric Angles and Figures

Engineers use various geometric figures in drawing bridge plans. Figures that have right angles are squares, rectangles, and right triangles. Figures that have acute angles and obtuse angles can be triangles and parallelograms.

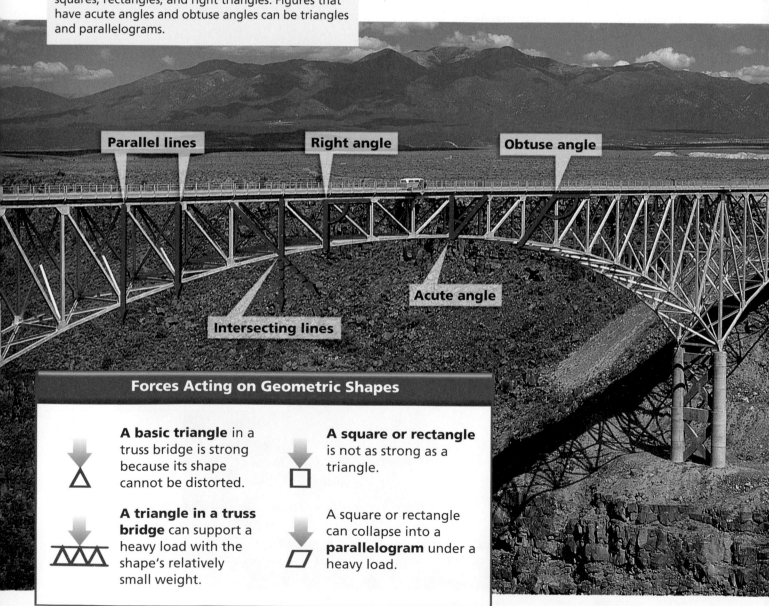

Parallel lines

Right angle

Obtuse angle

Acute angle

Intersecting lines

Forces Acting on Geometric Shapes

A basic triangle in a truss bridge is strong because its shape cannot be distorted.

A square or rectangle is not as strong as a triangle.

A triangle in a truss bridge can support a heavy load with the shape's relatively small weight.

A square or rectangle can collapse into a **parallelogram** under a heavy load.

Math Activity

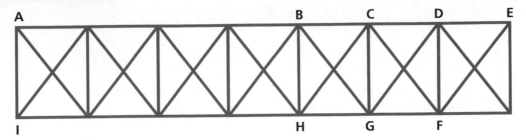

A   B   C   D   E

I   H   G   F

The chief building engineer has asked you to draw up exact plans for a new truss bridge. How well will you do as an assistant? Review the captions and labels on the previous page. Then answer these questions:

1. Which lines are parallel?

2. Which lines intersect?

3. What kind of figure is formed by *ABHI*?

4. What kind of figure is formed by *HCF*?

5. What kind of angle is *BGF*—obtuse or right?

6. What kind of angle is *CHG*?

7. What kind of triangle is *BHG*? What makes it this kind of triangle?

8. Why is a triangle stronger than a square?

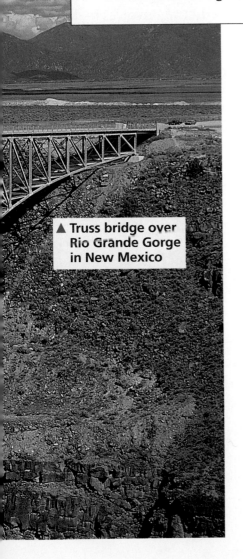

▲ **Truss bridge over Rio Grande Gorge in New Mexico**

Tie It Together

Work in small groups to build a model of a bridge out of a box of spaghetti and a roll of masking tape. Meet as a group to choose the type of bridge you will build. Each bridge should be strong enough to hold a brick. You can build

- a beam bridge
- a truss bridge
- an arch bridge
- a suspension bridge (This one is challenging.)

After drawing a sketch of the bridge design, assign jobs for each team member. Then

- decide how long the bridge span will be
- measure and cut the materials
- build the roadway first for beam, truss, and suspension bridges
- build the arch first in an arch bridge

When your bridge is complete, display it in the classroom. Test the strength of each bridge by placing a brick on the roadway. Discuss the difference in bridge structures. Determine which bridge design is the strongest.

Think Like a Scientist

Scientists have a particular way of looking at the world, or scientific habits of mind. Whenever you ask a question and explore possible answers, you use many of the same skills that scientists do. Some of these skills are described on this page.

Observing

When you use one or more of your five senses to gather information about the world, you are **observing.** Hearing a dog bark, counting twelve green seeds, and smelling smoke are all observations. To increase the power of their senses, scientists sometimes use microscopes, telescopes, or other instruments that help them make more detailed observations.

An observation must be an accurate report of what your senses detect. It is important to keep careful records of your observations in science class by writing or drawing in a notebook. The information collected through observations is called evidence, or data.

Inferring

When you interpret an observation, you are **inferring,** or making an inference. For example, if you hear your dog barking, you may infer that someone is at your front door. To make this inference, you combine the evidence— the barking dog—and your experience or knowledge—you know that your dog barks when strangers approach—to reach a logical conclusion.

Notice that an inference is not a fact; it is only one of many possible interpretations for an observation. For example, your dog may be barking because it wants to go for a walk. An inference may turn out to be incorrect even if it is based on accurate observations and logical reasoning. The only way to find out if an inference is correct is to investigate further.

Predicting

When you listen to the weather forecast, you hear many predictions about the next day's weather—what the temperature will be, whether it will rain, and how windy it will be. Weather forecasters use observations and knowledge of weather patterns to predict the weather. The skill of **predicting** involves making an inference about a future event based on current evidence or past experience.

Because a prediction is an inference, it may prove to be false. In science class, you can test some of your predictions by doing experiments. For example, suppose you predict that larger paper airplanes can fly farther than smaller airplanes. How could you test your prediction?

Activity

Use the photograph to answer the questions below.

Observing Look closely at the photograph. List at least three observations.

Inferring Use your observations to make an inference about what has happened. What experience or knowledge did you use to make the inference?

Predicting Predict what will happen next. On what evidence or experience do you base your prediction?

Classifying

Could you imagine searching for a book in the library if the books were shelved in no particular order? Your trip to the library would be an all-day event! Luckily, librarians group together books on similar topics or by the same author. Grouping together items that are alike in some way is called **classifying.** You can classify items in many ways: by size, by shape, by use, and by other important characteristics.

Like librarians, scientists use the skill of classifying to organize information and objects. When things are sorted into groups, the relationships among them become easier to understand.

Activity

Classify the objects in the photograph into two groups based on any characteristic you choose. Then use another characteristic to classify the objects into three groups.

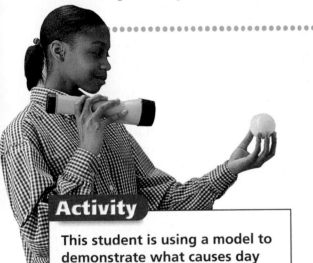

Activity

This student is using a model to demonstrate what causes day and night on Earth. What do the flashlight and the tennis ball in the model represent?

Making Models

Have you ever drawn a picture to help someone understand what you were saying? Such a drawing is one type of model. A model is a picture, diagram, computer image, or other representation of a complex object or process. **Making models** helps people understand things that they cannot observe directly.

Scientists often use models to represent things that are either very large or very small, such as the planets in the solar system, or the parts of a cell. Such models are physical models—drawings or three-dimensional structures that look like the real thing. Other models are mental models—mathematical equations or words that describe how something works.

Communicating

Whenever you talk on the phone, write a report, or listen to your teacher at school, you are communicating. **Communicating** is the process of sharing ideas and information with other people. Communicating effectively requires many skills, including writing, reading, speaking, listening, and making models.

Scientists communicate to share results, information, and opinions. Scientists often communicate about their work in journals, over the telephone, in letters, and on the Internet.

They also attend scientific meetings where they share their ideas with one another in person.

Activity

On a sheet of paper, write out clear, detailed directions for tying your shoe. Then exchange directions with a partner. Follow your partner's directions exactly. How successful were you at tying your shoe? How could your partner have communicated more clearly?

Making Measurements

By measuring, scientists can express their observations more precisely and communicate more information about what they observe.

Measuring in SI

The standard system of measurement used by scientists around the world is known as the International System of Units, which is abbreviated as SI (**Système International d'Unités,** in French). SI units are easy to use because they are based on powers of 10. Each unit is ten times larger than the next smallest unit and one tenth the size of the next largest unit. The table lists the prefixes used to name the most common SI units.

Length To measure length, or the distance between two points, the unit of measure is the **meter (m).** The distance from the floor to a doorknob is approximately one meter. Long distances, such as the distance between two cities, are measured in kilometers (km). Small lengths are measured in centimeters (cm) or millimeters (mm). Scientists use metric rulers and meter sticks to measure length.

Common Conversions	
1 km	= 1,000 m
1 m	= 100 cm
1 m	= 1,000 mm
1 cm	= 10 mm

Activity

The larger lines on the metric ruler in the picture show centimeter divisions, while the smaller, unnumbered lines show millimeter divisions. How many centimeters long is the shell? How many millimeters long is it?

Common SI Prefixes		
Prefix	Symbol	Meaning
kilo-	k	1,000
hecto-	h	100
deka-	da	10
deci-	d	0.1 (one tenth)
centi-	c	0.01 (one hundredth)
milli-	m	0.001 (one thousandth)

Liquid Volume To measure the volume of a liquid, or the amount of space it takes up, you will use a unit of measure known as the **liter (L).** One liter is the approximate volume of a medium-size carton of milk. Smaller volumes are measured in milliliters (mL). Scientists use graduated cylinders to measure liquid volume.

Activity

The graduated cylinder in the picture is marked in milliliter divisions. Notice that the water in the cylinder has a curved surface. This curved surface is called the *meniscus.* To measure the volume, you must read the level at the lowest point of the meniscus. What is the volume of water in this graduated cylinder?

Common Conversion
1 L = 1,000 mL

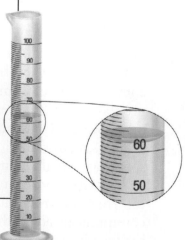

Mass To measure mass, or the amount of matter in an object, you will use a unit of measure known as the **gram (g).** One gram is approximately the mass of a paper clip. Larger masses are measured in kilograms (kg). Scientists use a balance to find the mass of an object.

Common Conversion

1 kg = 1,000 g

Activity

The mass of the potato in the picture is measured in kilograms. What is the mass of the potato? Suppose a recipe for potato salad called for one kilogram of potatoes. About how many potatoes would you need?

0.25 KG

Temperature To measure the temperature of a substance, you will use the **Celsius scale.** Temperature is measured in degrees Celsius (°C) using a Celsius thermometer. Water freezes at 0°C and boils at 100°C.

Time The unit scientists use to measure time is the **second (s).**

Activity

What is the temperature of the liquid in degrees Celsius?

Converting SI Units

To use the SI system, you must know how to convert between units. Converting from one unit to another involves the skill of **calculating,** or using mathematical operations. Converting between SI units is similar to converting between dollars and dimes because both systems are based on powers of ten.

Suppose you want to convert a length of 80 centimeters to meters. Follow these steps to convert between units.

1. Begin by writing down the measurement you want to convert—in this example, 80 centimeters.

2. Write a conversion factor that represents the relationship between the two units you are converting. In this example, the relationship is 1 meter = 100 centimeters. Write this conversion factor as a fraction, making sure to place the units you are converting from (centimeters, in this example) in the denominator.

3. Multiply the measurement you want to convert by the fraction. When you do this, the units in the first measurement will cancel out with the units in the denominator. Your answer will be in the units you are converting to (meters, in this example).

Example

80 centimeters = ■ meters

$$80 \text{ centimeters} \times \frac{1 \text{ meter}}{100 \text{ centimeters}} = \frac{80 \text{ meters}}{100}$$

$$= 0.8 \text{ meters}$$

Activity

Convert between the following units.

1. 600 millimeters = ■ meters
2. 0.35 liters = ■ milliliters
3. 1,050 grams = ■ kilograms

Conducting a Scientific Investigation

In some ways, scientists are like detectives, piecing together clues to learn about a process or event. One way that scientists gather clues is by carrying out experiments. An experiment tests an idea in a careful, orderly manner. Although experiments do not all follow the same steps in the same order, many follow a pattern similar to the one described here.

Posing Questions

Experiments begin by asking a scientific question. A scientific question is one that can be answered by gathering evidence. For example, the question "Which freezes faster—fresh water or salt water?" is a scientific question because you can carry out an investigation and gather information to answer the question.

Developing a Hypothesis

The next step is to form a hypothesis. A **hypothesis** is a possible explanation for a set of observations or answer to a scientific question. In science, a hypothesis must be something that can be tested. A hypothesis can be worded as an *If . . . then . . .* statement. For example, a hypothesis might be *"If I add table salt to fresh water, then the water will freeze at a lower temperature."* A hypothesis worded this way serves as a rough outline of the experiment you should perform.

Designing an Experiment

Next you need to plan a way to test your hypothesis. Your plan should be written out as a step-by-step procedure and should describe the observations or measurements you will make.

Two important steps involved in designing an experiment are controlling variables and forming operational definitions.

Controlling Variables In a well-designed experiment, you need to keep all variables the same except for one. A **variable** is any factor that can change in an experiment. The factor that you change is called the **manipulated variable**. In this experiment, the manipulated variable is the amount of table salt added to the water. Other factors, such as the amount of water or the starting temperature, are kept constant.

The factor that changes as a result of the manipulated variable is called the **responding variable**. The responding variable is what you measure or observe to obtain your results. In this experiment, the responding variable is the temperature at which the water freezes.

An experiment in which all factors except one are kept constant is called a **controlled experiment**. Most controlled experiments include a test called the control. In this experiment, Container 3 is the control. Because no salt is added to Container 3, you can compare the results from the other containers to it. Any difference in results must be due to the addition of salt alone.

Forming Operational Definitions Another important aspect of a well-designed experiment is having clear operational definitions. An **operational definition** is a statement that describes how a particular variable is to be measured or how a term is to be defined. For example, in this experiment, how will you determine if the water has frozen? You might decide to insert a stick in each container at the start of the experiment. Your operational definition of "frozen" would be the time at which the stick can no longer move.

Experimental Procedure
1. Fill 3 containers with 300 milliliters of cold tap water.
2. Add 10 grams of salt to Container 1; stir. Add 20 grams of salt to Container 2; stir. Add no salt to Container 3.
3. Place the 3 containers in a freezer.
4. Check the containers every 15 minutes. Record your observations.

Interpreting Data

The observations and measurements you make in an experiment are called **data.** At the end of an experiment, you need to analyze the data to look for any patterns or trends. Patterns often become clear if you organize your data in a data table or graph. Then think through what the data reveal. Do they support your hypothesis? Do they point out a flaw in your experiment? Do you need to collect more data?

Drawing Conclusions

A **conclusion** is a statement that sums up what you have learned from an experiment. When you draw a conclusion, you need to decide whether the data you collected support your hypothesis or not. You may need to repeat an experiment several times before you can draw any conclusions from it. Conclusions often lead you to pose new questions and plan new experiments to answer them.

Activity

Is a ball's bounce affected by the height from which it is dropped? Using the steps just described, plan a controlled experiment to investigate this problem.

Technology Design Skills

Engineers are people who use scientific and technological knowledge to solve practical problems. To design new products, engineers usually follow the process described here, even though they may not follow these steps in the exact order. As you read the steps, think about how you might apply them in technology labs.

Identify a Need

Before engineers begin designing a new product, they must first identify the need they are trying to meet. For example, suppose you are a member of a design team in a company that makes toys. Your team has identified a need: a toy boat that is inexpensive and easy to assemble.

Research the Problem

Engineers often begin by gathering information that will help them with their new design. This research may include finding articles in books, magazines, or on the Internet. It may also include talking to other engineers who have solved similar problems. Engineers often perform experiments related to the product they want to design.

For your toy boat, you could look at toys that are similar to the one you want to design. You might do research on the Internet. You could also test some materials to see whether they will work well in a toy boat.

Drawing for a boat design ▼

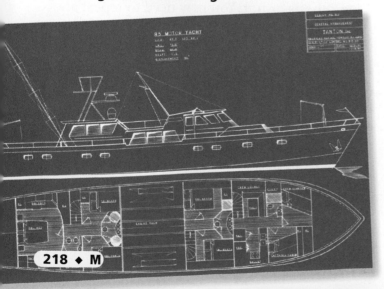

Design a Solution

Research gives engineers information that helps them design a product. When engineers design new products, they usually work in teams.

Generating Ideas Often design teams hold brainstorming meetings in which any team member can contribute ideas. **Brainstorming** is a creative process in which one team member's suggestions often spark ideas in other group members. Brainstorming can lead to new approaches to solving a design problem.

Evaluating Constraints During brainstorming, a design team will often come up with several possible designs. The team must then evaluate each one.

As part of their evaluation, engineers consider constraints. **Constraints** are factors that limit or restrict a product design. Physical characteristics, such as the properties of materials used to make your toy boat, are constraints. Money and time are also constraints. If the materials in a product cost a lot, or if the product takes a long time to make, the design may be impractical.

Making Trade-offs Design teams usually need to make trade-offs. In a **trade-off**, engineers give up one benefit of a proposed design in order to obtain another. In designing your toy boat, you will have to make trade-offs. For example, suppose one material is sturdy but not fully waterproof. Another material is more waterproof, but breakable. You may decide to give up the benefit of sturdiness in order to obtain the benefit of waterproofing.

Build and Evaluate a Prototype

Once the team has chosen a design plan, the engineers build a prototype of the product. A **prototype** is a working model used to test a design. Engineers evaluate the prototype to see whether it works well, is easy to operate, is safe to use, and holds up to repeated use.

Think of your toy boat. What would the prototype be like? Of what materials would it be made? How would you test it?

Troubleshoot and Redesign

Few prototypes work perfectly, which is why they need to be tested. Once a design team has tested a prototype, the members analyze the results and identify any problems. The team then tries to **troubleshoot,** or fix the design problems. For example, if your toy boat leaks or wobbles, the boat should be redesigned to eliminate those problems.

Communicate the Solution

A team needs to communicate the final design to the people who will manufacture and use the product. To do this, teams may use sketches, detailed drawings, computer simulations, and word descriptions.

Activity

You can use the technology design process to design and build a toy boat.

Research and Investigate

1. Visit the library or go online to research toy boats.

2. Investigate how a toy boat can be powered, including wind, rubber bands, or baking soda and vinegar.

3. Brainstorm materials, shapes, and steering for your boat.

Design and Build

4. Based on your research, design a toy boat that
   - is made of readily available materials
   - is no larger than 15 cm long and 10 cm wide
   - includes a power system, a rudder, and an area for cargo
   - travels 2 meters in a straight line carrying a load of 20 pennies

5. Sketch your design and write a step-by-step plan for building your boat. After your teacher approves your plan, build your boat.

Evaluate and Redesign

6. Test your boat, evaluate the results, and troubleshoot any problems.

7. Based on your evaluation, redesign your toy boat so it performs better.

Creating Data Tables and Graphs

How can you make sense of the data in a science experiment? The first step is to organize the data to help you understand them. Data tables and graphs are helpful tools for organizing data.

Data Tables

You have gathered your materials and set up your experiment. But before you start, you need to plan a way to record what happens during the experiment. By creating a data table, you can record your observations and measurements in an orderly way.

Suppose, for example, that a scientist conducted an experiment to find out how many Calories people of different body masses burn while doing various activities. The data table shows the results.

Notice in this data table that the manipulated variable (body mass) is the heading of one column. The responding variable (for

Calories Burned in 30 Minutes			
Body Mass	Experiment 1: Bicycling	Experiment 2: Playing Basketball	Experiment 3: Watching Television
30 kg	60 Calories	120 Calories	21 Calories
40 kg	77 Calories	164 Calories	27 Calories
50 kg	95 Calories	206 Calories	33 Calories
60 kg	114 Calories	248 Calories	38 Calories

Experiment 1, the number of Calories burned while bicycling) is the heading of the next column. Additional columns were added for related experiments.

Bar Graphs

To compare how many Calories a person burns doing various activities, you could create a bar graph. A bar graph is used to display data in a number of separate, or distinct, categories. In this example, bicycling, playing basketball, and watching television are the three categories.

To create a bar graph, follow these steps.

1. On graph paper, draw a horizontal, or *x*-, axis and a vertical, or *y*-, axis.

2. Write the names of the categories to be graphed along the horizontal axis. Include an overall label for the axis as well.

3. Label the vertical axis with the name of the responding variable. Include units of measurement. Then create a scale along the axis by marking off equally spaced numbers that cover the range of the data collected.

4. For each category, draw a solid bar using the scale on the vertical axis to determine the height. Make all the bars the same width.

5. Add a title that describes the graph.

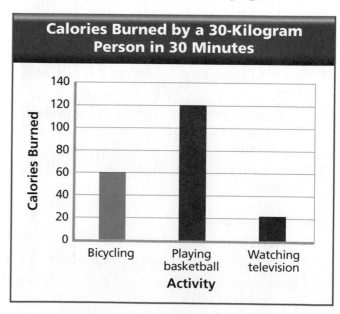

Line Graphs

To see whether a relationship exists between body mass and the number of Calories burned while bicycling, you could create a line graph. A line graph is used to display data that show how one variable (the responding variable) changes in response to another variable (the manipulated variable). You can use a line graph when your manipulated variable is **continuous,** that is, when there are other points between the ones that you tested. In this example, body mass is a continuous variable because there are other body masses between 30 and 40 kilograms (for example, 31 kilograms). Time is another example of a continuous variable.

Line graphs are powerful tools because they allow you to estimate values for conditions that you did not test in the experiment. For example, you can use the line graph to estimate that a 35-kilogram person would burn 68 Calories while bicycling.

To create a line graph, follow these steps.

1. On graph paper, draw a horizontal, or *x*-, axis and a vertical, or *y*-, axis.

2. Label the horizontal axis with the name of the manipulated variable. Label the vertical axis with the name of the responding variable. Include units of measurement.

3. Create a scale on each axis by marking off equally spaced numbers that cover the range of the data collected.

4. Plot a point on the graph for each piece of data. In the line graph above, the dotted lines show how to plot the first data point (30 kilograms and 60 Calories). Follow an imaginary vertical line extending up from the horizontal axis at the 30-kilogram mark. Then follow an imaginary horizontal line extending across from the vertical axis at the 60-Calorie mark. Plot the point where the two lines intersect.

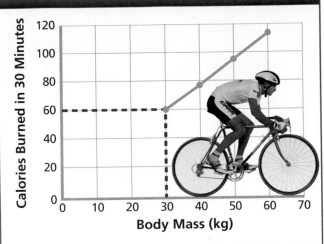

Effect of Body Mass on Calories Burned While Bicycling

5. Connect the plotted points with a solid line. (In some cases, it may be more appropriate to draw a line that shows the general trend of the plotted points. In those cases, some of the points may fall above or below the line. Also, not all graphs are linear. It may be more appropriate to draw a curve to connect the points.)

6. Add a title that identifies the variables or relationship in the graph.

Activity

Create line graphs to display the data from Experiment 2 and Experiment 3 in the data table.

Activity

You read in the newspaper that a total of 4 centimeters of rain fell in your area in June, 2.5 centimeters fell in July, and 1.5 centimeters fell in August. What type of graph would you use to display these data? Use graph paper to create the graph.

Circle Graphs

Like bar graphs, circle graphs can be used to display data in a number of separate categories. Unlike bar graphs, however, circle graphs can only be used when you have data for *all* the categories that make up a given topic. A circle graph is sometimes called a pie chart. The pie represents the entire topic, while the slices represent the individual categories. The size of a slice indicates what percentage of the whole a particular category makes up.

The data table below shows the results of a survey in which 24 teenagers were asked to identify their favorite sport. The data were then used to create the circle graph at the right.

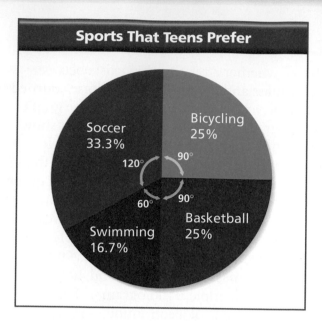

Sports That Teens Prefer

Favorite Sports

Sport	Students
Soccer	8
Basketball	6
Bicycling	6
Swimming	4

To create a circle graph, follow these steps.

1. Use a compass to draw a circle. Mark the center with a point. Then draw a line from the center point to the top of the circle.

2. Determine the size of each "slice" by setting up a proportion where x equals the number of degrees in a slice. (*Note:* A circle contains 360 degrees.) For example, to find the number of degrees in the "soccer" slice, set up the following proportion:

$$\frac{\text{Students who prefer soccer}}{\text{Total number of students}} = \frac{x}{\text{Total number of degrees in a circle}}$$

$$\frac{8}{24} = \frac{x}{360}$$

Cross-multiply and solve for x.

$$24x = 8 \times 360$$
$$x = 120$$

The "soccer" slice should contain 120 degrees.

3. Use a protractor to measure the angle of the first slice, using the line you drew to the top of the circle as the 0° line. Draw a line from the center of the circle to the edge for the angle you measured.

4. Continue around the circle by measuring the size of each slice with the protractor. Start measuring from the edge of the previous slice so the wedges do not overlap. When you are done, the entire circle should be filled in.

5. Determine the percentage of the whole circle that each slice represents. To do this, divide the number of degrees in a slice by the total number of degrees in a circle (360), and multiply by 100%. For the "soccer" slice, you can find the percentage as follows:

$$\frac{120}{360} \times 100\% = 33.3\%$$

6. Use a different color for each slice. Label each slice with the category and with the percentage of the whole it represents.

7. Add a title to the circle graph.

Activity

In a class of 28 students, 12 students take the bus to school, 10 students walk, and 6 students ride their bicycles. Create a circle graph to display these data.

Math Review

Scientists use math to organize, analyze, and present data. This appendix will help you review some basic math skills.

Mean, Median, and Mode

The **mean** is the average, or the sum of the data divided by the number of data items. The middle number in a set of ordered data is called the **median**. The **mode** is the number that appears most often in a set of data.

Example

A scientist counted the number of distinct songs sung by seven different male birds and collected the data shown below.

Male Bird Songs							
Bird	A	B	C	D	E	F	G
Number of Songs	36	29	40	35	28	36	27

To determine the mean number of songs, add the total number of songs and divide by the number of data items—in this case, the number of male birds.

$$\text{Mean} = \frac{231}{7} = 33 \text{ songs}$$

To find the median number of songs, arrange the data in numerical order and find the number in the middle of the series.

27 28 29 35 36 36 40

The number in the middle is 35, so the median number of songs is 35.

The mode is the value that appears most frequently. In the data, 36 appears twice, while each other item appears only once. Therefore, 36 songs is the mode.

Practice

Find out how many minutes it takes each student in your class to get to school. Then find the mean, median, and mode for the data.

Probability

Probability is the chance that an event will occur. Probability can be expressed as a ratio, a fraction, or a percentage. For example, when you flip a coin, the probability that the coin will land heads up is 1 in 2, or $\frac{1}{2}$, or 50 percent.

The probability that an event will happen can be expressed in the following formula.

$$P(\text{event}) = \frac{\text{Number of times the event can occur}}{\text{Total number of possible events}}$$

Example

A paper bag contains 25 blue marbles, 5 green marbles, 5 orange marbles, and 15 yellow marbles. If you close your eyes and pick a marble from the bag, what is the probability that it will be yellow?

$$P(\text{yellow marbles}) = \frac{15 \text{ yellow marbles}}{50 \text{ marbles total}}$$

$$P = \frac{15}{50}, \text{ or } \frac{3}{10}, \text{ or } 30\%$$

Practice

Each side of a cube has a letter on it. Two sides have *A*, three sides have *B*, and one side has *C*. If you roll the cube, what is the probability that *A* will land on top?

Area

The **area** of a surface is the number of square units that cover it. The front cover of your textbook has an area of about 600 cm².

Area of a Rectangle and a Square To find the area of a rectangle, multiply its length times its width. The formula for the area of a rectangle is

$$A = \ell \times w, \text{ or } A = \ell w$$

Since all four sides of a square have the same length, the area of a square is the length of one side multiplied by itself, or squared.

$$A = s \times s, \text{ or } A = s^2$$

Example

A scientist is studying the plants in a field that measures 75 m × 45 m. What is the area of the field?

$$A = \ell \times w$$
$$A = 75 \text{ m} \times 45 \text{ m}$$
$$A = 3{,}375 \text{ m}^2$$

Area of a Circle The formula for the area of a circle is

$$A = \pi \times r \times r, \text{ or } A = \pi r^2$$

The length of the radius is represented by r, and the value of π is approximately $\frac{22}{7}$.

Example

Find the area of a circle with a radius of 14 cm.

$$A = \pi r^2$$
$$A = 14 \times 14 \times \frac{22}{7}$$
$$A = 616 \text{ cm}^2$$

Practice

Find the area of a circle that has a radius of 21 m.

Circumference

The distance around a circle is called the circumference. The formula for finding the circumference of a circle is

$$C = 2 \times \pi \times r, \text{ or } C = 2\pi r$$

Example

The radius of a circle is 35 cm. What is its circumference?

$$C = 2\pi r$$
$$C = 2 \times 35 \times \frac{22}{7}$$
$$C = 220 \text{ cm}$$

Practice

What is the circumference of a circle with a radius of 28 m?

Volume

The volume of an object is the number of cubic units it contains. The volume of a wastebasket, for example, might be about 26,000 cm³.

Volume of a Rectangular Object To find the volume of a rectangular object, multiply the object's length times its width times its height.

$$V = \ell \times w \times h, \text{ or } V = \ell w h$$

Example

Find the volume of a box with length 24 cm, width 12 cm, and height 9 cm.

$$V = \ell w h$$
$$V = 24 \text{ cm} \times 12 \text{ cm} \times 9 \text{ cm}$$
$$V = 2{,}592 \text{ cm}^3$$

Practice

What is the volume of a rectangular object with length 17 cm, width 11 cm, and height 6 cm?

Fractions

A **fraction** is a way to express a part of a whole. In the fraction $\frac{4}{7}$, 4 is the numerator and 7 is the denominator.

Adding and Subtracting Fractions To add or subtract two or more fractions that have a common denominator, first add or subtract the numerators. Then write the sum or difference over the common denominator.

To find the sum or difference of fractions with different denominators, first find the least common multiple of the denominators. This is known as the least common denominator. Then convert each fraction to equivalent fractions with the least common denominator. Add or subtract the numerators. Then write the sum or difference over the common denominator.

> **Example**
>
> $$\frac{5}{6} - \frac{3}{4} = \frac{10}{12} - \frac{9}{12} = \frac{10 - 9}{12} = \frac{1}{12}$$

Multiplying Fractions To multiply two fractions, first multiply the two numerators, then multiply the two denominators.

> **Example**
>
> $$\frac{5}{6} \times \frac{2}{3} = \frac{5 \times 2}{6 \times 3} = \frac{10}{18} = \frac{5}{9}$$

Dividing Fractions Dividing by a fraction is the same as multiplying by its reciprocal. Reciprocals are numbers whose numerators and denominators have been switched. To divide one fraction by another, first invert the fraction you are dividing by—in other words, turn it upside down. Then multiply the two fractions.

> **Example**
>
> $$\frac{2}{5} \div \frac{7}{8} = \frac{2}{5} \times \frac{8}{7} = \frac{2 \times 8}{5 \times 7} = \frac{16}{35}$$

> **Practice**
>
> Solve the following: $\frac{3}{7} \div \frac{4}{5}$.

Decimals

Fractions whose denominators are 10, 100, or some other power of 10 are often expressed as decimals. For example, the fraction $\frac{9}{10}$ can be expressed as the decimal 0.9, and the fraction $\frac{7}{100}$ can be written as 0.07.

Adding and Subtracting With Decimals To add or subtract decimals, line up the decimal points before you carry out the operation.

> **Example**
>
> $$\begin{array}{r} 27.4 \\ + \ 6.19 \\ \hline 33.59 \end{array} \qquad \begin{array}{r} 278.635 \\ - \ 191.4 \\ \hline 87.235 \end{array}$$

Multiplying With Decimals When you multiply two numbers with decimals, the number of decimal places in the product is equal to the total number of decimal places in each number being multiplied.

> **Example**
>
> $$\begin{array}{r} 46.2 \text{ (one decimal place)} \\ \times \ 2.37 \text{ (two decimal places)} \\ \hline 109.494 \text{ (three decimal places)} \end{array}$$

Dividing With Decimals To divide a decimal by a whole number, put the decimal point in the quotient above the decimal point in the dividend.

> **Example**
>
> $$15.5 \div 5$$
> $$\begin{array}{r} 3.1 \\ 5\overline{)15.5} \end{array}$$

To divide a decimal by a decimal, you need to rewrite the divisor as a whole number. Do this by multiplying both the divisor and dividend by the same multiple of 10.

> **Example**
>
> $$1.68 \div 4.2 = 16.8 \div 42$$
> $$\begin{array}{r} 0.4 \\ 42\overline{)16.8} \end{array}$$

> **Practice**
>
> Multiply 6.21 by 8.5.

Ratio and Proportion

A **ratio** compares two numbers by division. For example, suppose a scientist counts 800 wolves and 1,200 moose on an island. The ratio of wolves to moose can be written as a fraction, $\frac{800}{1,200}$, which can be reduced to $\frac{2}{3}$. The same ratio can also be expressed as 2 to 3 or 2 : 3.

A **proportion** is a mathematical sentence saying that two ratios are equivalent. For example, a proportion could state that $\frac{800 \text{ wolves}}{1,200 \text{ moose}} = \frac{2 \text{ wolves}}{3 \text{ moose}}$. You can sometimes set up a proportion to determine or estimate an unknown quantity. For example, suppose a scientist counts 25 beetles in an area of 10 square meters. The scientist wants to estimate the number of beetles in 100 square meters.

Example

1. Express the relationship between beetles and area as a ratio: $\frac{25}{10}$, simplified to $\frac{5}{2}$.

2. Set up a proportion, with x representing the number of beetles. The proportion can be stated as $\frac{5}{2} = \frac{x}{100}$.

3. Begin by cross-multiplying. In other words, multiply each fraction's numerator by the other fraction's denominator.

$$5 \times 100 = 2 \times x, \text{ or } 500 = 2x$$

4. To find the value of x, divide both sides by 2. The result is 250, or 250 beetles in 100 square meters.

Practice

Find the value of x in the following proportion: $\frac{6}{7} = \frac{x}{49}$.

Percentage

A **percentage** is a ratio that compares a number to 100. For example, there are 37 granite rocks in a collection that consists of 100 rocks. The ratio $\frac{37}{100}$ can be written as 37%. Granite rocks make up 37% of the rock collection.

You can calculate percentages of numbers other than 100 by setting up a proportion.

Example

Rain falls on 9 days out of 30 in June. What percentage of the days in June were rainy?

$$\frac{9 \text{ days}}{30 \text{ days}} = \frac{d\%}{100\%}$$

To find the value of d, begin by cross-multiplying, as for any proportion:

$$9 \times 100 = 30 \times d \qquad d = \frac{900}{30} \qquad d = 30$$

Practice

There are 300 marbles in a jar, and 42 of those marbles are blue. What percentage of the marbles are blue?

Significant Figures

The **precision** of a measurement depends on the instrument you use to take the measurement. For example, if the smallest unit on the ruler is millimeters, then the most precise measurement you can make will be in millimeters.

The sum or difference of measurements can only be as precise as the least precise measurement being added or subtracted. Round your answer so that it has the same number of digits after the decimal as the least precise measurement. Round up if the last digit is 5 or more, and round down if the last digit is 4 or less.

Example

Subtract a temperature of 5.2°C from the temperature 75.46°C.

75.46 − 5.2 = 70.26

5.2 has the fewest digits after the decimal, so it is the least precise measurement. Since the last digit of the answer is 6, round up to 3. The most precise difference between the measurements is 70.3°C.

Practice

Add 26.4 m to 8.37 m. Round your answer according to the precision of the measurements.

Significant figures are the number of nonzero digits in a measurement. Zeroes between nonzero digits are also significant. For example, the measurements 12,500 L, 0.125 cm, and 2.05 kg all have three significant figures. When you multiply and divide measurements, the one with the fewest significant figures determines the number of significant figures in your answer.

Example

Multiply 110 g by 5.75 g.

110 × 5.75 = 632.5

Because 110 has only two significant figures, round the answer to 630 g.

Scientific Notation

A **factor** is a number that divides into another number with no remainder. In the example, the number 3 is used as a factor four times.

An **exponent** tells how many times a number is used as a factor. For example, $3 \times 3 \times 3 \times 3$ can be written as 3^4. The exponent 4 indicates that the number 3 is used as a factor four times. Another way of expressing this is to say that 81 is equal to 3 to the fourth power.

Example

$$3^4 = 3 \times 3 \times 3 \times 3 = 81$$

Scientific notation uses exponents and powers of ten to write very large or very small numbers in shorter form. When you write a number in scientific notation, you write the number as two factors. The first factor is any number between 1 and 10. The second factor is a power of 10, such as 10^3 or 10^6.

Example

The average distance between the planet Mercury and the sun is 58,000,000 km. To write the first factor in scientific notation, insert a decimal point in the original number so that you have a number between 1 and 10. In the case of 58,000,000, the number is 5.8.

To determine the power of 10, count the number of places that the decimal point moved. In this case, it moved 7 places.

$$58{,}000{,}000 \text{ km} = 5.8 \times 10^7 \text{ km}$$

Practice

Express 6,590,000 in scientific notation.

Reading Comprehension Skills

Each section in your textbook introduces a Target Reading Skill.
You will improve your reading comprehension by using the
Target Reading Skills described below.

Using Prior Knowledge

Your prior knowledge is what you already know before you begin to read about a topic. Building on what you already know gives you a head start on learning new information. Before you begin a new assignment, think about what you know. You might look at the headings and the visuals to spark your memory. You can list what you know. Then, as you read, consider questions like these.

• How does what you learn relate to what you know?

• How did something you already know help you learn something new?

• Did your original ideas agree with what you have just learned?

Asking Questions

Asking yourself questions is an excellent way to focus on and remember new information in your textbook. For example, you can turn the text headings into questions. Then your questions can guide you to identify the important information as you read. Look at these examples:

Heading: Using Seismographic Data

Question: How are seismographic data used?

Heading: Kinds of Faults

Question: What are the kinds of faults?

You do not have to limit your questions to text headings. Ask questions about anything that you need to clarify or that will help you understand the content. *What* and *how* are probably the most common question words, but you may also ask *why, who, when,* or *where* questions.

Previewing Visuals

Visuals are photographs, graphs, tables, diagrams, and illustrations. Visuals contain important information. Before you read, look at visuals and their labels and captions. This preview will help you prepare for what you will be reading.

Often you will be asked what you want to learn about a visual. For example, after you look at the normal fault diagram below, you might ask: What is the movement along a normal fault? Questions about visuals give you a purpose for reading—to answer your questions.

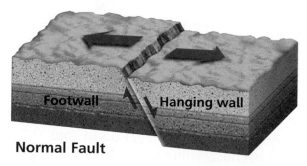

Footwall   Hanging wall

Normal Fault

Outlining

An outline shows the relationship between main ideas and supporting ideas. An outline has a formal structure. You write the main ideas, called topics, next to Roman numerals. The supporting ideas, called subtopics, are written under the main ideas and labeled A, B, C, and so on. An outline looks like this:

Technology and Society
I. Technology through history
II. The impact of technology on society
A.
B.

Identifying Main Ideas

When you are reading science material, it is important to try to understand the ideas and concepts that are in a passage. Each paragraph has a lot of information and detail. Good readers try to identify the most important—or biggest—idea in every paragraph or section. That's the main idea. The other information in the paragraph supports or further explains the main idea.

Sometimes main ideas are stated directly. In this book, some main ideas are identified for you as key concepts. These are printed in bold-face type. However, you must identify other main ideas yourself. In order to do this, you must identify all the ideas within a paragraph or section. Then ask yourself which idea is big enough to include all the other ideas.

Comparing and Contrasting

When you compare and contrast, you examine the similarities and differences between things. You can compare and contrast in a Venn diagram or in a table.

Venn Diagram A Venn diagram consists of two overlapping circles. In the space where the circles overlap, you write the characteristics that the two items have in common. In one of the circles outside the area of overlap, you write the differing features or characteristics of one of the items. In the other circle outside the area of overlap, you write the differing characteristics of the other item.

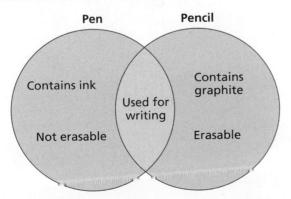

Table

Table In a compare/contrast table, you list the characteristics or features to be compared across the top of the table. Then list the items to be compared in the left column. Complete the table by filling in information about each characteristic or feature.

Blood Vessel	Function	Structure of Wall
Artery	Carries blood away from heart	
Capillary		
Vein		

Identifying Supporting Evidence

A hypothesis is a possible explanation for observations made by scientists or an answer to a scientific question. Scientists must carry out investigations and gather evidence that either supports or disproves the hypothesis.

Identifying the supporting evidence for a hypothesis or theory can help you understand the hypothesis or theory. Evidence consists of facts—information whose accuracy can be confirmed by testing or observation.

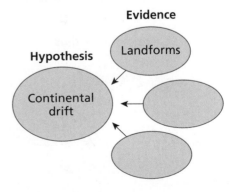

Sequencing

A sequence is the order in which a series of events occurs. A flowchart or a cycle diagram can help you visualize a sequence.

Flowchart To make a flowchart, write a brief description of each step or event in a box. Place the boxes in order, with the first event at the top of the chart. Then draw an arrow to connect each step or event to the next.

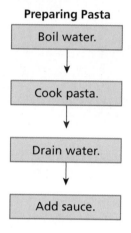

Preparing Pasta

Boil water.
↓
Cook pasta.
↓
Drain water.
↓
Add sauce.

Cycle Diagram A cycle diagram shows a sequence that is continuous, or cyclical. A continuous sequence does not have an end because when the final event is over, the first event begins again. To create a cycle diagram, write the starting event in a box placed at the top of a page in the center. Then, moving in a clockwise direction, write each event in a box in its proper sequence. Draw arrows that connect each event to the one that occurs next.

Seasons of the Year

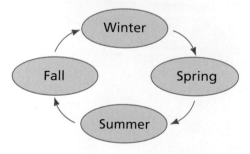

Relating Cause and Effect

Science involves many cause-and-effect relationships. A cause makes something happen. An effect is what happens. When you recognize that one event causes another, you are relating cause and effect.

Words like *cause, because, effect, affect,* and *result* often signal a cause or an effect. Sometimes an effect can have more than one cause, or a cause can produce several effects.

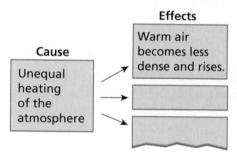

Cause — Unequal heating of the atmosphere

Effects — Warm air becomes less dense and rises.

Concept Mapping

Concept maps are useful tools for organizing information on any topic. A concept map begins with a main idea or core concept and shows how the idea can be subdivided into related subconcepts or smaller ideas.

You construct a concept map by placing concepts (usually nouns) in ovals and connecting them with linking words (usually verbs). The biggest concept or idea is placed in an oval at the top of the map. Related concepts are arranged in ovals below the big idea. The linking words connect the ovals.

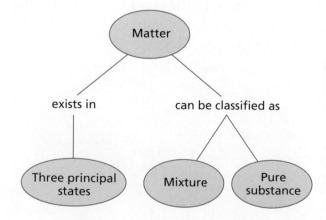

Matter
exists in — Three principal states
can be classified as — Mixture, Pure substance

Building Vocabulary

Knowing the meaning of these prefixes, suffixes, and roots will
help you understand the meaning of words you do not recognize.

Word Origins Many science words come to
English from other languages, such as Greek
and Latin. By learning the meaning of a few
common Greek and Latin roots, you can determine the meaning of unfamiliar science words.

Prefixes A prefix is a word part that is added
at the beginning of a root or base word to
change its meaning.

Suffixes A suffix is a word part that is added
at the end of a root word to change the meaning.

Greek and Latin Roots

Greek Roots	Meaning	Example
ast-	star	astronaut
geo-	Earth	geology
metron-	measure	kilometer
opt-	eye	optician
photo-	light	photograph
scop-	see	microscope
therm-	heat	thermostat

Latin Roots	Meaning	Example
aqua-	water	aquarium
aud-	hear	auditorium
duc-, duct-	lead	conduct
flect-	bend	reflect
fract-, frag-	break	fracture
ject-	throw	reject
luc-	light	lucid
spec-	see	inspect

Prefixes and Suffixes

Prefix	Meaning	Example
com-, con-	with	communicate, concert
de-	from; down	decay
di-	two	divide
ex-, exo-	out	exhaust
in-, im-	in, into; not	inject, impossible
re-	again; back	reflect, recall
trans-	across	transfer

Suffix	Meaning	Example
-al	relating to	natural
-er, -or	one who	teacher, doctor
-ist	one who practices	scientist
-ity	state of	equality
-ology	study of	biology
-tion, -sion	state or quality of	reaction, tension

Safety Symbols

These symbols warn of possible dangers in the laboratory and remind you to work carefully.

 Safety Goggles Wear safety goggles to protect your eyes in any activity involving chemicals, flames or heating, or glassware.

 Lab Apron Wear a laboratory apron to protect your skin and clothing from damage.

 Breakage Handle breakable materials, such as glassware, with care. Do not touch broken glassware.

 Heat-Resistant Gloves Use an oven mitt or other hand protection when handling hot materials such as hot plates or hot glassware.

 Plastic Gloves Wear disposable plastic gloves when working with harmful chemicals and organisms. Keep your hands away from your face, and dispose of the gloves according to your teacher's instructions.

 Heating Use a clamp or tongs to pick up hot glassware. Do not touch hot objects with your bare hands.

 Flames Before you work with flames, tie back loose hair and clothing. Follow instructions from your teacher about lighting and extinguishing flames.

 No Flames When using flammable materials, make sure there are no flames, sparks, or other exposed heat sources present.

 Corrosive Chemical Avoid getting acid or other corrosive chemicals on your skin or clothing or in your eyes. Do not inhale the vapors. Wash your hands after the activity.

 Poison Do not let any poisonous chemical come into contact with your skin, and do not inhale its vapors. Wash your hands when you are finished with the activity.

 Fumes Work in a ventilated area when harmful vapors may be involved. Avoid inhaling vapors directly. Only test an odor when directed to do so by your teacher, and use a wafting motion to direct the vapor toward your nose.

 Sharp Object Scissors, scalpels, knives, needles, pins, and tacks can cut your skin. Always direct a sharp edge or point away from yourself and others.

 Animal Safety Treat live or preserved animals or animal parts with care to avoid harming the animals or yourself. Wash your hands when you are finished with the activity.

 Plant Safety Handle plants only as directed by your teacher. If you are allergic to certain plants, tell your teacher; do not do an activity involving those plants. Avoid touching harmful plants such as poison ivy. Wash your hands when you are finished with the activity.

 Electric Shock To avoid electric shock, never use electrical equipment around water, or when the equipment is wet or your hands are wet. Be sure cords are untangled and cannot trip anyone. Unplug equipment not in use.

 Physical Safety When an experiment involves physical activity, avoid injuring yourself or others. Alert your teacher if there is any reason you should not participate.

 Disposal Dispose of chemicals and other laboratory materials safely. Follow the instructions from your teacher.

 Hand Washing Wash your hands thoroughly when finished with the activity. Use soap and warm water. Rinse well.

 General Safety Awareness When this symbol appears, follow the instructions provided. When you are asked to develop your own procedure in a lab, have your teacher approve your plan before you go further.

Science Safety Rules

General Precautions
Follow all instructions. Never perform activities without the approval and supervision of your teacher. Do not engage in horseplay. Never eat or drink in the laboratory. Keep work areas clean and uncluttered.

Dress Code
Wear safety goggles whenever you work with chemicals, glassware, heat sources such as burners, or any substance that might get into your eyes. If you wear contact lenses, notify your teacher.

Wear a lab apron or coat whenever you work with corrosive chemicals or substances that can stain. Wear disposable plastic gloves when working with organisms and harmful chemicals. Tie back long hair. Remove or tie back any article of clothing or jewelry that can hang down and touch chemicals, flames, or equipment. Roll up long sleeves. Never wear open shoes or sandals.

First Aid
Report all accidents, injuries, or fires to your teacher, no matter how minor. Be aware of the location of the first-aid kit, emergency equipment such as the fire extinguisher and fire blanket, and the nearest telephone. Know whom to contact in an emergency.

Heating and Fire Safety
Keep all combustible materials away from flames. When heating a substance in a test tube, make sure that the mouth of the tube is not pointed at you or anyone else. Never heat a liquid in a closed container. Use an oven mitt to pick up a container that has been heated.

Using Chemicals Safely
Never put your face near the mouth of a container that holds chemicals. Never touch, taste, or smell a chemical unless your teacher tells you to.

Use only those chemicals needed in the activity. Keep all containers closed when chemicals are not being used. Pour all chemicals over the sink or a container, not over your work surface. Dispose of excess chemicals as instructed by your teacher.

Be extra careful when working with acids or bases. When mixing an acid and water, always pour the water into the container first and then add the acid to the water. Never pour water into an acid. Wash chemical spills and splashes immediately with plenty of water.

Using Glassware Safely
If glassware is broken or chipped, notify your teacher immediately. Never handle broken or chipped glass with your bare hands.

Never force glass tubing or thermometers into a rubber stopper or rubber tubing. Have your teacher insert the glass tubing or thermometer if required for an activity.

Using Sharp Instruments
Handle sharp instruments with extreme care. Never cut material toward you; cut away from you.

Animal and Plant Safety
Never perform experiments that cause pain, discomfort, or harm to animals. Only handle animals if absolutely necessary. If you know that you are allergic to certain plants, molds, or animals, tell your teacher before doing an activity in which these are used. Wash your hands thoroughly after any activity involving animals, animal parts, plants, plant parts, or soil.

During field work, wear long pants, long sleeves, socks, and closed shoes. Avoid poisonous plants and fungi as well as plants with thorns.

End-of-Experiment Rules
Unplug all electrical equipment. Clean up your work area. Dispose of waste materials as instructed by your teacher. Wash your hands after every experiment.

English and Spanish Glossary

A

absolute zero The temperature at which no more energy can be removed from matter. (p. 178)
cero absoluto Temperatura a la cual no se puede quitar más energía a la materia.

acceleration The rate at which velocity changes. (p. 22)
acelaración Razón a la que cambia la velocidad.

air resistance The fluid friction experienced by objects falling through the air. (p. 49)
resistencia del aire Fricción de fluido experimentada por los objetos que caen a través del aire.

Archimedes' principle The rule that the buoyant force on an object is equal to the weight of the fluid the object displaces. (p. 84)
principio de Arquímedes Regla que enuncia que la fuerza de flotación que actúa sobre un objeto es igual al peso del líquido que desaloja.

average speed The overall rate of speed at which an object moves; calculated by dividing the total distance an object travels by the total time. (p. 11)
rapidez media Velocidad general a la que se mueve un objeto; se calcula dividiendo la distancia total recorrida por el tiempo total empleado.

B

balanced forces Equal forces acting on an object in opposite directions. (p. 38)
fuerzas equilibradas Fuerzas iguales que actúan sobre un objeto en direcciones opuestas.

barometer An instrument used to measure atmospheric pressure. (p. 80)
barómetro Instrumento que se usa para medir la presión atmosférica.

Bernoulli's principle The rule that a stream of fast-moving fluid exerts less pressure than the surrounding fluid. (p. 96)
principio de Bernoulli Regla que enuncia que la corriente de un fluido de rápido movimiento ejerce menor presión que el fluido del entorno.

boiling Vaporization that occurs on and below the surface of a liquid. (p. 193)
ebullición Evaporación que ocurre sobre y bajo la superficie de un líquido.

buoyant force The upward force exerted by a fluid on a submerged object. (p. 83)
fuerza de flotación Fuerza ascendente que ejerce un líquido sobre un objeto sumergido.

C

Celsius scale The temperature scale on which water freezes at 0 degrees and boils at 100 degrees. (p. 178)
escala Celsius Escala de temperatura en la cual el agua se congela a los 0 grados y hierve a los 100 grados.

centripetal force A force that causes an object to move in a circle. (p. 65)
fuerza centrípeta Fuerza que causa que un objeto se mueva en círculos.

change of state The physical change of matter from one state to another. (p. 192)
cambio de estado Cambio físico de la materia de un estado a otro.

chemical energy The potential energy stored in chemical bonds. (p. 154)
energía química Energía potencial almacenada en los enlaces químicos.

combustion The process of burning a fuel to produce thermal energy. (p. 168)
combustión Proceso de quemado de un combustible para producir energía térmica.

compound machine A device that combines two or more simple machines. (p. 135)
máquina compuesta Dispositivo que combina dos o más máquinas simples.

condensation The change from the gaseous to the liquid state of matter. (p. 193)
condensación Cambio de la materia del estado gaseoso al estado líquido.

conduction The transfer of heat from one particle of matter to another. (p. 184)
conducción Transferencia de calor desde una partícula de materia a otra.

conductor A material that conducts heat well. (p. 187)
conductor Material que puede conducir bien el calor.

convection The transfer of heat by the movement of currents within a fluid. (p. 184)
convección Transferencia del calor a través del movimiento de las corrientes dentro de un líquido.

convection current A current caused by the rising of heated fluid and sinking of cooled fluid. (p. 184)
corriente de convección Movimiento circular causado por el ascenso de un líquido calentado y el descenso de un líquido enfriado.

D

density The mass of a substance contained in a unit of volume. (p. 85)
densidad Masa de una sustancia contenida en una unidad de volumen.

E

efficiency The percentage of the input work that is converted to output work. (p. 119)
eficiencia Porcentaje del trabajo aportado que se convierte en trabajo producido.

elastic potential energy The energy of stretched or compressed objects. (p. 150)
energía elástica potencial Energía de los objetos estirados o comprimidos.

electrical energy The energy of electric charges. (p. 154)
energía eléctrica Energía de las cargas eléctricas.

electromagnetic energy The energy of light and other forms of radiation. (p. 155)
energía electromagnética Energía de la luz y otras formas de radiación.

energy The ability to do work or cause change. (p. 147)
energía Capacidad para realizar trabajo o causar un cambio.

energy transformation The process of changing one form of energy to another. (p. 158)
transformación energética Proceso de cambio de una forma de energía a otra.

evaporation Vaporization that occurs at the surface of a liquid. (p. 193)
evaporación Vaporización que ocurre en la superficie de un líquido.

external combustion engine An engine powered by fuel burned outside the engine. (p. 196)
motor de combustión externa Motor alimentado por combustible que se quema fuera del motor.

F

Fahrenheit scale The temperature scale on which water freezes at 32 degrees and boils at 212 degrees. (p. 178)
escala Fahrenheit Escala de temperatura en la cual el agua se congela a los 32 grados y hierve a los 212 grados.

fluid A material that can easily flow. (p. 76)
fluido Sustancia que puede fluir con facilidad.

fluid friction Friction that occurs as an object moves through a fluid. (p. 44)
fricción de fluido Fricción que ocurre cuando un objeto se mueve a través de un fluido.

force A push or pull exerted on an object. (p. 36)
fuerza Empuje o atracción que se ejerce sobre un objeto.

fossil fuel A material such as coal that forms over millions of years from the remains of ancient plants and animals; burned to release chemical energy. (p. 166)
combustible fósil Material, como el carbón de piedra, que se forma durante millones de años a partir de los restos de animales y vegetales; se quema para liberar la energía química.

free fall The motion of a falling object when the only force acting on it is gravity. (p. 48)
caída libre Movimiento de un objeto que cae cuando la única fuerza que actúa sobre el mismo es la gravedad.

freezing The change from the liquid to the solid state of matter. (p. 192)
congelación Cambio de la materia del estado líquido al estado sólido.

friction The force that one surface exerts on another when the two surfaces rub against each other. (p. 43)
fricción Fuerza que ejerce una superficie sobre otra cuando se frotan una contra otra.

fulcrum The fixed point around which a lever pivots. (p. 128)
fulcro Punto fijo en torno al cual gira una palanca.

gravitational potential energy Potential energy that depends on the height of an object. (p. 149)
energía potencial gravitatoria Energía potencial que depende de la altura de un objeto.

gravity The force that pulls objects toward each other. (p. 46)
gravedad Fuerza que atrae objetos entre sí.

heat Thermal energy that is transferred from matter at a higher temperature to matter at a lower temperature. (p. 179)
calor Energía térmica que se transfiere desde una materia a mayor temperatura a una materia a menor temperatura.

heat engine A device that converts thermal energy into mechanical energy. (p. 195)
motor térmico Máquina que convierte la energía térmica en energía mecánica.

hydraulic system A system that multiplies force by transmitting pressure from a small surface area through a confined fluid to a larger surface area. (p. 93)
sistema hidráulico Sistema que multiplica la fuerza transmitiendo la presión de un área total pequeña a un área total mayor a través de un fluido confinado.

inclined plane A simple machine that is a flat, sloped surface. (p. 125)
plano inclinado Máquina simple que consiste en una superficie plana con pendiente.

inertia The tendency of an object to resist any change in its motion. (p. 52)
inercia Tendencia de un objeto a resistir cualquier cambio en su movimiento.

input force The force exerted on a machine. (p. 115)
fuerza aplicada Fuerza que se ejerce sobre una máquina.

input work The work done on a machine as the input force acts through the input distance. (p. 115)
trabajo aportado Trabajo realizado sobre una máquina mientras la fuerza aplicada actúa a lo largo de la distancia de aplicación.

instantaneous speed The speed of an object at one instant of time. (p. 11)
rapidez instantánea Velocidad de un objeto en un instante de tiempo.

insulator A material that does not conduct heat well. (p. 187)
aislante Material que no conduce bien el calor.

internal combustion engine An engine that burns fuel inside cylinders within the engine. (p. 196)
motor de combustión interna Motor que quema el combustible dentro de cilindros, dentro del motor.

International System of Units (SI) A system of measurement based on multiples of ten and on established measures of mass, length, and time. (p. 9)
Sistema Internacional de Unidades (SI) Sistema de medidas basado en múltiplos de diez y en medidas establecidas de masa, longitud y tiempo.

joule A unit of work equal to one newton-meter. (p. 111)
julio Unidad de trabajo igual a un newton-metro.

Kelvin scale The temperature scale on which zero is the temperature at which no more energy can be removed from matter. (p. 178)
escala Kelvin Escala de temperatura en la cual el cero es la temperatura a la cual no se puede quitar más energía de la materia.

kinetic energy Energy that an object has due to its motion. (p. 147)
energía cinética Energía que tiene un objeto debido a su movimiento.

law of conservation of energy The rule that energy cannot be created or destroyed. (p. 162)
ley de la conservación de la energía Regla que dice que la energía no se puede crear ni destruir.

law of conservation of momentum The rule that in the absence of outside forces the total momentum of objects that interact does not change. (p. 59)
ley de la conservación del momento Regla según la cual en ausencia de fuerzas externas, el momento total de los objetos no cambia en su interacción.

lever A simple machine that consists of a rigid bar that pivots about a fixed point. (p. 128)
palanca Máquina simple que consiste en una barra rígida que gira en torno a un punto fijo.

lift An upward force. (p. 97)
fuerza de elevación Fuerza ascendente.

machine A device that changes the amount of force exerted, the distance over which a force is exerted, or the direction in which force is exerted. (p. 115)
máquina Dispositivo que altera la cantidad de fuerza ejercida, la distancia sobre la que se ejerce la fuerza o la dirección en la que se ejerce la fuerza.

mass The amount of matter in an object. (p. 46)
masa Cantidad de materia en un objeto.

matter Anything that has mass and takes up space. (p. 163)
materia Cualquier cosa que tiene masa y ocupa un espacio.

mechanical advantage The number of times a machine increases a force exerted on it. (p. 118)
ventaja mecánica Número de veces que una máquina amplifica la fuerza que se ejerce sobre ella.

mechanical energy Kinetic or potential energy associated with the motion or position of an object. (p. 151)
energía mecánica Energía cinética o potencial asociada con el movimiento o posición de un objeto.

melting The change from the solid to the liquid state of matter. (p. 192)
fusión Cambio en el estado de la materia de sólido a líquido.

meter The basic SI unit of length. (p. 9)
metro Unidad básica de longitud del SI.

momentum The product of an object's mass and velocity. (p. 58)
momento Producto de la masa de un objeto por su velocidad.

motion The state in which one object's distance from another is changing. (p. 7)
movimiento Estado en el que la distancia entre un objeto y otro va cambiando.

English and Spanish Glossary

N

net force The overall force on an object when all the individual forces acting on it are added together. (p. 37)
fuerza neta Fuerza total que actúa sobre un objeto cuando se suman las fuerzas individuales que actúan sobre él.

newton A unit of measure that equals the force required to accelerate 1 kilogram of mass at 1 meter per second per second. (p. 37)
newton Unidad de medida que es igual a la fuerza necesaria para acelerar 1 kilogramo de masa 1 metro por segundo cada segundo.

nuclear energy The potential energy stored in the nucleus of an atom. (p. 155)
energía nuclear Energía potencial almacenada en el núcleo de un átomo.

O

output force The force exerted on an object by a machine. (p. 115)
fuerza desarrollada Fuerza que una máquina ejerce sobre un objeto.

output work The work done by a machine as the output force acts through the output distance. (p. 115)
trabajo producido Trabajo que una máquina efectúa mientras la fuerza desarrollada actúa a lo largo de la distancia desarrollada.

P

pascal A unit of pressure equal to 1 newton per square meter. (p. 75)
pascal Unidad de presión igual a 1 newton por metro cuadrado.

Pascal's principle The rule that when force is applied to a confined fluid, the increase in pressure is transmitted equally to all parts of the fluid. (p. 91)
principio de Pascal Regla que enuncia que cuando se aplica una fuerza a un fluido confinado, el aumento en la presión es transmitida por igual a todas las partes del fluido.

plate One of the major pieces that make up Earth's upper layer. (p. 18)
placa Una de las partes principales que forman la capa exterior de la Tierra.

potential energy Stored energy that results from the position or shape of an object. (p. 149)
energía potencial Energía almacenada que es el resultado de la posición o forma de un objeto.

power The rate at which work is done. (p. 111)
potencia Razón a la que se realiza trabajo.

pressure The force exerted on a surface divided by the total area over which the force is exerted. (p. 75)
presión Fuerza ejercida sobre una superficie dividida por el área total sobre la cual se ejerce la fuerza.

projectile An object that is thrown. (p. 50)
proyectil Objeto que es lanzado.

pulley A simple machine that consists of a grooved wheel with a rope or cable wrapped around it. (p. 132)
polea Máquina simple que consiste en una rueda con un surco en el que entra una cuerda o cable.

R

radiation The transfer of energy by electromagnetic waves. (p. 184)
radiación Transferencia de energía a través de ondas electromagnéticas.

reference point A place or object used for comparison to determine if an object is in motion. (p. 7)
punto de referencia Lugar u objeto usado como punto de comparación para determinar si un objeto está en movimiento.

refrigerant The substance that absorbs and releases heat in a cooling system. (p. 199)
refrigerante Sustancia que absorbe y elimina calor en un sistema de enfriamiento.

rolling friction Friction that occurs when an object rolls over a surface. (p. 44)
fricción de rodamiento Fricción que ocurre cuando un objeto rueda sobre una superficie.

S

satellite Any object that orbits around another object in space. (p. 65)
satélite Cualquier objeto que orbita alrededor de otro objeto en el espacio.

screw A simple machine that is an inclined plane wrapped around a central cylinder to form a spiral. (p. 127)
tornillo Máquina simple que consiste en un plano inclinado enrollado en un cilindro central para formar una espiral.

sliding friction Friction that occurs when one solid surface slides over another. (p. 44)
fricción de deslizamiento Fricción que ocurre cuando una superficie sólida se desliza sobre otra.

slope The steepness of a line on a graph, equal to its vertical change divided by its horizontal change. (p. 14)
pendiente Inclinación de una recta en una gráfica, igual a su cambio vertical dividido por su cambio horizontal.

specific heat The amount of heat required to raise the temperature of 1 kilogram of a material by 1 kelvin. (p. 180)
calor específico Cantidad de calor que se requiere para elevar la temperatura de 1 kilogramo de material 1 grado Kelvin.

speed The distance an object travels per unit of time. (p. 10)
rapidez Distancia que viaja un objeto por unidad de tiempo.

state One of the three forms—solid, liquid, or gas—in which most matter on Earth exists. (p. 191)
estado Una de las tres formas (sólido, líquido o gas) en las que existe la materia en la Tierra.

static friction Friction that acts on objects that are not moving. (p. 44)
fricción estática Fricción que actúa sobre los objetos que no se mueven.

 T

temperature The measure of the average kinetic energy of the particles in matter. (p. 176)
temperatura Medida de la energía cinética promedio de la partículas de la materia.

terminal velocity The greatest velocity a falling object can achieve. (p. 49)
velocidad terminal La máxima velocidad que puede alcanzar un objeto que cae.

theory of plate tectonics The theory that pieces of Earth's outer layer are in constant motion. (p. 19)
teoría de la tectónica de placas Teoría que enuncia que las partes de la capa exterior de la Tierra están en constante movimiento.

thermal energy The total potential and kinetic energy of the particles in an object. (p. 153)
energía térmica Energía cinética y potencial total de las partículas de un objeto.

thermal expansion The expansion of matter when it is heated. (p. 194)
expansión térmica Expansión de la materia cuando se calienta.

 U

unbalanced forces Forces that produce a nonzero net force, which changes an object's motion. (p. 38)
fuerzas desequilibradas Fuerzas que producen una fuerza neta diferente de cero, lo cual cambia el movimiento de un objeto.

 V

velocity Speed in a given direction. (p. 12)
velocidad Rapidez en una dirección dada.

 W

wedge A simple machine that is an inclined plane that moves. (p. 126)
cuña Máquina simple que consiste en un plano inclinado en movimiento.

weight The force of gravity on an object at the surface of a planet. (p. 47)
peso Fuerza de gravedad ejercida sobre un objeto en la superficie de un planeta.

wheel and axle A simple machine that consists of two attached circular or cylindrical objects that rotate about a common axis, each one with a different radius. (p. 130)
rueda y eje Máquina simple que consiste en dos objetos circulares o cilíndricos unidos, de diferente radio, que giran en torno a un eje común.

work Force exerted on an object that causes it to move. (p. 108)
trabajo Fuerza ejercida sobre un objeto para moverlo.

Index

Page numbers for key terms are printed in **boldface** type.
Page numbers for illustrations, maps, and charts are printed in *italics*.

A

absolute zero **178**
acceleration **22**–27
  calculating 24–25
  change in direction and 22, 23
  changes in force and mass and 54
  in free fall *48*
  graphing 26–27
  gravity and *46*, 48
  Newton's second law and 52–54
action force **56**–57
action-reaction pairs **56**–57
actual mechanical advantage **121**
air conditioners 199
aircraft
  flight of 95, 97, 100–101
  helicopters 100–101
airplane wing, Bernoulli's principle
  and 97
air pressure. *See* atmospheric
  pressure
air resistance **49**
Archimedes' principle **84**
area **224**
  pressure and 75
artificial satellite **65**
atmospheric pressure **76**–80
  elevation and *78, 79*
  measuring 80
  at sea level 77
average speed **11**
  of Earth's plates 21
axle, wheel and *130*–132

B

balanced forces **38**–39
  falling objects and 49
balanced pressure 77
barometer *80*
Bernoulli's principle **96**–99
  applying 97–99
biomechanical engineer xii–3
block and tackle 132
body, simple machines in 134
boiling 193
boiling point **193**
bonds in chemical compounds,
  chemical energy in *154*
bones and muscles, levers of 134
brainstorming **218**
bridges 204–211
buoyant force **83**–84
  Archimedes' principle and *84*
  changing density of submarine
    and 86, *87*
  gravity and 83

C

calculating, skill of **215**
Celsius scale **178**, 215
centimeter (cm) 9
centripetal force **65**
change of state **192**–193
chemical compounds, bonds in 154
chemical energy *154*
  in fossil fuels 167, 168
circular motion 23, 65
classifying, skill of **213**
collisions, momentum in 61
combustion **168**
  external combustion engines *196*
  in heat engines 195
  internal combustion engines 196
communicating, skill of **213**
compound machines **135**
conclusion **217**
condensation *193*
conduction **184**, *185*
conductors **186**, **187**
conservation 59
  of energy *162*–163
  of momentum, law of **59**–61
constraint **218**
continents, motion of *20*
controlled experiment **217**
convection **184**, *185*
convection current **184**
conversion factor 9
cooling systems 198–199

D

data **217**
degrees Celsius (°C) **178**
degrees Fahrenheit (°F) **178**
density 84, **85**–86
  changing 86, *87*
  comparing densities of
    substances 85
depth, water pressure and *78, 79*–80
direction
  acceleration and change in **22**, 23
  of flow of heat 186
  of force, machines that change
    116, *117*
  friction and 43
  mechanical advantage of machine
    that changes 119
  net force and **37,** 38–39
  velocity and **12**–13
  work and force in same 109

distance
  calculating amount of work based
    on 110–111
  calculating speed based on *10*–11
  gravitational force and 47
  input 115, 116, *117*
  machines that change input 116, *117*
  measuring 9
  mechanical advantage of machine
    that increases 118
  output 115
distance-versus-time graph 14, 27

E

Earth
  gravity and 47
  plates of **18**–21
efficiency *119*
  calculating 120
  friction and 119, 120, 121
  of machines 119–121
Einstein, Albert 163
elastic potential energy *150*, 161
electrical energy **154**
  fossil fuels used to produce 168–*169*
electromagnetic energy **155,** 167
electromagnetic waves, transfer of
  energy by 155, 184
elevation, atmospheric pressure and
  78, 79
energy 146, *147*
  chemical **154**, 167, 168
  conservation of *162*–163
  electrical **154**, 168–*169*
  electromagnetic **155,** 167
  fossil fuels and **166**–169
  friction and 162
  kinetic. *See* **kinetic energy**
  matter transformed to 163
  mechanical **151**–152, 162, 195–196
  nuclear **155,** 167
  potential. *See* **potential energy**
  power and 147
  from the sun 167
  thermal. *See* **thermal energy**
  work and 147
energy transformations **158**–161
  combustion and **168**
  conservation of energy and *162*–163
  energy from sun 167
  multiple transformations 159
  between potential and kinetic
    energy 160–161
  single transformations 159
evaporation **193**
exponent 148, **227**
external combustion engines *196*

Index

F

Fahrenheit scale 178
falling objects. *See also* **gravity**
    air resistance and *49*
    free fall *48*
fixed pulley 132, *133*
flight
    of aircraft 95, 97, 100–101
    Bernoulli's principle and 97
floating
    buoyant force and *83*–84
    density and 84, *85*–86, *87*
fluid 76
    air as 86
fluid friction 44, *45*
    air resistance *49*
fluid motion 95, 96
    Bernoulli's principle and **96**–99
fluid pressure 76–80
    air pressure as 76
    balanced pressure 77
    cause of 76
    of moving fluid 96
    Pascal's principle and **91**–94
    on submerged object *83*–84
    transmitting pressure in fluid 91–92
    variations in *78,* 79–80
food, energy transformations in 159
force(s) 36. *See also* **friction; gravity; input force; output force; pressure**
    action-reaction 56–57
    balanced *38*–*39, 49*
    buoyant *83*–84, 86, 87
    calculating amount of work based on 110–111
    centripetal **65**
    combining 37–39
    machines that change amount of input 116, *117*
    mechanical advantage of machine that increases 118
    motion and *37,* 38–39
    net *37,* 38–39, 53–54
    Newton's first law of motion and 51–52
    Newton's second law of motion and 53–54
    unbalanced *38, 39,* 48, 51
    work and *108,* 109
fossil fuels 166–169
    formation of 166–167
    use of 168–*169*
four-stroke engines 196, *197*
fraction 225
free fall 48
freezing 192

freezing point 192, 193
friction 42, *43*–44, *45*
    causes of 43
    efficiency and *119,* 120, 121
    energy and 162
    types of 44, *45*
fulcrum 128

G

Galileo Galilei 51, 52
gases 191
    liquid-gas changes of state 193
gram (g) 215
graph(s)
    acceleration 26–27
    motion 14–15
gravitational potential energy 149, 160, 161
gravity 42, **46**–50
    acceleration due to *46,* 48
    buoyant force and *83*
    factors affecting 46–47
    law of universal gravitation 46
    motion and 42, 48–50
    projectile motion and *50*
    satellites in orbit around Earth and 66

H

heat *179*
    specific *180*–181
    uses of 195–199
heat engines 195–196, *197*
heat transfer 183–187
    by conduction **184,** *185*
    conductors in 186, **187**
    by convection **184,** *185*
    in cooling systems 198–199
    direction of flow 186
    insulators in 186, **187**
    by radiation **184,** *185*
height, gravitational potential energy and *149*
helicopters 100–101
Hickam, Homer 64
horsepower 113
hydraulic device 92
hydraulic systems 93–94
    hydraulic brakes 94
    hydraulic lifts 93
hypothesis 216

I

iceberg 82, *86*
ideal machines 121
ideal mechanical advantage. *See* **mechanical advantage**

incisors 134
inclined plane *125*
    wedge as *126*
inertia 52
    satellite motion and 66
inferring, skill of 212
input distance 115
    machines that change 116, *117*
input force 115
    on inclined plane *125*
    on lever *128*
    machines that change 116, *117*
    mechanical advantage and *118*–119
    on pulley 132
    on screw *127*
    on wedge *126*
    on wheel and axle 131
input work 115
    efficiency of machine and *119*
instantaneous speed 11
insulators 186, *187*
internal combustion engines 196
internal energy. *See* **thermal energy**
International System of Units 9. *See also* **units of measurement**

J

Joule, James Prescott 111
joule (J) 111, 113, 147, 179
juggling, energy in 160

K

Kelvin scale 178
kelvins (K) 178
kilogram 46
kilometers (km) 9
kinetic energy 147–148, 176
    calculating 148
    electrical energy as form of **154**
    factors affecting 148
    mechanical energy and 152
    temperature as measure of average **176**–178
    transformation between potential energy and 160–161

L

laboratory safety 232–233
law
    of conservation of energy 162–163
    of conservation of momentum 59–61
    of universal gravitation 46
levers 128, 129
    living, in body 134
    types of 128, *129*
lift, Bernoulli's principle and 97, 99

Index

Page numbers for key terms are printed in **boldface** type.
Page numbers for illustrations, maps, and charts are printed in *italics*.

liquids 191
  liquid-gas changes of state 193
  solid-liquid changes of state
    192–193
liter (L) 214

M

machines 114, **115**–121
  automation in workplace, debate
    over 138–139
  compound *135*
  efficiency of *119*–121
  ideal 121
  mechanical advantage of *118*–119
  real 121
  work made easier by 114,
    115–116, *117*
making models, skill of 213
manipulated variable 217
mass 46
  conservation of momentum and 61
  gravity and 46–47
  inertia and *52*
  kinetic energy and 148
  momentum of moving object and
    58–59
  Newton's second law of motion
    and 53–54
  per unit volume, density as **85**
  weight and *47*
matter 163
  energy and 163
  states of 190–194
mean 223
measurement, units of. *See* units of
    measurement
mechanical advantage *118*–119
  actual 121
  ideal 121
  of inclined plane *125*
  of lever *128*
  of pulley *132*
  of screw *127*
  of wedge *126*
  of wheel and axle 132
mechanical energy 151–152
  heat engines and **195**–196
  transformed to thermal energy by
    friction 162
median 223
melting *192*
melting point 192, 193
meter (m) **9**, 214
millimeter (mm) 9
mode 223
momentum **58**–59
  conservation of **59**–61

motion 6, **7**–15
  acceleration and **22**–27
  circular 23, 65
  describing 7–9
  detecting 56
  of Earth's plates **18**–21
  fluid 95, 96
  force and *37*, 38–39
  friction and 42, *43*–44, *45*
  graphing 14–15
  gravity and 42, **46**–50
  kinetic energy and **147**–148
  measuring distance and 9
  Newton's first law of 51–52
  Newton's second law of 52–54
  Newton's third law of 55–61, 65
  projectile *50*, 66
  relative 8
  satellite 66
  velocity and 12–13
movable pulleys 132, *133*

N

net force **37**
  balanced forces and **38**–39
  Newton's second law of motion
    and 53–54
  unbalanced forces and **38**
Newton, Isaac 37, 46, 58, 66
  first law of motion 51–*52*
  second law of motion 52–54
  third law of motion 55–61, 65
newton (N) **37**, 53, 75
nuclear energy *155*, 167
nuclear fission 155
nuclear fusion 155, 167
nuclear power plants 163

O

observing, skill of 212
operational definition 217
orbit of satellite 65–67
output distance 115
output force 115
  inclined plane and *125*
  lever and *128*
  mechanical advantage and *118*–119
  pulley and 132
  screw and *127*
  wedge and *126*
  wheel and axle and 131
output work 115
  efficiency of machine and *119*

P

Pascal, Blaise 91
pascal (Pa) **75**

Pascal's principle 90, **91**–94
  hydraulic device and 92
  hydraulic systems and **93**–94
  using 92–94
pendulum, energy in 160–161
percentage 226
plane, inclined *125*
plates, Earth's **18**–21
  reasons for movement of 19
  speed of motion 21
  theory of plate tectonics **19**
plate tectonics, theory of **19**
pole vault, energy in 161
potential energy **149**–150. *See also*
    fossil fuels
  chemical energy as *154*
  elastic *150*, 161
  gravitational *149*, 160, 161
  mechanical energy and 152
  nuclear energy *155*, 167
  transformation between kinetic
    energy and 160–161
power *111*
  calculating 112
  energy and *147*
  units of 113
  work and 111–113
power plants 168–*169*
  nuclear 163
precision 226
predicting, skill of 212
pressure 74, *75*–80
  area and 75
  atmospheric 76–80
  balanced 77
  calculating 75
  fluid. *See* **fluid pressure**
  measuring 80
  moving fluids and 95, 96
  transmitted in fluid, Pascal's
    principle of **91**–94
  unbalanced 77
probability 223
projectile *50*, 66
proportion 226
prototype 219
pulley 132
  types of 132, *133*

R

radiation 184, *185*
ratio 226
reaction force 56–57
real machines 121
reference point *7*, 8
  relative motion and 8
refrigerant 199
refrigerators 198–199

Index

relative motion 8
relativity, theory of 163
responding variable 217
rockets 64
rolling friction 44, 45

S

safety in the laboratory 232–233
satellite(s) 64, 65–67
  artificial 65
  location 67
  motion 66
scales, temperature 178
scientific notation 227
screws 127
second (time) 215
ship, ability to float of 82, 84, 85
significant figures 227
SI units of measurement 9, 214. See also units of measurement
simple machines 124–134
  in body 134
  inclined plane 125
  lever 128, 129
  pulley 132, 133
  screw 127
  wedge 126
  wheel and axle 130–132
sinking. See also buoyant force
  density and 84, 85–86, 87
  of ship 82
sliding friction 44, 45
slope(s) 14
  calculating 14
  different 15
  of distance-versus-time graph 14, 27
  of speed-versus-time graph 26
solid-liquid changes of state 192–193
solids 191
space shuttle 65
specific heat 180–181
speed 10
  acceleration and change in 22–27
  average 11
  calculating 10–11
  decreasing 23
  increasing 23
  instantaneous 11
  of object in orbit around Earth 66
  velocity and 12–13
speed equation 10
speed-versus-time graph 26
states 191
states of matter 190–194
  changes of 192–193
  thermal expansion and 193–194
  three 191
static friction 44, 45

steam engine 196
submarine, changing density of 86, 87
sun, energy from 167
Système International (SI) 9. See also units of measurement

T

temperature 176–178. See also heat transfer
  measuring 177
  specific heat and 180–181
temperature scales 178
terminal velocity 49
theory of plate tectonics 19
thermal energy 153, 178–179
  calculating changes in 181
  changes of state and absorption or release of 192–193
  combustion and transformation of chemical energy to 168
  cooling systems to transfer 198–199
  heat as transferred 179
  heat engine and transformation of 195–196
  heat transfer and 186
  mechanical energy transformed by friction to 162
  specific heat and 181
  states of matter and 190–194
thermal expansion 193–194
thermometer 177
thermostats 194
time
  in distance-versus-time graphs 14, 27
  power and 111
  in speed-versus-time graph 26
Titanic (ship), sinking of 82
trade-offs 218
troubleshoot 219

U

unbalanced forces 38, 39, 51
unbalanced pressure 77
units of measurement 9
  of acceleration 24, 53
  for area 75
  for energy 147
  for heat 179
  joules 111, 113, 147, 179
  of mass 46
  for momentum 58
  newton (N) 37, 53, 75
  pascal (Pa) 75
  for power 113
  for pressure 75
  for specific heat 180

universal gravitation, law of 46

V

vaporization 193
variable 217
velocity 12
  acceleration and change in 22–27
  air resistance and 49
  conservation of momentum and 61
  describing 12–13
  kinetic energy and 148
  momentum of moving object and 58–59
  terminal 49

W

water
  density of ice compared to 86
  freezing and boiling points of 178
  specific heat of 181
  three states of 191
water pressure, depth and 78, 79–80
Watt, James 113
watt (W) 113
waves 155
  electromagnetic 155, 184
wedge(s) 126
  in body 134
weight 47
  of air 76
  buoyant force and 83–84
  gravitational potential energy and 149
  pressure of 75
wheel and axle 130–132
wing of airplane, Bernoulli's principle and 97
work 108
  calculating 110–111
  energy as transfer of 147
  input 115, 119
  made easier by machines 114, 115–116, 117
  meaning of 108–109
  mechanical energy as ability to do 152
  output 115, 119
  power and 111–113
Wright, Wilbur and Orville 95, 97

X

x-rays 155

Z

zero, absolute 178

Acknowledgments

Staff Credits

Diane Alimena, Michele Angelucci, Scott Andrews, Jennifer Angel, Laura Baselice, Carolyn Belanger, Barbara A. Bertell, Suzanne Biron, Peggy Bliss, Stephanie Bradley, James Brady, Anne M. Bray, Sarah M. Carroll, Kerry Cashman, Jonathan Cheney, Joshua D. Clapper, Lisa J. Clark, Bob Craton, Patricia Cully, Patricia M. Dambry, Kathy Dempsey, Leanne Esterly, Emily Ellen, Thomas Ferreira, Jonathan Fisher, Patricia Fromkin, Paul Gagnon, Kathy Gavilanes, Holly Gordon, Robert Graham, Ellen Granter, Diane Grossman, Barbara Hollingdale, Linda Johnson, Anne Jones, John Judge, Kevin Keane, Kelly Kelliher, Toby Klang, Sue Langan, Russ Lappa, Carolyn Lock, Rebecca Loveys, Constance J. McCarty, Carolyn B. McGuire, Ranida Touranont McKneally, Anne McLaughlin, Eve Melnechuk, Natania Mlawer, Janet Morris, Karyl Murray, Francine Neumann, Baljit Nijjar, Marie Opera, Jill Ort, Kim Ortell, Joan Paley, Dorothy Preston, Maureen Raymond, Laura Ross, Rashid Ross, Siri Schwartzman, Melissa Shustyk, Laurel Smith, Emily Soltanoff, Jennifer A. Teece, Elizabeth Torjussen, Amanda M. Watters, Merce Wilczek, Amy Winchester, Char Lyn Yeakley. **Additional Credits** Tara Alamilla, Louise Gachet, Allen Gold, Andrea Golden, Terence Hegarty, Etta Jacobs, Meg Montgomery, Stephanie Rogers, Kim Schmidt, Adam Teller, Joan Tobin.

Illustration

David Corrente: 105; **John Edwards and Associates:** 66, 92, 197; **Andrea Golden:** 204–211; **Kevin Jones Associates:** 94; **Rob Schuster:** 97; **J/B Woolsey Associates:** 1, 3, 49, 70b; **All other artwork developed by Morgan Cain & Associates.**

Photography

Photo Research Sue McDermott

Cover Image top, David Madison/Getty Images, Inc.; **net,** Ian Walton/Getty Images, Inc.; **ball,** Royalty-Free/Corbis.

Page vi t, Richard Haynes; **vi-vii b,** Prisma Dia/Index Stock Imagery, Inc.; **vii t,** Richard Haynes; **viii,** Richard Haynes; **ix,** Richard Haynes; **xi,** Richard Haynes; **xii,** Courtesy of Museum of Science; **1,** Stephen G. Maka/DRK Photo; **2l,** Brian Smale/Discover Magazine; **2r,** Helen Ghiradella/Discover Magazine; **3,** Courtesy of Museum of Science.

Chapter 1

Pages 4–5, Mark Barrett/Index Stock Imagery/PictureQuest; **5r,** PhotoDisc/Getty Images, Inc.; **6t,** Richard Haynes; **6–7b,** Prisma Dia/Index Stock Imagery, Inc.; **7t,** Sat Yip/SuperStock; **8t,** Chris Sorensen; **8b,** Digital Vision/Getty Images Inc.; **9,** Kim Taylor/Bruce Coleman Inc.; **10–11,** Robert LaBerge/Getty Images, Inc.; **12t,** Topham/The Image Works; **12m,** North Wind Picture Archives; **12b,** National Motor Museum, Beaulieu, England; **13l,** Bettmann/Corbis; **13r,** Fritz Hoffmann/documentCHINA; **14,** Bob Daemmrich Photography; **17,** Richard Haynes; **18t,** Russ Lappa; **18b,** Earth Imaging/Getty Images, Inc.; **21,** Richard Haynes; **22t,** Richard Haynes; **22b,** Jamie Squire/Getty Images Inc.; **23l,** Ezra Shaw/Getty Images Inc.; **23m,** Adam Pretty/Getty Images Inc.; **23r,** Nick Wilson/Getty Images Inc.; **25,** Kwame Zikomo/SuperStock; **26,** Eyewire Collection/Getty Images Inc.; **28,** Richard Haynes; **29,** Lou Jones/Image Bank/Getty Images, Inc.; **30,** Robert LaBerge/Getty Images, Inc.

Chapter 2

Pages 34–35, Stephen Munday/Getty Images, Inc.; **35r,** Richard Haynes; **36,** Richard Haynes; **37,** Duomo/Corbis; **38 all,** Richard Haynes; **39,** Richard Haynes; **40,** Richard Haynes; **41,** Ken O'Donaghue; **42t,** Richard Haynes; **42b,** Kindra Clineff/Index Stock Imagery, Inc.; **43t,** B & C Alexander/Photo Researchers, Inc.; **43b,** Jan Hinsch/Photo Researchers, Inc.; **44,** Russ Lappa; **45tl,** Michael Newman/PhotoEdit; **45tr,** Michael Newman/PhotoEdit; **45bl,** David Young-Wolff/PhotoEdit; **45br,** Kelly-Mooney Photography/Corbis; **46,** Joe McBride/Corbis; **47,** NASA; **48,** Megna/Peticolas/Fundamental Photographs; **50,** Richard Megna/Fundamental Photographs; **51t,** Russ Lappa; **51b,** Bettmann/Corbis; **52 all,** Richard Haynes; **53,** David Madison Sports Photography; **54,** Richard Haynes; **55,** Richard Haynes; **56tl,** David Madison Sports Photography; **56tr,** Omni Photo Communicatons, Inc./Index Stock Imagery, Inc.; **56b,** Lawrence Manning/Corbis; **57l,** Syracuse/Dick Blume/The Image Works; **57r,** Michael Devin Daly/Corbis Stock Market; **58,** Superstock; **59tl,** David Davis/Index Stock Imagery, Inc.; **59tr,** Image Source/Alamy Images; **59b,** Russ Lappa; **63,** Richard Haynes; **64t,** Richard Haynes; **64b,** Courtesy of Homer Hickam; **65,** Jeff Hunter/Getty Images, Inc.; **66,** Richard Haynes; **68,** David Young-Wolff/PhotoEdit.

Chapter 3

Pages 72–73, Getty Images, Inc.; **73r,** Richard Haynes; **74t,** Richard Haynes; **74bl,** Milton Feinberg/Stock Boston; **74br,** Chlaus Lotscher/Stock Boston; **75 all,** Richard Haynes; **76,** PhotoDisc/Getty Images, Inc.; **77 both,** Richard Megna/Fundamental Photographs; **80,** Paul Seheult-Eye Ubiquitous/Corbis; **82t,** Russ Lappa; **82b,** Ken Marshall/Madison Press. Ltd.; **83,** Bill Wood/Bruce Coleman, Inc.; **84 both,** Richard Haynes; **85,** Runk/Schoenberger/Grant Heilman Photography, Inc.; **86t,** Russ Lappa; **86b,** Ralph A. Clevenger/Corbis; **89,** Richard Haynes; **90t,** Richard Haynes; **90b,** Stephen Frink/Corbis; **91,** Richard Haynes; **95t,** Richard Haynes; **95b,** Mercury Archives/Getty Images, Inc.; **96 both,** Richard Haynes; **99,** Maxime Laurent/Digital Vision; **102t,** Stephen Frink/Corbis; **102b,** Paul Seheult-Eye Ubiquitous/Corbis; **104,** Russ Lappa.

Chapter 4

Pages 106–107, The G. R. "Dick" Roberts Photo Library; **107r,** Corbis; **108 both,** Richard Haynes; **109 all,** Richard Haynes; **110 both,** Richard Haynes; **111 both,** MVR Photo; **112,** Shelley Rotner/Omni-Photo Communications, Inc.; **113,** The Granger Collection, NY; **114t,** Corel Corp.; **114b,** Jim West/The Image Works; **115,** PhotoDisc/Getty Images, Inc.; **116,** Richard Haynes; **117t,** Thinkstock/SuperStock; **117m,** Richard Haynes; **117b,** MVR Photo; **118,** Sergio Piumatti; **119,** Richard Haynes; **120,** Russ Lappa; **121,** Charles D. Winters/Photo Researchers, Inc.; **122,** Richard Haynes; **124t,** Richard Haynes; **124b,** Russ Lappa; **125,** Richard Haynes; **126t,** Tony Freeman/PhotoEdit; **126b,** Russ Lappa; **127l,** Russ Lappa; **127r,** Richard Haynes; **129t,** Richard Haynes; **129m,** David Brownell; **129b,** Karl Weatherly/Corbis; **130l,** Sylvain Grandadam/Getty Images, Inc.; **130r,** Gerard Champion/Getty Images, Inc.; **131l,** Michael S. Yamashita/Corbis; **131m,** Jeffrey Aaronson/Network Aspen; **131r,** Ortelius; **132,** Prentice Hall School Division; **133,** Sandra Baker/Getty Images, Inc.; **134t all,** Richard Haynes; **134b,** David Young-Wolff/PhotoEdit; **135,** Russ Lappa; **136,** Cleo Photography/PhotoEdit; **137,** Richard Haynes; **138t,** Mark Gibson; **138m,** Royalty-Free/Corbis; **138b,** Bettmann/Corbis; **139,** Mark Gibson; **140,** Russ Lappa.

Chapter 5

Pages 144–145, Reuters/Toshiyuki Aizawa/Corbis; **145r,** Richard Haynes; **146t,** Richard Haynes; **146b,** Corel Corp./Mike Chambers; **147,** Paul and Lindamarie Ambrose/Getty Images, Inc.; **150,** Andy Wheeler/Alamy Images; **151,** AP/Wide World Photos; **151 football,** Reuters/Corbis; **152l,** AP/Wide World Photos; **152r,** Paine Stock Photos; **153,** Soames Summerhays/Photo Researchers, Inc.; **154t,** William L. Wantland/Tom Stack & Associates, Inc.; **154b,** Dorling Kindersley; **155t,** NASA; **155b,** Howard Sochurek/Corbis; **157,** Richard Haynes; **158t,** Richard Haynes; **158b,** Ken Straiton/Corbis; **160t,** Richard Haynes; **160b,** Richard Megna/Fundamental Photographs; **161,** Gilbert Iundt; TempSport/Corbis; **162t,** Russ Lappa; **162b,** Brand X Pictures/Getty Images, Inc.; **163,** Courtesy of the Archives, California Institute of Technology; **164,** Richard Haynes; **165,** Richard Haynes; **166,** Russ Lappa; **167t,** Glenn Short/Getty Images, Inc.; **167b,** Melvin Grubb/Grubb Photo Service, Inc.; **168l,** Robert Harding Picture Library/Alamy Images; **168m,** Richard M. Busch; **168r,** Nicholas DeVore/Bruce Coleman, Inc.; **169tl,** Brownie Harris/Corbis; **169tr,** Don Klumpp/Photographer's Choice/Getty Images, Inc.; **169b,** Clive Streeter/Dorling Kindersley; **170,** Brand X Pictures/Getty Images, Inc.; **172,** Globus, Holway & Lobel/Corbis.

Chapter 6

Pages 174–175, Roy Ooms/Masterfile; **175r,** Russ Lappa; **176,** Richard Haynes; **177,** Russ Lappa; **178,** Spencer Grant/PhotoEdit; **179,** Richard Haynes; **180,** IT International, Ltd./eStock Photo; **182,** Richard Haynes; **183t,** Russ Lappa; **183b,** Michael Mancuso/Omni-Photo Communications, Inc.; **185,** Melanie Acevedo/Getty Images, Inc.; **186t,** Russ Lappa; **186b,** Richard Haynes; **189,** Richard Haynes; **190,** Wayne Eastep/Getty Images, Inc.; **191,** David Stoecklein/Corbis; **192,** Richard Haynes; **193,** R. Knolan Benfield, Jr./Visuals Unlimited; **197,** Xenophon A. Beake/Corbis; **200,** Michael Mancuso/Omni-Photo Communications, Inc.

Page 204t, Martin Puddy/Getty Images, Inc.; **204–205b,** Chris Warren/International Stock; **205t,** PhotoDisc/Getty Images, Inc.; **206–207t,** David Lawrence; **206–207b,** Mitchell Funk/Photographer's Choice/Getty Images, Inc.; **207r,** Richard Haynes; **208l,** Corbis; **208r,** Joseph Pobereskin/Getty Images, Inc.; **209,** Bettmann/Corbis; **210–211,** Richard Weiss/Peter Arnold, Inc.; **212,** Tony Freeman/PhotoEdit; **213t,** Russ Lappa; **213m,** Richard Haynes; **213b,** Russ Lappa; **214,** Richard Haynes; **216,** Richard Haynes; **218,** Tanton Yachts; **219,** Richard Haynes; **221t,** Dorling Kidersley; **221b,** Richard Haynes; **223,** Image Stop/Phototake; **226,** Richard Haynes; **233,** Richard Haynes; **234,** Paul Seheult-Eye Ubiquitous/Corbis; **235,** David Stoecklein/Corbis; **237,** Richard Haynes; **239l,** Russ Lappa; **238b,** Stephen Frink/Corbis; **234,** Paul Seheult-Eye Ubiquitous/Corbis; **235,** David Stoecklein/Corbis; **237,** Richard Haynes; **238b,** Stephen Frink/Corbis; **239l,** Russ Lappa.